JUSTICE BETWEEN GENERATIONS

The Growing Power of the Elderly in America

MATTHEW C. PRICE

PRAEGER

Westport, Connecticut
London

Library of Congress Cataloging-in-Publication Data

Price, Matthew C., 1962–
    Justice between generations : the growing power of the elderly in
America / Matthew C. Price.
        p.   cm.
    Includes bibliographical references and index.
    ISBN 0–275–96012–9 (alk. paper)
    1. Senior power—United States.   2. Intergenerational relations—
Political aspects—United States.   3. Aged—United States—Social
conditions.   4. Social security—United States.   5. Poor children—
United States.   I. Title.
HQ1064.U5P695   1997
305.26′0973—dc21   97–19234

British Library Cataloguing in Publication Data is available.

Library of Congress Catalog Card Number: 97–19234
ISBN: 0–275–96012–9

First published in 1997

Praeger Publishers, 88 Post Road West, Westport, CT 06881
An imprint of Greenwood Publishing Group, Inc.

Printed in the United States of America

The paper used in this book complies with the
Permanent Paper Standard issued by the National
Information Standards Organization (Z39.48–1984).

10 9 8 7 6 5 4 3 2 1

Contents

Introduction

Being old in America has meant different things at different times, but today it means wealth and power. This shift reflects one of the most dramatic demographic transitions in human history: in the span of a few generations, "oldness" itself has undergone a transformation that exceeds in scope the changes affecting aging during all the preceding generations of American history.

Qualitatively and quantitatively, the nature of "old age" has been tranformed beyond recognition. People now live longer into their "golden years." Much longer. And they live better as well.

What has produced this demographic revolution? Several factors have been crucial. Technological developments have meant that most people will live longer, and have dramatically improved the quality of life for those that do. A half-century of economic expansion, as well as a number of public policies adopted during that period, have greatly increased the personal wealth of the average older citizen. Just as important, greater access to medical care has enabled the vast majority of older Americans to benefit from medical breakthroughs that otherwise would have been prohibitively expensive. Society now pays for what the elderly citizen alone would be unable to afford.

Things change. Being 70 years old at the end of the twentieth century means that an individual enjoys prospects for good health, a comfortable retirement income, and the actuarial probability of a number of fruitful years ahead. Such an individual may not consider himself or herself "old" at all, and may not be considered old in the terms of the surrounding culture. We frequently hear people of that age refer to themselves as "70 years young."

In 1790, when the first national census was taken, fewer than 20% of the population lived to age 70. "Retirement," moreover, did not exist then: men worked until their bodies were no longer physically able, and went through life fearing for their economic welfare should that day come. In this respect, the prospect of growing "old" has become a more reasonable expectation, and an infinitely more hopeful one. We are more likely to grow old, and things are likely to go better for us when we do.

But, along with the benefits that have proceeded from extending longevity, there have been new challenges as well. As life spans were prolonged, the elderly began to pose a growing economic burden for the country, even putting stress upon the traditional family structure which had once cared for the aged. By the middle of the nineteenth century, old age was being increasingly portrayed in the popular culture as a time of neglect and loneliness, as reflected in these lyrics of the era:

The Lonely Old Wife

Long ago, when her bosom was swelling with pride,
The lonely old wife was a gay young bride
And the rose on her cheek wore its richest bloom,
When she gave her hand to the joyous groom.

Faded and worn is her beauty now,
Gray are the hairs on her wrinkled brow
Silent she sits by the old hearth stone
Sad are her thoughts
She is there alone,
Sad are her thoughts
She is there alone.[1]

By 1862 Ralph Waldo Emerson would hint at the growing tensions in the public attitudes toward the elderly:

Youth is everywhere in place. Age, like woman, requires fit surroundings. Age is comely in churches, in chambers of State and Ceremony, in council-chambers, in courts of justice and historical societies. . . . But in the rush and uproar of Broadway . . . few envy the consideration enjoyed by the oldest inhabitant. . . . In short the creed of the street is, Old Age is not disgraceful, but immensely disadvantageous.[2]

By the twentieth century, older Americans had become, as a group, neglected and impoverished. Gradually society began to reexamine its attitudes toward older Americans. They had, after all, spent their lives working to produce national prosperity: was it right for the nation to ignore them once they had become unable to work? It was a tortuous dilemma for an individualist culture, and would require decades to resolve. The resulting breakthroughs in public policy for the elderly—particularly Social Security and Medicare—were vital elements in establishing a new quality of life for seniors.

Now, a generation later, those programs are under attack as never before. They take from the poor and give to the rich, it is charged. They divert vital resources away from the young, and give them to those in their twilight years.

More young people believe in UFOs than believe that the Social Security system will be solvent when they retire. But the elderly know the value of those programs to their welfare, and they have the resources, the political clout, and the determination to defend those programs. The battle over the future of old age is just heating up, but it promises to shape America's future for the next century.

"It's a great time to be silver," goes the television advertisement, one of the growing number of marketing efforts aimed specifically at elderly Americans. It is indeed a great time to be silver. But what about those who won't be silver for thirty more years? Or 50 more? Will the future still hold the "golden years" for them that it once held for their parents? Do their parents care?

The saga of how older Americans came from the margins of society to a position of predominance in American politics reveals much about the stunning changes that have shaken society, and hints at the earthquake to come.

1

From Veneration to Burden

What is rare is valued. Veneration comes more easily when a thing is scarce. During the early years of the American republic, old people were scarce. And since they made no great material demands upon society, it was not difficult for early Americans to revere the elderly. Older Americans being so few, it was a reverence that existed largely in the abstract. The elderly worked until they were no longer able, and then became the wards of their own families. Care for the aged was an integral part of the overall fabric of social cooperation and obligation. The obligation of support normally did not last long, either. Shorter life expectancy meant that the time lag between one becoming incapacitated and the time of death was likely to be relatively brief.

History gives frequent examples of groups that are revered as long as they remain fairly unobtrusive, and make few demands on the population. Often, when these groups begin to grow in numbers, or begin to ask more of society, sentiment becomes more strained. It is easier to venerate the idea of a thing than the actual thing itself. In America's early years (with a median age of 16, the new United States was young in every sense), it was not a demanding social norm to treat the elderly with "respect" and "veneration." These consisted mainly of rhetorical assertions of sentiment rather than of substantial material sacrifice.

It is one thing to revere what one knows only as an abstraction, to venerate the elderly when one knows none. It is quite another thing to venerate an elderly relation who has become unable to care for himself, requires constant attention, and has moved in. Because there were relatively so few older citizens in young America, showing respect for the elderly generally required little positive action or personal sacrifice. Expression of deference toward the elderly consisted, for the most part, in the expression of sentiments of deference.

Yet, such sentiments were socially requisite. Gerontologist W. Andrew Achenbaum cites a *Webster's Dictionary* from the nineteenth century to indicate how pervasive this attitude of reverence toward the elderly was: "We venerate an old faithful magistrate; we venerate parents and elders; we venerate men consecrated of sacred office; we venerate old age or gray hairs; we venerate, or ought to venerate, the gospel and its precepts."[1]

An attitude of solemn respect toward the elderly was presumed to be so implicit and widespread that it was actually used as part of a definition for a term connoting solemn respect. In fact, of the five definitions given, three explicitly referred to longevity, the other two, tellingly, to sacred duties. And in the definitions, it is presumed that Americans venerate the elderly, whereas they "ought to" do so for the gospel.

Being part of a group which was venerated, however, did not relieve the elderly individual of the need to make a living. It was expected that one would remain economically productive as long as physically possible. And since age was widely taken to be a sign of wisdom and advanced understanding of one's craft, it was generally considered to be counterproductive to withdraw an individual from employment just at that time when he or she was best able to contribute.

Indeed, the deterioration sometimes associated with age was typically attributed not to any physical characteristics associated with the aging process itself, but to lack of use. To prevent someone from participating in their own profession simply due to some arbitrary age barrier was not to spare the elderly from hard labor in the twilight years, but to doom them to social neglect and personal decay. Youngness, not oldness, was regarded as being, of itself, a disqualifier for certain important tasks. While there are numerous limitations on the youthfulness of aspiring political candidates written into the American Constitution, there are none for old age.

Retirement is a new invention. People were expected to work as long as they were able, to prevent becoming a burden to their families and to society. However, in the agrarian culture (nearly two-thirds of Americans were still employed in agriculture at the time of the Civil War),[2] there existed a heritage of tight family bonds which freed the elderly farmer from the need for doing the most strenuous activity. In addition, the goodwill and filial obligation felt by children toward aging parents were often supplemented by more concrete considerations: in particular, the elderly parent's ownership of the family land was of paramount interest to the children. By retaining land ownership until near the end of their lives, elderly parents could insure a degree of economic security that might not have been guaranteed by filial piety alone. In an agrarian world, control of the land was itself the possession of power, and the calculated release of land to the next generation was a way that the older generation could retain power until the end was near. Thus, material inducements combined with social tradition to insure that children observed due veneration toward their elderly parents, and helped to provide a kind of old-age security. That security enabled the aging farmer to expect that the heavier tasks would be taken up by younger family members; but "retirement" in the modern sense, of entirely abandoning one's occupation, was never part of the equation.

Because of the widespread distribution of freeheld land in the United States, there may have even been a greater degree of authority retained by the elderly in the young republic than there had been in Europe, where most American farmers had their roots. In contrast to European farmers, most American parents could hold out the prospect of inheritance to their faithful sons. Even wealthy men, therefore, who could have easily afforded to distribute their land to their sons, were reluctant to do so before old age, because by retaining land they retained control, and security. "Land was an instrument of generational politics," writes David Hackett Fischer, "a way of preserving both the power and authority of the elderly. Sons were bound to their fathers by ties of economic dependency; youth was the hostage of age."[3] Genuine personal financial independence of one's father often came only after his death. Veneration had a material as well as a moral aspect.

MOVE TO THE CITY

Traditional filial obligations eroded under the social acid of industrialization. The economic milieu of the factory is very different from that of the farm. The social environment of the city is a world away from the countryside. Life changed for every group, but for the elderly most of all. The technological advancements that accompanied industrialization would make old age more common; the social changes that accompanied urbanization would make old age more unpleasant.

In the latter part of the nineteenth century, as industrialism progressed and materialism advanced, the traditional respect for old age became less forthcoming. This was particularly true for the elderly lower down the economic ladder, those who lacked the material resources that were, increasingly, the measure of one's worth to society.

With urbanization, the extended family began to contract. Where it had once been possible to support several generations on the same piece of farmland, the more confined living conditions and unpredictable working conditions of city life served to spread families apart, to break them up.

In an agrarian culture, at least, individuals could survive by living off of the land. They were also more likely to be surrounded by a supportive network of family and community. On moving to the city, it became necessary to have a constant source of money income in order to survive; and people were living, more than ever before in history, among strangers.

Unlike the aging farm owner counting on the beneficence and self-interest of his own children to see him through the latter years, workers in the city knew they could rely on no such beneficence from the factory owner. Every laborer knew that if (when) age slowed him down, he would quickly be replaced by a younger, more vigorous worker. Industrialism brought generations into direct conflict in a way that they had not been earlier.

Meanwhile, in the move to the city, most gradually surrendered the ties which had once bound extended families together so strongly. There were no longer three or four interdependent generations living together, each caring for the other. More than ever before, it was every generation for itself; the younger worker needing to work, the older worker fearing being supplanted by the younger. In agrarian culture, one's children were the only retirement plan that existed. When urbanization eroded that bond, it eroded that limited retirement security.

Industrialism meant that unemployment was becoming an inevitable consequence of aging. "Superannuation," a word which had once been used to describe animals and farm implements that had become too old to be useful, was now coming to be used to refer to workers who had grown to old to remain productive, too old to be employed. In the profit-and-loss world of the factory and the city, the economic factor was becoming the central consideration in the calculus of human value. The limitations of the "veneration" which American society had held for the elderly began to manifest themselves, as the abstract pronouncements of social goodwill began to bump up against the material realities of clashing interests.

In the period between the end of the Civil War and the dawn of the twentieth century, America was transformed from an agricultural to an industrial nation. With the shift in lifestyles came a change of emphasis. While Americans had always been oriented toward the aim of material prosperity, the dawn of a "Gilded Age" established new heights of materialism and individualism. It was the elevation to new prominence of what Henry James referred to as the "Bitch-Goddess success." These changes in attitude were accelerated, and their effects enhanced, by a move away from the community life of rural, agrarian America, to the life of the urban centers. The dynamics of urban life simply seem to produce different values than those of country life.

And America was urbanizing rapidly. In 1790, 5.1% of the population lived in cities; by 1850 the figure was still only 15.3%; but by 1910, the proportion of the population living in urban areas had jumped to 45.7%.[4] In 1840, 70% of America's GNP was agricultural; by 1890, barely 33% still was.[5]

Industrialization and urbanization were advancing at breakneck speeds, and both would have dramatic, often traumatic, effects on the lives of the elderly. As urbanization progressed, the size of cities grew correspondingly, so that Americans were not only living more in cities, but living in bigger, more crowded ones. In 1800 the largest city in the country had a population of fewer than 100,000, and even in 1860 just nine cities had more than 100,000 residents: six between 100,000 and 250,000, and only three had between 250,000 and 1 million inhabitants.[6]

Explosive industrial expansion spurred the growth of the cities. As late as the 1880s, agriculture generated more income in the United States than manufacturing. By 1910 the value of U.S. manufacturing output was double that of agriculture. American industry comprised over one-third of total world manufacturing output.[7] The tide of industrialism lifted the American standard of living to unprecedented levels and drew millions to the cities from the coutryside.

Industrialization and the promise of jobs in the new factories lured Americans from the countryside to the city, but it also attracted a wave of immigration from abroad. Between 1821 and 1830 a total of 143,438 immigrants were admitted to the United States by the Immigration and Naturalization Service; between 1851 and 1860 the number had risen to over 2.5 million; and between 1901 and 1910 immigration peaked, jumping to 8.8 million.[8]

Immigrants did not move to rural areas but "toward where the jobs were, the cities." Historian James MacGregor Burns describes this period of explosive growth of the nation's cities, in which immigrants "commingled with another vast migration of Americans from rural to urban areas. The desolate New England farms, with their sagging fences, broken windows, and overgrown pastures, hinted of earlier decisions to desert century-old houses for the rumored shorter hours and higher pay of factory life."[9]

The U.S. population quadrupled between 1850 and 1910, from 23.2 million to 92 million,[10] reflecting an astonishing average increase of nearly 30% in each decade. Burns describes the unprecedented growth, industrialization, and urbanization which transformed the United States in the latter half of the nineteenth century:

> The population explosion in American cities was phenomenal; between 1860 and 1900, New York City grew from 1 million to 3.5 million, Philadelphia from half a million to 1.3 million, Boston from 170,000 to over half a million, Chicago from a small city to almost 1.7 million. Equally spectacular was the rise in the number of cities with more than 100,000 persons—from nine to fifty between 1860 and 1910. People talked about the ever-growing midwestern and eastern metropolises, but smaller cities of the West also underwent rapid growth, as did some in the South—Birmingham, Louisville, Memphis, the bustling cities of Texas. In sum, the American people were becoming more numerous, more diversified ethnically, more urbanized, older. . . .[11]

"A very populous city," wrote Aristotle in *The Politics,* "can rarely, if ever, be well governed." America's cities were becoming more and more populous and held a growing proportion of the population. Cities would be found to have much higher rates of crimes against persons, and were least conducive to the well-being of individuals in their later years, who, seeming more vulnerable, might make appealing targets.

The greater threat to one's welfare, though, was not of being deprived of one's income by force, but by age. In rural areas there had typically been a network of family and friends upon whom one could rely when things got tough. In the city, a community of strangers, there was often no such safety net. And, lacking that social network, there was frequently none at all. Public services for the needy in the Gilded Age, the zenith of the individualistic ethic and its ideal of unrestrained capitalism, were negligible relative to the growing problem. Poverty was widely considered to be the result of character defects. Older people, then, were doubly vulnerable in America's large urban centers where they lived in growing numbers.

Just as it had fundamentally altered socioeconomic relationships, industrialism would spark a reappraisal of the place of the elderly in society, and would produce what Achenbaum calls "the obsolescence of old age." In the utilitarian world of early industrialism, what was not productive was not worthwhile. The tradition of veneration eroded; taking its place was the growing feeling that old people were a burden—to their families and to society. Achenbaum identifies the period between 1865 and 1914, the era of rapid industrialization, as marking a change in the ideas most Americans held about aging and the aged:

> With growing frequency after the Civil War, Americans began to challenge nearly every favorable belief about the usefulness and merits of age . . . instead of depicting the elderly as stately and healthy, more and more observers described them as ugly and disease-ridden. Instead of extolling the aged's moral wisdom and practical sagacity, popular and scientific commentators increasingly concluded that old people were incapable of contributing anything to society.[12]

Partly responsible for the growing perceptions of the elderly as a public burden were the growing numbers of old people themselves. As life expectancy was extended, there were greater absolute numbers of older Americans, and they constituted a growing portion of the population.

With more old people, it was now profitable to begin to single them out as an identifiable socioeconomic group, a phenomenon that would later take on enormous marketing importance. One early manifestation of this trend was the emergence of a new genre in book publishing: books and magazine articles began to proliferate, giving advice for maintaining well-being into old age. In 1881 Dr. Joseph Richardson noted that a decline of physical vigor and mental alertness frequently accompanied the aging process. Richardson's solution: "a judicious change of occupation and of scene, particularly in foreign travel." The "danger signals" of failure of memory or "loss of reasoning power" might serve as symptoms, Dr. Richardson maintained, that could arouse the elderly individual to take remedial action. If no preventative action is taken (and, according to Richardson it usually wasn't) the individual "falls into a condition of decay which renders long life a grievous burden, not only to the sufferer himself but also to the loving relatives and anxious friends who surround him."[13]

Dr. S.G. Lathrop edited a work entitled *Fifty Years and Beyond.* (The title hints at shifting views about aging: someone who is fifty years old today is still widely considered to be in middle age.) The message of the book: you can live a happy, healthy life if you take care of yourself—even after 50. Lathrop argued that old age was made a gratifying time of life by the tradition of respect for the elderly, which even then still persisted as a powerful social norm, although he noted that it seemed to be eroding with the rising generation. "There are, it must be acknowledged and lamented, some foolish and ill-educated young persons who do not pay the veneration which is due to the hoary head."[14]

Many writers of the period stressed the need for the elderly to put their faith in a higher source to endure the hardships unique to that time of life, and to prepare to pass away from this life to the next. "Crowned with (piety)," wrote one, "old age is always beautiful."[15] "To the child of God," wrote another, "death is the birthday of everlasting life."[16]

For many, old age did not always seem beautiful. Oliver Wendell Holmes saw it as a time of yearning for things past, a time of regret. He put the feeling of nostalgic recollection and wistfulness into poignant verse:

> O for one hour of youthful joy!
> Give back my twentieth spring!
> I'd rather laugh a bright-haired boy,
> Than reign a grey-beard king!
>
> Off with the wrinkled spoils of age!
> Away with learning's crown!
> Tear out life's wisdom written page,
> And dash its trophies down!
>
> One moment let my life-blood stream
> From boyhood's fount of fame!
> Give me one giddy, reeling dream
> Of life all love and flame![17]

Henry Ward Beecher wrote that old age invariably is accompanied by greater—at least different—sorrows than those of youth, but that these could give life a greater understanding and fullness if borne with grace. Still, the emphasis seems to have shifted from the almost unqualified encomiums to aging and the aged that had predominated in the new republic. Reverend Beecher compared the cycle of life to the annual rhythm of the changing seasons, and here again there is the hint of regret. "After the days in summer begin to grow short, I cannot help sighing often; and as they still grow shorter and shorter, I look upon things, not with pain, but with a melancholy eye." Old age was being transformed in the civic mind from an unmitigated blessing to be rejoiced, to a trial which had to be endured, a test to be overcome. "There are sorrows that are not painful, but are of the nature of some acids, and give piquancy to life."[18]

Old age was increasingly perceived to be a time of greater disconsolation and sadness. This shift in attitudes may have reflected the real conditions of the elderly, in the shift from the agrarian to the urban, where little indeed is venerated but aspects of the commercial. Maria Child's "moral hint" for the elderly: keep those negative sentiments inside. In *Looking Toward Sunset* she wrote, "it is unkind to add the weight of your own despondency to the burdens of another." Instead, try to occupy your later years with industrious effort. Michaelangelo, Handel, Haydn, Linnaeus and Wesley, she pointed out, did some of their best work later in life. Also, the aged should surround themselves with "pleasant external objects."[19]

Old age was considered, more and more, something to be dreaded. External manifestations of this condition should be avoided, if possible. It was a theme that would pick up momentum in the next decades. Shortly after the turn of the century, a number of works began to appear on precisely that topic, anticipating the boom in the "Stay Young Forever" genre that has persisted and burgeoned until present times.

With growing numbers of Americans living longer and longer, doctors were devoting more attention to the problems of aging. Old age was, increasingly, treated as a period of problems rather than of promise. The Reverend W.X. Ninde described the popular conception of aging at the dawn of the twentieth century:

> We rarely hear old age referred to as beautiful. . . . Even ripened manhood and womanhood have superior charms; but we gloomily anticipate age as the period of mental degeneracy and physical decay. The freshness of life wasted; the bloom gone from the cheek; the light from the eye; the vigor from the step . . . in the common estimation, old people are a burden to themselves, and, however much the faithful heart may revolt at confessing it, a burden to their friends.[20]

Given such public conceptions of aging, it is no wonder that individuals would want to defer it, or hide it. Physician Arnold Lorand wrote *Old Age Deferred* in 1923, suggesting that it was perfectly natural that individuals should wish to avoid, or delay, the effects of the aging process: and not only the deterioration in health and physical vigor that frequently accompanied old age, but also the purely external manifestations of aging. Thus, Dr. Lorand warned, drink plenty of water or your skin will suffer from premature wrinkling. "The face will appear lean and haggard, the skin shrivelled and folded, and lines and wrinkles will appear already in the faces of young women." Nutrition was critical for acting young as well as looking young, containing, as it does, "a most important substance, called 'vitamines,' which, as its name shows, conveys a kind of vitality to the tissues."[21]

The superficial preoccupation with youthful appearance is not a modern development. In the early part of this century, writers such as Lorand were already describing ways to camouflage the external effects of age: "A Few Cosmetic Hints for the Remedying of Old Looks" contained the following words of advice:

> In persons of certain age and also in younger persons with a fading expression of the face and beginning wrinkles I have found, as efficacious in producing an immediate improvement, the gentle application to the face of any kind of fats of pure quality and the rubbing thereon of some reliable preparation of white powder.[22]

Even the external indicators of the aging process had become something to be covered up, dyed, downplayed. Even the appearance of youthfulness was something to be pursued:

As gray hairs create, even in persons still young, an elderly appearance, it might appear to their advantage to color them. It is best to use such coloring only in regions of small extent rather than in a general way. As the most inoffensive coloring of gray hair among dark hair, I would consider the preparations containing nitrate of silver.[23]

Age and its attributes were becoming socially unattractive. If one could not prevent growing old, one should at least have the good social sense to avoid the appearance of old age. The desire to avoid looking old is not a recent phenomenon. Its roots are deep in American and Western culture. But the preoccupation seems to have accelerated, especially at the mass level, at around the time that has been described as the period of the "obsolescence of old age"; meaning, when age declined in the general perception as something to be admired, respected, venerated, and became something to be pitied or ignored. The very depth of experience of the elderly, once the source of veneration, had itself become a kind of liability. "Passions, grief and sorrow may prove detrimental," wrote Lorand, "as they often leave lines and wrinkles in the face."[24]

It would be inaccurate to speak of discrete phases in attitudes toward the elderly. We cannot point to a time when one sentiment (veneration, tolerance, respect, pity, etc.) operated to the exclusion of all others. At the time when the elderly were more widely venerated, for example, there were surely those who regarded them as burdensome. Yet central themes can be identified as running throughout the historical record. The theme of veneration for the elderly ("respect your elders") never died out altogether, but continued to play a prominent part in much social discourse. Nor are expressions of regret over the physical afflictions that can accompany the aging process anything new.

Nevertheless, there can be identified the waxing and waning of these themes over time in the popular usage. There have always been those, for example, who have celebrated youth as opposed to old age. Emerson was reiterating this timeless theme when he wrote, in 1862, that "youth is everywhere in place."[25] The notion is found much earlier in Western civilization, in Greek and Roman thought. Yet it has been only in the relatively recent past, the last hundred years or so, that the social emphasis (it has been called an obsession) has come to be placed so starkly on the advantages of youngness and the disadvantages of age. Whether this preoccupation is reversed as the elderly move into positions of even greater social and economic influence remains to be seen.

Youngness had always been an American preoccupation. For much of its brief history America had been a young nation filled with young people. "The youth of America is their oldest tradition," wrote Oscar Wilde in *A Woman of No Importance*. "It has been going on now for three hundred years."[26] What was changing was not the absorption with youth—it persisted, and grew. What had evolved was the public conception of the elderly.

Industrialism accentuated the limiting aspects of the aging process, promoted the growing vulnerability of the elderly, and made them more open to the charges that they were not pulling their own weight. In a society focused on present productivity and prosperity, past contributions are of little significance. The question always is: "what are you doing for us now?" By the turn of the century, most Americans felt that the elderly were not making significant contributions to society.[27] Aging and the aged had undergone a remarkable transition in the public mind: from objects of veneration and respect, to ones of pity and even resentment. As their numbers grew, and as they became more concentrated in America's cities, older people were becoming difficult to ignore as a group. Lumped together, they seemed to constitute a national problem.

Hopeful works did appear. Writing in 1923, psychologist G. Stanley Hall wrote that "a rich old age" is the reward of a life well-lived. Individuals can, and should, prepare for old age. Those who do, and are prepared for it when it comes

do sometimes attain vision and even prophetic power, and their last words to the world they are leaving are not like the inane babblings of the dying, which friends so often cherish, but are often the best and most worth heeding by their juniors of all their counsels. . . . Nietzsche was right in making Zarathustra old and he himself was the overman whose message he brought to the world. He was intent on the future of man and not on his present, still less his past. Thus, the ideal man will be chiefly concerned for what is yet to be. . . .

In fine, it cannot be too strongly urged or too often repeated that at present we know little of old age and that little is so predominantly of its inferior specimens, its unfavorable traits and defects and limitations, that the old have been prone to repudiate their years.[28]

Dr. Lillien Martin, writing in 1930, noted that, in addition to the physical impairments that often accompany aging, social attitudes were equally limiting. "Small wonder that people turned away from facing this entirely unattractive future." Martin described the views of her university students, who regarded the elderly as the "unburied dead."[29] A society which abandons its elderly as America was doing, Martin insisted, not only deprives the elderly of the chance to remain productive, but also loses the potential contributions the elderly might have made if allowed to do so. Lives are diminished, and society is the poorer for it. Only reeducation, of the elderly, and of society, could produce the changes required to permit older Americans to contribute, and enable society to accept that contribution. Only after attitudes had been substantially altered would the old "at last, take the important and distinct place so long denied them."[30] The sentiment remains as powerful today.

THE EMERGING CRISIS

When Robert Hunter published his important study, *Poverty,* in 1904, he cited "the aged" first among those groups in need of public assistance. Private charities were inadequate at the time, and public assistance was worse. "It seems an almost hopeless outlook," Hunter wrote. "And it would be if there were not means at hand to meet some of these stern facts, other than those offered by the ordinary charitable activities.[31] Government had the capacity, and the obligation, to step in, he argued. It should establish a system of public insurance that would protect against the times of life when an individual may be incapable of work. "The poverty of today is in great measure unnecessary."[32] It was a contrarian message during the heyday of rugged-individualist capitalism. And, while the work attracted the attention of prominent social critics (H.G. Wells wrote that the book should be "compulsory reading for every prosperous adult in the United States"[33]), it made no impact on policy. The times were not yet ready for such a change.

Yet Hunter's study, and its claim that 10 million Americans lived in poverty, ultimately proved to be seminal in raising national consciousness. The plight of impoverished Americans was slowly—very slowly—coming to be regarded as a national public problem, not merely a problem for private institutions to address. In the early decades of the twentieth century, an emerging body of literature would bring problems of poverty in America out of the national closet, and into the light of public discourse.

Writing in 1916, Dr. Maurice Parmelee noted that, because of low wages, it was difficult for many workers to make it from paycheck to paycheck, and imposssible for most to save for the time when they would be too old to work. "It is easy to belive," he wrote, "that many workers reach old age without being able to make any provision for the time when they can no longer work."[34]

America was in the midst of the Progressive movement, and the prevailing dogmas of the Protestant Ethic, dominant for centuries, were now being called into question. Principles such as rugged individualism and self-reliance (and their corollary doctrine that society has little responsibility for the needy) were coming under attack. A landmark work in this area came in 1929, a scathing attack upon social neglect by Robert Kelso, director of the St. Louis Community Fund and Council. "Poverty in the social order," Kelso wrote in his *Poverty,* "stands out like a fungus upon the surface of decay."[35] Kelso explicitly rejected the dominant notion that poverty was an inescapable consequence of social life, a manifestation of personal inadequacies. He observed that, in 1920, there were nearly 5 million Americans who, because of their age, were "naturally helpless," and unable to provide for their own welfare. Surely it was not the fault of the elderly man, willing to work, that the changes brought about by industrialization had rendered him incapable to do so. "The problem of old age in the modern world is a problem of industrial superannuation. It is the problem of the jobless, propertyless man, not a feeble old body. He may be fairly vigorous, but for the purpose of modern industry controlled by automatic machinery, he is too old to be useful."[36]

According to Kelso, science had made the problem worse, not better. The problem he identified has become an ongoing challenge for medicine: how to increase longevity while maintaining quality of life. Science, Kelso noted, had added 15 years to life expectancy without adding 15 years to productivity. And, in a society preoccupied with utilitarian tabulations, "economic harmony would demand that the worker die as soon as he is superannuated, too old to carry his own weight in industry."[37]

Since this is obviously undesireable, society must respond to the economic dislocation that inevitably occurs when age has made individuals unable to provide for their own economic welfare. Yet, since society did not respond to these needs, aging had become a burden—impoverishing not only the aged themselves, but their families as well.[38] Aging was a cause for fear, and for resentment. "Old age," Kelso concluded, "is a synonym for poverty in the modern industrial world. . . . In the modern world, when a person reaches 65, he is practically discarded."[39]

Thus, by the 1920s, when Robert and Helen Lynd undertook their historic study of "Middletown" (selected for being as representative as possible to the larger national picture), there was little talk any longer of the veneration that accompanied aging. Instead, the industrial revolution had shifted the measure of worth to economic productivity, and the elderly did not measure up to this new standard. The old lived in poverty, the young lived in fear of old age.

Of the three machine shops in Middletown, only one made some effort to retain older workers. However, that particular plant, the Lynds explained, "dates back to the end of the eighties" and did not reflect the general trend. They held out little hope that things would get better for elderly workers in town: in the two major industrial plants, only 1-2% percent of workers were elderly, a figure considerably below the demographics of the community at large. (And "elderly" referred to anyone in their 50s). Comments by one of the factory managers shed light on the new problems facing older workers in the modern age:

I think there's less opportunity for older men in industry now than there used to be. The principal change I've seen in the plant here has been the speeding up of machines and the eliminating of the human factor by machinery. The company has no definite policy of firing men when they reach a certain age, nor of hiring men under a certain age, but in general we find that when a man reaches fifty he is slipping down in production.[40]

Another plant manager reported how he went out of his way to help the elderly: "We try to find a place for these older men when they are as old as fifty-five if there is no danger in their working near machinery."[41] The emergence of an industrial economy that held out little hope of productive employment beyond 50 years of age must have made the prospect of growing old a mixed blessing.

Predictably, the Lynds found a great deal of anxiety over getting older among the wives of workers as well. The wife of a 40-year-old laborer bewailed: "Whenever you get old they are done with you." The wife of a pattern maker reported: "He is forty and in about ten years now will be on the shelf. A pattern maker really isn't that much wanted after forty-five. They always put in the young men. What will we do? Well, that is just what I don't know."

The wife of a 46-year-old machinist looked to the future with similar unease: "I worry about what we'll do when he gets older and isn't at the factories and I am unable to work. We can't expect our children to support us and we can't seem to save any money for that time."[42] By early in the twentieth century, after two generations of industrial progress, the twilight years of life had become the nightmare years.

2

Voices in the Wilderness

For the first 150 years of the American republic, the public commitment to the needs of the elderly was insignificant. The role of the federal government in addressing any of the fundamental problems of poverty was virtually nonexistent.[1] This policy of laissez-faire, of a public sphere largely uninvolved in the economic sphere, was a product of centuries of the essential American principles of minimalist government and individual self-sufficiency. Americans did not expect, or want, government looking out for them.

The individualist ethic took root early in the settlements of the New World, where the small size and close-knit social organization of the communities meant that voluntary assistance was generally adequate to meet the needs of those who were unable to care for themselves. A cohesive family structure and pervasive church system were important in this regard.

Thus, the problems of economic insufficiency were seen as being outside of the political sphere altogether. They were the responsibility of civil society. (In fact, the first laws to address the problem of poverty were those designed to restrict entry to a community by individuals who might pose such problems. During the 1630s, Boston and Plymouth enacted "restrictions on the sale of property and visitation by strangers . . . to control the influx of the poor, the criminal, and those of incompatible religions.")[2] And through the nineteenth century, there was little that the political sphere, with its limited scope and powers, was capable of doing to address the causes of poverty, even had it desired to do so.

Although developers and speculators, attempting to lure immigrants across the ocean, painted a picture of the new world as a place of abundance and prosperity for all who could make the journey, the reality was one of hardship for the great majority of newcomers. The roads, it turned out, were not paved with gold.

The immigrants, of course, did not bring much wealth with them, either, being drawn largely from the lower classes of European society. After all, those willing to uproot themselves from the security of home and fatherland, endure a difficult voyage across the ocean, and face uncertain prospects in a strange land, were not from the upper crust of Europe. They brought with them few resources, but a belief that America offered new opportunities that they would not have back home. They were not wrong: America did provide opportunities for prosperity that had not existed for most immigrants in their homelands. However, it was a demanding existence, and while some did achieve great wealth, many others, already living on the razor's edge of subsistence, were easily driven into poverty by illness or other misfortune.[3]

While the epic transformation of the industrial revolution made it easier for individuals to slip into poverty, unyielding social opinion continued to regard with skepticism the plight of the poor. "Self-reliance" was the credo of the day.

It was the age of Social Darwinism, and Yale sociologist William Graham Sumner was not alone in his belief that

if we let nature alone she cures vice by the most frightful penalties . . . a drunkard in the gutter is just where he ought to be. Nature is working away at him to get him out of the way, just as she sets up her processes of dissolution to remove whatever is a failure in its own line.[4]

The era seemed to be summed up neatly by English Social Darwinist Herbert Spencer's phrase "survival of the fittest." There was little room in that paradigm for public welfare. Indeed, it was a view positively antithetical to philanthropy on behalf of the needy. If society's least capable, unable to support themselves, are supported by the artificial means of public beneficence, they would only continue to procreate, thereby undermining the vitality of the species as a whole. What is mercy to the poor may be injustice to the species.

Still under the sway of the laissez-faire calculus of Adam Smith a century after the publication of *The Wealth of Nations*, advocates for the poor sought to create a more systematic process for caring for the poor. In the latter part of the nineteenth century, proponents of a new "scientific philanthropy" saw little need for government involvement in addressing the problem of poverty. Public systems tended to be inefficient, and corrupted their beneficiaries; lacking systematic screening which could be better performed by private institutions, public ones might seduce workers away from work with easy access to free food and shelter.

While most of the charitable institutions, such as the numerous Charity Organization Societies that sprang up in cities throughout the United States, continued to be affiliated with religious organizations, there was, during the late nineteenth century, for the first time a widespread effort to dissociate evangelism from philanthropy and focus mainly on the material problems of poverty. Not that questions of ethics ceased to be a central consideration; the question of the

moral character of the poor remained an important problem for the charity societies. There continued to be an emphasis on the regeneration of the individual's
moral rather than material condition. As one advocate observed, "alms are like
drugs, and are as dangerous. Very often they create an appetite which is more
harmful than the pain which they relieve."[5] It has remained an enduring criticism in America of public welfare programs for the poor.

Nevertheless, the "scientific philanthropy" of the nascent charity organizations of the latter nineteenth century undertook something never done before in
this country: to systematically address the full range of social problems relating
to poverty and, importantly, to prevent poverty rather than simply to address its
consequences.

In the years immediately following the Civil War, "prevention" was direc-
ted toward individual character. Mrs. Josephine Shaw Lowell, founder of the
New York Charity Organization Society, expressed the prevailing sentiment
when she wrote that "the usual cause of poverty is to be found in some deficiency—moral, mental, or physical—in the person who suffers."[6] It was the
dominant view in America in the mid-nineteenth century, as it had been for
countless generations earlier. But the search for the sources of poverty had led
some reformers, by the 1890s, to a broader view. By the end of the nineteenth
century, workers in what was becoming the profession of social work were
taking case histories, compiling statistical charts, and exploring social conditions
associated with the experience of poverty.[7] Even good people, they were dis-
covering, could become poor.

Increased immigration and an economic downturn in 1893 made the efforts
of the social workers all the more vital, and by the turn of the century the
inchoate practice of social work had begun to coalesce as a professional and
political force, in conjunction with other "social scientists."[8] The first school for
the training of social workers was established in 1898, and before long, volunteers were being supplanted by professionals. Within two decades, professional
associations were sprouting up, and a set of standards was emerging for the
practice of social work and the "scientific" treatment of poverty and the poor.[9]

By the dawn of the twentieth century, the welfare professionals were
increasingly vocal in calling for a greater public role in the care for the needy.
Prominent social welfare workers led the way in publicly advocating greater
governmental responsibility, and by 1908 they had succeeded in convincing
activist President Theodore Roosevelt to hold a White House Conference on
Dependent Children. Roosevelt invited 200 national leaders for a two-day conference in Washington, reversing Franklin Pierce's edict of half a century earlier
that government had no role in solving social welfare problems.[10]

The conference, and the subsequent public attention it focused on the problems of dependent children, forced Congress to act on a child welfare bill which
had been languishing in committee for years. Welfare reformers came to Congress to testify at hearings that were receiving widespread national attention. The
U.S. government spent more each year on animal husbandry, it was reported,

than on problems of the nation's children. The result was a higher mortality rate for young children than for young animals. The proposed solution: creation of a Children's Bureau to address social welfare problems relating to the nation's youth.

Over the months that followed, a broad spectrum of groups came out in support of the proposed legislation, and for a greater public role in social welfare. Parent-teacher organizations, labor unions, social workers, and a variety of other groups actively supported the bill. And, despite arguments that the bill's supporters were "socialists" or communist sympathizers, it was finally signed into law by President William Howard Taft on April 9, 1912. The newly established U.S. Children's Bureau was commissioned to report on "all matters pertaining to the welfare of children and child life among all classes of our people"; its first-year appropriation of $25,640[11] marked an early commitment by the federal government to systematic social welfare policy, and indicated the emerging influence of those advocating public welfare programs.

The growth and professionalization of the social work industry continued apace in the ensuing years, reformers in the field actuated by the drive to increase the government's role. The American Association for the Study and Prevention of Infant Mortality, composed of physicians, educators, and social workers, proposed, in 1917, a plan of "public protection of maternity and infancy" whereby federal aid would be offered to states providing health assistance to needy mothers of newborn babies. Critics of the proposal warned that it would make the expanded Children's Bureau "the ruling power in the United States," and that it would result in "female celibates instructing mothers on how to bring up their babies."[12]

After years of intense, often vitriolic dispute, the measure finally passed, and on November 19, 1921, and was signed into law by President Warren G. Harding. It authorized the sizeable expenditure of $1,252,000 for each of the first five years, and marked a major new commitment by the federal government to social welfare. Some 3,000 child and maternal health centers in 45 states were created between 1921 and 1929, when Hoover's opposition resulted in the program being discontinued. But while the federal government lagged, many states had already been moving ahead with public assistance for the needy, prompted by many of the same reformers who had found minimal success at the national level.

The reformers' argument, that children can grow up to be productive adults only if they are raised in homes with a minimum level of income, frequently found a more receptive audience among state legislatures than it had in the U.S. Congress. In April 1911, Missouri became the first state to pass a law providing benefits to mothers who had become widows; by 1919, 35 states had; and in 1935, when Congress passed the Social Security Act, only Georgia and South Carolina lacked Widows' Pension laws.[13] By 1929, when the federal government's program for needy mothers was cancelled, state widow pension programs were distributing $30 million.

Infants were the most clearly identifiable target group, but the logic of public support for the vulnerable inexorably expanded the scope of state welfare assistance. By 1930, 12 states and Alaska had established programs to assist the elderly. The disgrace once associated with being indigent, and in need of aid, was beginning to erode. It was argued that infants on the one hand, and old people on the other, were not impoverished because of their own moral failings, nor were they the unfit members of the species, being weeded out by some unseen process of natural selection. Instead, they were simply fellow citizens in need of assistance. It was becoming legitimate for the government to give that assistance, and no longer shameful to receive it.

The 1920s were a period of growing state activity on behalf of seniors. In California, which provided them a $30 monthly pension, a minister observed: "The (California) law is reasonably liberal, generous, and helpful. . . . The outlook (elsewhere) is hopeful. Justice for the aged seems to be on the way. Since industry does not look after workers in their old age, the counties and states will do it and pay the bill out of public taxes."[14] Justice for the aged, however, would take some time.

One of the most forceful advocates for a national old-age pension plan was publicist Abraham Epstein. In his work as director of the Pennsylvania Commission to Investigate Old Age Pensions, Epstein came to realize that a genuinely comprehensive and fair policy to protect the elderly would require a national approach. In 1927 he established the American Association for Old Age Security to promote that goal. (In 1932 the organization changed its name to The American Association for Social Security, helping to popularize the term that would become the title for the government's welfare program for the elderly.)

In addition to policy activism, Epstein attempted to influence mass opinion. In 1922 he published *Facing Old Age,* compiling an impressive collection of data to demonstrate the plight of the elderly in the United States. In seeing to the basic welfare needs of its oldest citizens, he argued, America lagged far behind other industrialized nations. In every English-speaking country, and in most civilized nations of the world, "the nineteenth-century doctrine of laissez-faire, as applied to aged and superannuated wage-earners, has been practically discarded. . . . Instead, a definite policy of social legislation has superceded the chaotic and degrading practices of alms-giving and poor relief."[15] The United States, the most prosperous nation in the world, was the one most negligent of its vulnerable older citizens.

In earlier eras, Epstein explained, growing old had been no reason for distress. The patriarchal society revered the elderly as sources of social wisdom, and recognized their welfare as a matter of first importance to the social unit. The feudal lord was obligated to care for those under his dominion, even past their productive years. The medieval worker was typically able to remain productive into his late years, and familial duty would generally insure that the disabled elderly were cared for. The agricultural economy likewise allowed individuals to make some economic contribution until late in life, and even during the early years of the factory system, lifelong labor contracts often gave an incentive for the employer to take an interest in the welfare of the worker.

But with the spread of industrialism and the rise of the "modern wage system" the common worker subsisted largely from paycheck to paycheck, becoming physically worn down by the harsh demands of factory life. Standardized production lines made the individual worker easily replaceable; as soon as age started to slow one down, a younger, more productive replacement was easily found. The job was more important than the individual performing it. And industrialization had not only made old workers obsolete, but also created a ready supply of substitutes with the structural unemployment that it produced. No need for the factory boss to cope with older, slower workers, when there was an endless supply of younger ones eager for the chance to work.

Society's definition of an "older" worker was not especially old, either. Epstein cited studies showing that skilled workers had trouble securing employment much past the age of 40. The result: a growing number of older Americans thrown onto the "industrial scrap heap." Having made their contribution to society, these older men and women were now discarded, no different from any other resource which has outlived its usefulness.[16]

The insecurity of old age did not only affect older Americans, however, Epstein argued. It hung like a dark cloud over the lives of younger workers as well.[17]

In his 1933 book *Insecurity: A Challenge to America,* Epstein wrote that little had changed. Barely 5% of those over 65 were employed, and few had sufficient provisions for their own welfare.[18] Public and private efforts on behalf of the elderly remained woefully inadequate.

That sentiment was shared by Isaac Rubinow, a statistician at the U.S. Bureau of Labor Statistics, and lecturer at the New York School of Philanthropy. As early as 1913, Rubinow had been arguing that the only way to seriously address the needs of the elderly was to establish a national insurance program. Two decades later, there was still no such national policy in place. America stood out in the industrialized world for this distinction. "Why has the movement for health insurance made such little progress in the country?" he asked in his 1934 book *The Quest For Security.*[19]

The answer had to do with the American ethic of individual self-reliance, and on the opposition of a wide range of interests such as employers and the American Medical Association.[20] In support were social work professionals, university groups, and political progresives, but there was "very little support beyond these circles."[21] Thus, by the mid-1930s, Rubinow could argue that the United States was the only industrialized nation in the world lacking any national policy for the welfare of the elderly.[22] That was the case despite the elderly having, for awhile, a most improbable advocate.

Herbert Hoover "believed in old age pensions," wrote Hoover's friend and confidante Ray Wilbur. "His original belief was that they should be established by the states. After later study he felt that the subject must extend further than dependence upon the states."[23]

In fact, Hoover's interest was not merely a passing fancy. Lacking the elaborate advisory apparatus available to modern presidents, he wrote, in September 1929, to the chairmen of a number of life insurance companies, asking them to calculate the costs of a national old-age pension plan.

> I am wondering if it would be too much trouble for you to have your actuaries prepare a table for me, indicating what the cost of an old age pension would be, assuming that there are no repayments of any kind except the pension itself—that is, take some basis, say $1200 a year payable in two cases, one at 60 years of age and another at 70, and tabulate the annual payments the policy holders of different ages must make, say from 21 years onward.
>
> It would also be of great interest to know what sort of lump sum payment would need to be made at 21 and other ages in order to secure such pension.[24]

Hoover was informed that for a retirement pension of $50 monthly, lump sum payment would be required as follows:[25] age at which lump sum payment is made:

21	$ 775
31	1,010
41	1,540
51	2,450

Or, if the payments were annualized, payments for persons of different ages would be:

21	$ 39
31	58
41	110
51	250

These studies were the earliest high-level analyses of the practical realities concerning a public old-age pension program. A correspondence with Frederick Ecker, president of Metropolitan Life Insurance Company, quietly ensued. When, on October 11, a competing insurance company publicly revealed the president's interest in the problem of old-age pensions, the entire industry reacted: insurance companies began to calculate potential pension programs.[26]

Lee Frankel, an insurance analyst at Metropolitan, suggested to Ecker that the company might be able to take advantage of the relationship Ecker had developed with the president: why not have Metropolitan promote the idea of legislation regarding state or federal support for an old age pension plan? Given Hoover's feelings on the issue, Frankel wrote Ecker, "we could secure the heartiest support for such a plan."[27] What is more American than doing well by doing good?

Frankel's belief that the issue was important to Hoover was not ill-founded. Hoover's assistant, French Strother, reported to one inquirer that Hoover had given the question of old-age pensions "a great deal of study." Hoover had, in fact, requested the Committee on Recent Social Trends to "make a special and searching investigation of facts and of methods by which this problem can be met." Strother said to another, "The President feels strongly that it is a duty of society by some means to solve this problem, so as to remove the fear of old age from the minds of every member of society."[28]

The president himself took concrete action on the issue. On October 26-27, 1929, he invited publicist/writer Samuel Crowther to stay at the White House, to help formulate a plan to promote the issue of old-age pensions. A March 1930 *Ladies Home Journal* article followed: "Insurance for Old Age: It Should Be Possible for Every Man to Carry His Income on His Back." Crowther was subsequently urged by Hoover to write a book on the subject.

The timing was, to put it mildly, not good. Within a week after Crowther's stay at the White House to discuss old-age pensions, Black Monday shook the stock market, and the nation began its free fall into the Great Depression. Hoover's attention turned away from the needs of the elderly, not to return. "Every effort had to be concentrated on restoring jobs," recalled Hoover aide Ray Wilbur. "The matter [of old age pensions] was deferred until times should improve."[29] For Hoover, as it turned out, the times did not improve.

3

A Social Contract Between Generations

The Great Depression changed everything. It jolted the nation, and more than just economically. Ideas and policy proposals once sustained on the fringes of political discourse by a handful of dedicated proponents now came alive as viable policy options. Something had to be done, and the old ways hadn't worked. Prevailing values were called into question. Even the doctrine of rugged individualism, the fundamental American orthodoxy since time immemorial, was coming under attack. Social Darwinism may have made sense when those in economic distress could be cast as the losers in the stiff competition of life. It made less sense when everyone knew someone who was unemployed and impoverished, when many or most people seemed to be losers in the process.

In one day, the value of American stocks fell $14 billion. By 1932, the *New York Times* Industrial Index, which had risen from 83 points in 1921 to 443 just before the crash, plunged to 85 points. By 1932 the common stock index had fallen from its precrash level of 260 to 90; 5,000 banks and 90,000 businesses had failed. A 25% drop in employment accompanied the economic collapse.[1] The traditional argument that anyone who really wanted to work could find work, that destitution was the result of moral failures, was no longer credible. The Great Depression taught Americans the limits of "rugged individualism."

Herbert Hoover's first reaction, and second, was to do nothing. But he was not alone in this. The Congress, and the American people as a whole, drawing upon centuries of philosophical tradition, believed that the role of government should be modest. A majority of members of both parties in Congress saw the "economic downturn" as an inescapable consequence of the business cycle. Bust follows boom. Boom follows bust. Most believed that the current downturn would, in due course, be remedied by the natural functioning of the free market.[2] Thus, when the Second Session of the Seventy-first Congress convened following Black Monday, the emerging economic crisis was ignored. Instead,

Congress took up consideration of legislation it had been working on in the previous session: a bill to drastically increase import tarriffs, a move designed to protect a number of critical constituencies, ranging from farming to textiles to manufacturing, from foreign competition. The resulting Smoot-Hawley bill would come to be widely viewed as extending the Depression abroad, and deepening it at home.

Despite such political economics as Smoot-Hawley, Congress maintained the ideology that politics ought to stay out of the economic sphere. It agreed with Hoover that government could not legislate the economy into recovery, any more than it could "exorcize a Caribbean hurricane by statutory law."[3] Government had not created the problem, therefore it could not resolve it.

Instead, most of Hoover's energy was placed in securing the cooperation of the business sector in restoring the economy. He saw himself as a "well-placed cheerleader" in this process,[4] having no power himself to determine events on the field, but doing his part by urging business to take the steps necessary for recovery (maintaining levels of employment and production, etc.). In the meantime, he would assuage public concerns. Hoover tried to instill faith in the system with occasional statements on the fundamental soundness of the American economy. Occasionally, perhaps, he even invented statistics to promote that confidence.[5]

Hoover's inaction can be overstated. Biographer Martin Fausold argues that Hoover took a number of decisive steps in addressing the crisis, and that no presidential action would have proved adequate to resolve the problem during the time remaining in Hoover's term. Furthermore, it seems likely that any president in office during the onset of the Depression would have been denied a second term in which to complete the remedial process.

Among the steps eventually undertaken by Hoover: urging the Federal Reserve to loosen credit; expanding government spending so as to create a Federal deficit; and launching the Agriculture Relief Act, "the largest peacetime relief effort in United States history," in an effort to address the crisis in the agriculture sector. Fausold praises Hoover's response: "One must describe as uncanny Hoover's antidepression efforts in those areas that historians have singled out as being the principal causes for the economic plight that came on the heels of the great stock-market crash of 1929."[6]

The response was, in any case, inadequate. And as the Depression ground on, the age-old American ideology of minimalist government was slowly being ground down. Notwithstanding Hoover's steady stream of optimistic pronouncements, it was becoming increasingly clear that the government was not making headway in solving the problem. Indeed, things were getting worse. Such steps as the government did take were designed to address macroeconomic problems, and largely overlooked the economic plight of the individual citizen. Charity groups had insufficient funds to deal with the massive problem of homelessness and destitution.

Hoover did not waver. He remained true to his minimalist view of government, and unresponsive to growing public demands for direct aid to the needy. At the same time, he was setting the stage for government activism: by discrediting the doctrine of laissez-faire in the public mind, he made it possible for his successors to undertake policies that he would not. Government passivity in the face of individual suffering was no longer licensed. Thus, the greater willingness of Americans to rely on government was, paradoxically, the legacy not only of his successors but, unwittingly, of Hoover himself. Achenbaum writes:

Hoover's inability to solve the nation's problems, despite his assiduous application of time-tested political tenets, had the unintentional effect of predisposing Americans to welcome the forceful use of Federal power that his Democratic opponent promised to employ if elected President.[7]

A NEW DEAL FOR THE ELDERLY

Franklin Roosevelt's New Deal was based on the premise, reiterated by Democratic candidates at all levels, that the hands-off policy pursued by the Republicans had not been sufficient; government owed more to its people than it had been delivering; and the public sector had a responsibility to the citizenry which consisted of more than maintaining an economic climate by which big business might pursue unbounded profitability. There was an obligation to the welfare of the ordinary citizen as well.

In his acceptance speech at the Democratic National Convention, July 2, 1932, in Chicago, Roosevelt declared that the alternative visions presented to voters had never been so stark. It was a choice between government concern for the individual, and the continued neglect that was becoming associated with existing laissez-faire policies.

Our Republican leaders tell us economic laws—sacred, inviolable, unchangeable—that these laws cause panics which no one could prevent. But while they prate of economic laws, men and women are starving. We must lay hold of the fact that economic laws are not made by nature. They are made by human beings. . . .

Never before, never before in modern history have the essential differences between the two major American parties stood out in such striking contrast as they do today. Republican leaders not only have failed in material things, they have failed in National vision, because in disaster they have held out no hope, they have pointed out no path for the people below to climb back to places of security and of safety in our American life.

Throughout the nation, men and women, forgotten in the political philosophy of the government of the last years look to us here for guidance and for more equitable distribution of national wealth.[8]

When the time came for the American public to make the monumental choice between Republican minimal government or a Democratic "New Deal," and a vastly expanded government role, the result was a watershed election which would shape American politics for decades.

In the election of 1932, the choice was, emphatically, for an expanded public sphere. Roosevelt won a 22,800,000 to 15,750,000 popular vote landslide over Hoover. The electoral votes were 472 to 59. Hoover carried only six states, suffering the worst election defeat of any Republican in history, other than 1912, when the party was split. Roosevelt took 282 counties that had never voted for a Democratic presidential candidate before, and won more counties than any candidate ever. The election marked a revolution in American political life and public policy.

"Plenty is at our doorstep," said Roosevelt in his first inaugural address. "But a generous use of it languishes in the very sight of the supply. Primarily this is because rulers of the exchange of mankind's goods have failed through their own stubbornness and their own incompetence, have admitted their failure, and have abdicated."[9] The new approach he proposed would be a modification, though not an abandonment, of the free-market model. It would pave the way for an explosion of government activity.

In the first three months after taking office, the celebrated "one hundred days," Roosevelt pushed through the new Congress an unprecedented succession of relief measures. During that early period, the president supervised the enactment of landmark legislation, including passage of the Emergency Banking Act, creation of the Civilian Conservation Corps, the Federal Emergency Relief Act, the Agricultural Adjustment Act, the Emergency Farm Mortgage Act, the Homeowners' Loan Act, the National Industrial Recovery Act, the Federal Deposit Insurance Corporation, and the Farm Credit Act. In terms of sheer legislative productivity, it was unprecedented. As Roosevelt sat in the White House to sign a number of bills at the close of the whirlwind session, he said, "More history is being made today than in [any] one day of our national life." "During all time, added Oklahoma Senator Thomas Gore."[10]

Millions were given jobs under the proliferating "alphabet agencies." Yet those who were unemployable, either from age or physical disbility, remained outside the scope of the government's assistance. They remained dependent upon the highly variable state assistance. The elderly and the infirm continued to suffer from public neglect, but now something had changed: a situation which just a few years earlier might have seemed consistent with the accepted order of minimal government now began to seem less intolerable.

An effort was made to remedy this situation in June 1934. Roosevelt, recognizing the plight of elderly Americans in the Depression, created the Committee on Economic Security, to investigate what could be done. The committee was to be chaired by Labor Secretary Frances Perkins, the first woman on the cabinet.[11] Others on the Committee included Treasury Secretary Henry Morgenthau, Jr., Attorney General Homer Cummings, Secretary of Agriculture Henry Wallace, and Federal Emergency Relief Administrator Harry Hopkins. Perkins selected Second Assistant Secretary of Labor Arthur Altmeyer to be chairman of the Technical Board. Edwin Witte, chairman of the Economics Department at the University of Wisconsin, was appointed executive director of the committee.

Executive Order 6757, dated June 29, 1934, established the Committee on Economic Security. It called for the Committee to "study the problems relating to the economic security of individuals and shall report to the President not later than December 1, 1934, its recommendations concerning proposals which in its judgement will promote greater economic security."[12]

From the outset it was clear that the Committee would be more than a fact-finding body—it would take an advocacy role. The Committee's initial statement, of August 1934, opened with the words "Economic security is a much broader concept than social insurance, embracing all measures to promote recovery and to develop a more stable economic system, as well as assistance to the victims of insecurity and maladjustment."[13] The statement went on to explain that the Committee's task would be to address the problem of "protection of the individual against dependency and distress."[14]

For Perkins and the other members of the Committee, drawn from academia, business, and government, their job would be to establish a concrete legislative proposal which the president could present to the next Congress, and which could be acted upon while the issue was still prominent in the public mind. The members were chosen for their support of the concept of social insurance, and felt that they had a mandate to deliver such a policy. Roosevelt had "sold himself" to the public, Perkins would later write, on the promise of "cradle to grave" insurance, and had been elected on the basis of that promise. The president wanted it, the public wanted it, and the Committee would deliver it.[15] Executive Director Witte would later record that, contrary to the Committee's publicly stated mission of fact-finding, he "assumed that the primary function of the Committee on Economic Security was not research, but the development of a legislative program to be presented to the next Congress."[16]

This was all to the growing consternation of the business community. When, in an August speech, Roosevelt praised the notion of social security, saying that it provided for "a wider opportunity for the average man," the stock market dropped several points. The concern among business leaders was that private industry would wind up paying the bill for any expansion of social welfare programs.[17] At a time of tremendous economic instability, it was essential to antagonize the business community as little as possible. For the Committee, then, the question of means was as important as that of ends. The broad parameters of the policy goals, after all, were already fairly clear, at least to those inside the process, before the Committee ever met; the problem was how to pay for those goals.

Perkins came upon the solution accidentally, at a social event attended by Supreme Court Justice Harlan Stone. In a conversation with Stone, Perkins told him that the Committee was attempting to develop a system of national social insurance, but was having trouble settling upon a method of paying for it. "Your court," she told him, "tells us what the constitution permits." The justice's casual response would shape the course of American history. Perkins recalled the conversation in her memoirs:

> Stone had whispered, "The taxing power of the Federal government, my dear; the taxing power is sufficient for everything you need."
> This was a windfall. I told the President but bound him to secrecy as to the source of my sudden superior legal knowledge. I insisted in Committee on the taxing power as the method for building up the fund and determining its expenditure for unemployment and old-age benefits to be paid in the future.[18]

Confirmation of the constitutional viablility of the taxing method must have been heartening to Roosevelt, who already considered that as being the most propitious means for implementing the policy and insuring its long-term survival. From the outset, he had decried the notion of one-sided relief, the "dole," wherein citizens would feel they were being given something for nothing. By employing the insurance paradigm, and taxing citizens now for benefits to be received later, Roosevelt would be able to advocate the program as being consistent with the age-old American values of individual autonomy and responsibility.

Use of the payroll tax to pay for the Social Security program would prove to be a critical juncture in the history of American social policy. Citizens would see taxes being taken out of each paycheck for the explicit purpose of paying for the program, creating a sense of individual entitlement. At the individual level that entitlement would become a powerful motivating issue. At the mass level, it would become an inexorable political force.

Roosevelt believed that the sense of personal entitlement would protect his controversial program from politicians who, even as the program was being considered, vowed to abolish it. He was right. Taxes were the answer. With remarkable political foresight, Roosevelt predicted the political inviolability of the program he was creating: "We put those payroll contributions there so as to give the contributors a legal, moral, and political right to collect their pensions and their unemployment benefits. With those taxes in there, no damn politician can ever scrap my social security program."[19]

The president could not have been more right. Once workers had begun paying into the program, it became their own, and no political meddling with it would be tolerated. Even during periods of severe fiscal constraint, when programs for education, for the poor, and for the nation's highways were being cut back, Social Security would remain untouched. It would come to be called the "sacred cow" of American politics. And that modest payroll with which it began would one day absorb more revenue than the federal income tax.

The Committee's report was submitted to the President on the morning of January 17, 1935. By that time there was no surprise regarding either the Committee's focus or its recommendations. The report called for a system of unemployment insurance as a first objective, "since most people must live by work." Unemployment compensation would be a "front line of defense," and was to be administered by the states with funding support from the federal government. A nationally uniform payroll tax would remove the "unfair competitive advantage" employers would have by transferring operations to states which had not adopted a compensation system. The Committee acknowledged that there were risks involved with embarking on such a dramatic new agenda of federal responsibility. The unemployment plan, it acknowledged, would be "frankly experimental." But the greater danger was to do nothing. If government were to delay until there were greater unanimity on the proper course of action, "there will be a long and unwarranted postponement of action."

Old-age security was the second major aspect of the proposal. The Committee recommended a combination of measures: "Noncontributory old age pensions, compulsory old age annuities, and voluntary contributory annuities, all to be applicable on retirement at age of 65 or over." Funds for the old-age pension program were not to be taken from general government revenues, but from a separate reserve created solely for the old-age pensions from contributed funds. The reserve would have to be maintained at about $15,250,000,000, from individual payroll taxes not to exceed $15 monthly per individual. It was a modest beginning, especially in contrast to what it would become.

No benefits would be paid out until after the system had been in operation five years, and none would be paid out to those who had not made at least 200 payments.

The voluntary old-age annuity system would serve as a supplement to the other programs, allowing workers to build up a more comprehensive protection "than it is possible to achieve with pensions based upon a means test."

The Committee also touched upon the question of public health, stating that, although "we are not prepared at this time to make recommendations for a system of health insurance," a nationwide preventive health program would be an initial step. First things first; national health insurance could come later.[20] Roosevelt feared that even the mention of a study on health insurance might jeopardize the entire Social Security program. To avoid the politically sensitive issue altogether, he sent the proposed Social Security legislation to Congress with a message explicitly stating that study of a national health insurance program was not planned at that time. As Witte recalled:

When in 1934 the Committee on Economic Security announced that it was studying health insurance it was at once subjected to misrepresentation and vilification. In the original Social Security bill there was only one line to the effect that the Social Security Board should study the problem and make a report to Congress. That little line was responsible for so many telegrams to members of Congress that the entire social security program seemed endangered until the Ways and Means Committee unanimously struck it out of the bill.[21]

Public health insurance was an incendiary issue in 1934. For decades thereafter, politicians would approach the subject warily. And when a national health insurance program finally was passed, it had been pared down to include only the elderly. The question of comprehensive national health insurance would remain political quicksand half a century later.

SOCIAL SECURITY LEGISLATION

On the same day that the Committee's report was made public, Roosevelt transmitted to Congress the details of his proposed social security program. These policies, he insisted, were at the core of the New Deal's efforts to provide Americans with a "more abundant life." Characteristically, Roosevelt began by pressing for immediate enactment of the program, writing to Congress of the urgency of the issue:

It is my best judgement that this legislation should be brought forward with a minimum of delay. Federal action is necessary to and conditioned upon the actions of the States. Forty four legislatures are meeting or will meet soon. In order that the necessary State action may be taken promptly it is important that the Federal Government proceed speedily.

Roosevelt praised the Committee for avoiding extravagant policy recommendations. It limited itself, he said, to "proposals that will appeal to the sound sense of the American people." By establishing a program of social insurance on a limited scale, Roosevelt noted, the United States would establish it on a firm foundation, but would, nonetheless, be lagging behind "most of the other advanced countries of the world."

Regarding the public's commitment to the elderly, Roosevelt set forth three "principles" which must direct government policy:

First, noncontributory old-age pensions for those who are now too old to build up their own insurance. . . .

Second, compulsory contributory annuities, which in time will establish a self-supporting system for those now young and for future generations.

Third, voluntary contributory annuities by which individual initiative can increase the annual amounts received in old age. It is proposed that the Federal Government assume one-half of the cost of the old-age pension plan, which ought ultimately to be supplanted by self-supporting annuities.

He concluded by saying that the nation was now paying "for the dreadful consequence of economic insecurity" and urged Congress not to "neglect the painful duty before us."[22]

Immediately after clerks had read the presidential message, Representative David Lewis (D-MD) in the House and Senator Robert Wagner (D-NY) in the Senate offered matching bills in their respective chambers. These were immediately referred to the House Ways and Means and the Senate Finance Committees.[23] The proposed legislation closely mirrored the work of the Committee on

Economic Security and, thus, the policy preferences of the President. The principal components were:

1. Protection of the economically distressed elderly (those over 65 years) in the immediate term by means of state pensions, financed half each by the state and Federal governments;
2. A national old-age insurance system, financed through compulsory contributions in equal parts by employers and employees;
3. A government voluntary annuity system for those in higher income categories;
4. Unemployment insurance, financed by a 3% payroll tax;
5. Federal grants to the states for providing widows and children with needed health services.
6. Creation of a Social Insurance Board to oversee the old age and unemployment systems. A Federal Relief Adminstration to oversee direct benefits to the elderly and other dependents. Public Health Service to oversee the distribution of health benefits.[24]

The Economic Security Act, the most important piece of social welfare legislation in American history, was a 13,000-word blueprint for the foundation of a welfare state. In introducing the bill, Senator Wagner called it the "most substantial evidence to date that our twin objectives of recovery and reform are fused in an inseparable unity of purpose and action." The Depression had made a national public commitment to the welfare of the elderly possible and, finally, inevitable. "Old age is a natural phenomenon that descends upon mankind everywhere with unfailing regularity," Wagner explained. "Therefore the bill . . . sets up a Federal system of compulsory old-age insurance . . . which will provide at least the minimum requirements for health and decency to every worker who has reached 65 years of age."[25]

A shift of revolutionary proportions had transpired in the nation's political outlook in the months and years just prior to the creation of the new social welfare program for the elderly. A decade earlier, the members of the Committee on Economic Security had been among the voices in the political wilderness calling for greater social compassion for the elderly. Now, their report was anxiously received by millions of Americans who demanded that government take a greater role. Senator Wagner noted the remarkable transformation of public opinion: "If one contrasts the Economic Security Bill with the public apathy toward the unfortunate that predominated a few years ago, he finds it hard to realize that he is living in the same world."[26]

By the time that Social Security legislation was being considered, the fundamental division in Congress was not over whether there should be a federal commitment to aid the elderly and the needy. Instead, the question had become one of degree: did this bill go far enough?

The divisions that did exist did not fall neatly along party lines. Senator William Borah (R-ID) criticized the plan for inadequately addressing the needs of the elderly: "I am not satisfied to make an outlay of nearly a billion dollars for armaments and $15 for old age."

Senator Charles McNary (R-OR) held a similar view, calling the federal contribution of $15 a month for old-age pensions "an inadequate sum."

Senator James Couzens (R-MI) complained that the bill was "too limited in financial scope."

The expectation of members from both parties was that the Social Security bill would quickly prevail. They were right. Republican Representative Everett Dirksen (IL) seemed to reflect the changed mood of Congress and the nation. "I am for social security," he said. "Why not?"[27]

The day after the bill was introduced, leaders in both houses of Congress began setting into motion the plan whereby the legislation could be passed with a minimum of deliberation and a maximum of haste. In the House, Speaker Joseph Byrns (D-TN) and Appropriations Committee Chairman James Buchanan (D-TX) announced a plan by which the bill would be considered during the next week under a "gag rule" stricly limiting debate. House Ways and Means Committee Chairman Robert Doughton (D-NC) said that deliberations would begin in that committee on the next Monday, and compilation of a list of witnesses was already under way.[28]

It seemed that every Congressman wanted to play a leading role in the unfolding Social Security drama. Witte reported that there was nearly as much friction over who would get prominent roles in directing the bill's passage as there was over the content of the bill itself. When the Speaker of the House referred it to the Ways and Means Committee, Labor Committee Chairman William Connory (D-MA) strenuously objected, insisting that it should pass through his committee instead. Members of Congress were conscious of the historical importance of the legislation, and wanted a place in that history if possible. When it was learned that the Senate Finance Committee intended to begin hearings on Tuesday, January 22, members of the House Ways and Means Committee demanded that hearings begin there one day earlier.[29]

In the process of its deliberations, Congress made a number of modifications of the original draft of the Social Security bill. Of great concern to the Southern members, led by Senator Harry Byrd (D-VA), was the possibility that giving the federal government authority to instruct the states as to who should be paid pensions, might increase the government's control over state racial policies. Southern states, in short, wished to remain free from Washington's interference on issues of racial discrimination.

The Roosevelt administration was pursuing a program of economic, not social, reform in 1935. It did not object when the plan was amended to allow states to determine their own additional qualifications for old-age assistance. On the surface, the nature of these requirements could have dealt with anything: those involved in the process, however, knew that it was a question of race. "The Southern members," Witte wrote, "did not want to give authority to anyone in Washington to deny aid to any state because it discriminated against Negroes in the administration of old age assistance."[30]

On the advice of House legislative counsel Middleton Beaman, the House Ways and Means Committee dropped references to the old-age insurance fund which would have been established under the original bill. Beaman argued that without a separation between the taxing and the benefit program, the already questionable constitutionality of a federal old-age pension plan would be seriously jeopardized. References to an "insurance fund" were dropped from the bill, and a Trust Fund was established in the Treasury to maintain the revenues.

It was a momentous decision. The Social Security program would not be, as originally proposed, a genuine pension system. All connection between funds paid in and benefits received were deleted. Instead, Social Security was to be simply a benefit plan for the elderly. This severing of the connection between taxes paid into the system and benefits taken out would become of vital importance for future generations.

Finally, at the urging of Treasury Secretary Morgenthau, the tax rate structure for the program was altered. Treasury department accountants had calculated that, under proposed payroll tax rates, the program would already be bankrupt by 1965. To solve the problem, tax rates were raised: they would begin at 1% on employers and employees, increasing .5% every three years until a maximum of 3% both on employers and employees was reached in 1949.[31] It was a proposed tax increase to preserve the solvency of a program that had not yet even been enacted into law. It was an omen of things to come.

In the end, conservative opponents of the new legislation were unable even to slow the Social Security juggernaut. What a century before had been inconceivable, and a decade before had been unachievable, was now inevitable. Without roll-call votes, the House, on August 8, 1935, and the Senate, on August 9, passed the Social Security Act. When President Roosevelt signed the bill into law on August 14, he remarked, "If the Senate and the House of Representatives in this long and arduous session had done nothing more than pass this bill, the session would be regarded as historic for all time."[32] America had made a public commitment to its elderly that it had never made before. That commitment would alter the course of American history, and transform the nature of American political life.

4

National Health Care
(For the Elderly)

Decades before the subject was politically viable in the United States, a nationalized policy of health care was put into practice in Germany, under Otto von Bismarck, in 1883. By the first decade of the twentieth century, a dozen European countries had some form of national health insurance. American advocates for national health insurance reforms, meanwhile, were meeting with little success.

Even the modest proposal by the Committee on Economic Security, recommending a study of the possibility of a national health insurance program, provoked such a fierce public reaction that Roosevelt feared it would jeopardize his entire Social Security program. His response, therefore, was to send the Social Security bill to Congress with an explicit assurance that study of a national health insurance program was not planned at that time. The issue has proved to be no less contentious in present times.

TRUMAN'S ADVOCACY FOR HEALTH CARE

Although national health insurance made little headway under Roosevelt, its supporters feared that, with his death, the issue would die altogether. Harry Truman, they believed, was too conservative to provide forceful advocacy for the issue. They were wrong. Truman took up the challenge of national health care more forcefully than his predecessor. In fact, it would be his advocacy that would lay the groundwork for the program that ultimately did prevail.

On November 19, 1945, Truman surprised the nation by asking Congress for a law creating a national health insurance program. His five-point plan called for a compulsory insurance plan nationally, disability pay to replace part of earnings lost due to sickness, expansion of the existing grants-in-aid program to states for the construction of hospital facilites, and the expansion of funding for medical research.

Truman knew that he was dealing with one of the hot-button issues of American politics, and would have to proceed cautiously. From the outset, the president knew that he would have to confront the widespread fear that public involvement in insurance would constitute "creeping socialism." To offset those concerns, he presented the program as reflecting the highest capitalist ideals. Americans, Truman said in presenting the plan, are "the most insurance-minded people in the world," they

will not be frightened off from health insurance because some people have misnamed it "socialized medicine."

I am in favor of the broadest possible coverage for this insurance system. I believe that all persons who work for a living and their dependents should be covered under such an insurance plan.[1]

A Republican majority in Congress doomed any such initiative during years immediately following the Second World War, and the issue slipped to the background. With the election of 1948, however, Truman believed that the time for his insurance program had come. It will be recalled that in that election, Truman, who had been counted out for most of the campaign, rallied to defeat Dewey, and carried with him a substantial Democratic majority in Congress. Democratic political prospects had seemed to make a U-turn, moving from 188 seats in the House of Representatives in the preceding 80th Congress, to 263 seats after the election. National health care had been an important part of the campaign. In his State of the Union message that year, Truman had vigorously renewed the call for a national health program, linking it with the existing Social Security system:

The greatest gap in our Social Security structure is the lack of adequate provision for the nation's health. We are rightly proud of the high standards of medical care we know how to provide in the United States. The fact is, however, that most of our people cannot afford to pay for the care they need.

I have often and strongly urged that this condition demands a national health program. The heart of the program must be a system of payment for medical care based on well-tried insurance principles. This great nation cannot afford to allow its citizens to suffer needlessly from the lack of proper medical care.

Our proper aim must be a comprehensive insurance system to protect all our people equally against insecurity and ill-health.[2]

Despite vigorous presidential advocacy, intense opposition by the powerful American Medical Association (AMA) meant that, even with a 263-171 Democratic partisan advantage, Truman got nowhere with the issue. If the measure could not pass under those conditions, advocates wondered, would it ever pass?

These concerns were accentuated in the 1950 elections. The AMA launched a massive nationwide campaign to warn of the perils of compulsory "socialized medicine," and the issue of a nationalized health insurance program became a central focus of the campaign. Governor Thomas Dewey of New York, still a leading figure in the Republican party following his defeat in the 1948 presidential race, remained an active critic of the administration. He promised to make Truman's proposal for "socialized medicine" a "central issue" in American politics. It was an issue on which Republicans were highly unified and Democrats were deeply divided. Asserting that he had no further interest in running for national office, Dewey insisted that it was possible to provide health care for all Americans, "without the taint of socialized medicine."[3]

The AMA, meanwhile, was launching a $3 million campaign to oppose what was regarded as a serious threat to the interests of its members. It worked. Opposition by the organization in the 1950 election was cited as making a critical difference in several elections. The AMA successfully targeted for defeat several senators who had been most prominent in promoting Truman's program.[4] The message was clear: advocate national insurance at your own risk.

The battle was waged fiercely by on both sides. The AMA charged that the Committee for the Nation's Health (an important national advocacy group which included as members Eleanor Roosevelt and future Supreme Court Justice Abe Fortas), had taken on a "pinkish pigmentation," and "definite hues of red."[5] These were serious allegations at a time when Senator Joe McCarthy had made the "red scare" a prominent national issue.

Some physicians, meanwhile, charged that the AMA was conducting a campaign of intimidation to keep its own members in line. Dr. Theodore Sanders of New York, attending the mid-term Democratic convention in New York, complained that the AMA "has succeeded in convincing the average physician that a kind word about the national health insurance program is a mighty risky gesture, which could well jeopardize his practice, his hospital positions, his opportunity to socialize, and even lay him open to malicious attack. Given this kind of intimidation, it is hard to know what a doctor really thinks, or as a matter of fact if he has thought the problem through."[6] The Democratic platform ultimately supported the president's plan, but only after a bitter and divisive political struggle.[7] The AMA wielded clout in both parties.

As a tax-exempt entity, the American Medical Association was not able to become directly involved in the 1950 congressional campaigns. Instead, physicians throughout the nation formed "local committees" to defeat candidates who supported Truman's health programs. Among those they helped to defeat was the influential Florida Senator Claude Pepper. In his autobiography, Pepper recalled that his support of federal programs for Truman's health insurance proposal drew charges from the medical lobby that he was a communist. In his 1950 Senate race, Pepper's opponent George Smathers capitalized on the AMA's smear campaign, circulating reports that "Red Pepper" had been endorsed by the Communist *Daily Worker*. A "Red Record" was distributed, depicting

Pepper as anxious to squander the nation's resources and betray American secrets to the Soviets.[8] "Crimson," Smathers told Florida voters "just happened to be Harvard's color" (Harvard was Pepper's alma mater).[9]

Pepper attributed his defeat to his support for national health insurance. The AMA, wrote Pepper, "poured money into the Florida race to help Smathers win, or rather to make certain that Pepper lost."[10]

Unable to campaign openly, the AMA launched an unsubtle covert campaign against national health insurance a month before the 1950 election. The campaign took the guise of a drive to increase enrollments in private health insurance plans. Advertisements were placed in every major newspaper and weekly magazine in the nation, warning of encroachments from the "enemies of free enterprise." Some 1,600 radio stations broadcast similar advertisements.[11]

If the election returns were any measure, the AMA was effective in promoting its views. The off-year election produced a record turnout of 40 million voters, and gave Republicans—who, with 47 seats already had effective control of the issue in the Senate—greater influence in the House. The party's strength there increased from a 171-263 disadvantage to a more competitive legislative balance of 199-234. In combination with conservative Southern Democrats, it would be more than enough to assure defeat for any efforts at major health care reform.

The final blow came in April 1951, when the now conservative-dominated House passed a measure, termed by its sponsors an "antipropaganda amendment," aimed specifically at Federal Security Administrator Oscar Ewing, who had been making speeches promoting the president's plan. The provision, proposed by Lawrence Smith (R-WI) stated that no funds in the year's appropriations bill could be used for "publicity or propaganda not heretofore authorized by Congress." Representative Smith singled out Ewing, criticizing him for "constantly propagandizing the country on socialized medicine."[12]

The president's advisors admitted defeat, sort of. A comprehensive national health insurance program seemed politically dead for the time being, but the issue was not buried altogether. Instead, Federal Security Administrator Ewing suggested to Truman that a more limited plan might have better legislative prospects. A program, specifically, targeting the elderly, the same group that already benefited from the existing Social Security system.

The idea had come to Ewing one evening while having cocktails at the house of William Randolph Hearst. Ewing was complaining to Hearst that the existing plan was at a political impasse. Hearst responded that, rather than trying for the whole ball of wax in one round, a more modest initial tack might be more successful. Instead, suggested Hearst, a "pilot plan" might be tried on a limited segment of the population. In that way it could be shown to work effectively and gradually be expanded to more universal coverage.

A few days later, another part of the puzzle was suggested to Ewing while he visited Louis Pink, head of the Blue Cross hospital insurance system in New York. Pink suggested that the plan could be most helpful to the over-65 age group. Combining the two, Ewing came up with an idea for a nationalized health insurance plan for the elderly.[13] It would be a way, he hoped, of getting the camel's nose under the tent. Once the elderly had been insured, the plan could be gradually expanded, as had happened in other countries. Fewer in number, and in more clearly legitimate need, senior citizens would be an easier sell to Congress, and could thus be used to pave the way for a broader program.[14]

By shifting the plan's focus from the general population to the elderly, the administration hoped that it would receive a more favorable hearing in Congress. While a plan of general health insurance for all Americans might be caricatured as a "socialist encroachment," who could oppose 60 days of medical care for elderly Americans? At a press conference announcing the scaled-down plan, Wilbur Cohen, senior advisor to Federal Security Agency chief Ewing, put it in precisely those terms: "It is difficult for me to see how anyone with a heart can oppose this."[15] The elderly were not selected to be the beneficiaries of Medicare for their political power, but for their sympathetic appeal. The political power would come in due time.

Older Americans were the ultimate vulnerable population. They were, through no fault of their own, less able to earn an income, less able to procure insurance, and more prone to illness. Cohen would later say that the amassed aggregate data became a "steamroller," crushing opponents' arguments.[16] Ewing was right: seniors could be portrayed as a group which had contributed to the nation's prosperity, and now needed the nation's help. Once the program had been established on behalf of the elderly, it could be expanded to cover other groups. Theodore Marmor, the noted analyst of the Medicare program, puts it bluntly: "The concentration on the burdens of the elderly was a ploy for sympathy."[17]

REPUBLICAN PARTY OPPOSITION

But the opposition was not impressed by the reduced scale of the proposed program. With the 1952 presidential campaign season now getting into full swing, the issue had become a hot election topic, and one which the Republicans felt they could use to their advantage. In announcing his candidacy for the presidency on October 16, 1951, Republican Senator Robert Taft (OH) promised to run on the "principles of liberty of the individual . . . of economic freedom and not on the New Deal philosophy of constant increase in Federal government power and Federal government spending." According to Taft, "growing socialism and government control" was "the greatest domestic issue before the people." He warned of the "concealed socialism" in Truman's health insurance proposal. "Socialized medicine not only violates the principle of extending aid only to those unable to pay, but it also proposes to nationalize the whole medical profession and completely destroys the power of our cities and counties to control the distribution of care."[18] From the outset of the campaign season, the issue promised to take center stage in American politics, and once again to put Truman on the defensive.

General Dwight D. Eisenhower, now candidate Eisenhower, also sensed the political utility of the issue, and put it center stage in his own campaign. In his first major press conference as presidential candidate, Eisenhower joined the chorus of voices warning against national health insurance, even of the scaled-down variety. "Beyond pure socialism, I believe, lies pure dictatorship and you can't escape it. . . . [The health insurance plan] was the first step toward the socialization of medicine and I'm against it."[19]

Private insurance companies, meanwhile, did what they could to undermine Truman's public health insurance initiative. Prudential Insurance Company of America, for example, the second largest insurer in the country, announced in June 1951 that it would begin selling "catastrophic" medical insurance. The new program was intended, according to company President Carrol Shanks, "to combat the possibility of socialized medicine." Until then, Shanks admitted, the insurance industry had "largely ignored its responsibilities to provide . . . complete protection in this regard." Through its oversight, it had unwittingly been "playing into the hands of advocates of Government insurance and socialized medicine." It would now begin to remedy this neglect.[20]

In addition, the AMA continued its alliance with the Republicans. At the Republican National Convention that year, it submitted a plank that summed up everything that people feared about the proposed program: "We reaffirm our vigorous opposition to national compulsory health insurance or another form of socialized medicine which would institute governmental control over both patients and doctors, lower the quality of medical care, impose heavy new tax burdens on all the people and undermine the American system of enterprise."[21]

The broad national coalition of interests arrayed against Truman's proposed insurance program was having its effect, even among Democrats. Governor Adlai Stevenson of Illinois, having clinched the Democratic nomination by late summer, recognized the political power of the forces opposing the plan, and was unwilling to take them on. Instead, Stevenson hedged: "I am against socialization of the practice of medicine as much as I would be against the socialization of my own profession," he explained.[22]

Even before the end of Truman's term, then, his legacy of forceful advocacy on behalf of national health care for the elderly seemed to be for naught. His own party was not even taking up the struggle. The 1952 Democratic party platform, issued in July, seemed to be a backstep from the party's previous commitment. It called for "modern medicine" and greater government control over spiraling health care costs. "We recognize that the costs of medical care have grown prohibitive for millions of Americans."[23] No solution was offered. The attacks of the AMA and other groups had had the desired effect.

The AMA, meanwhile, was undergoing an attack of its own. In the October edition of *The Atlantic,* Dr. James Means, professor of medicine at Harvard University and Chief of Medical Services at Massachussetts General Hospital, wrote an article on the organization's waging of the campaign against Truman's health insurance proposal. As an interest group, Means wrote, the AMA (from which he had resigned his membership the previous year) was uniquely positioned to advocate its own interests, almost to monopolize the field of discussion of medical policy. Doctor knows best. Indeed, not only did the AMA dominate discussion, but the leadership of the Association typically acted in an authoritarian manner within the AMA itself. Thus, when the organization's legislative body, the "House of Delegates," voted in December 1948 to assess a fee of $25 to each member to raise the $3.5 million "political war chest" with which to fight the Truman plan, "there was some fuzziness as to whether this assessment was to be obligatory or voluntary, although the word is hardly interpretable as 'voluntary.'"[24]

A learned profession has sunk, or been dragged, in its political sphere, to a distressingly low level. Individually the American doctor of medicine is, in most instances, an honest, sincere, and generous person. . . . When he organizes, however, his collective behavior is, at times, less noble than that which he displays when acting on his own initiative.[25]

The *Journal of the American Medical Association* had refused to accept an advertisement from *The Atlantic* touting the upcoming issue in which the Means article was to appear. This caused D.B. Snyder, the magazine's publisher, to assert that the Association "is hostile to discussion of present-day medical services, even by one of the foremost medical men in America."[26]

Pointing to the oligarchic nature of the Association, Truman called it a "little clique" that was attempting to use tactics of political intimidation to protect its special interests. At a speech in Sedalia, Missouri, he read a memo from a local doctor's committee giving instructions on how to rally support at an upcoming parade for Republican vice-presidential candidate Richard Nixon: "In order to make the best possible impression on the general public," the memo had said, "we are asking you to use a small car if that is at all possible." The Democrats would win the election, Truman predicted, with the "small car vote, from the genuine small car people . . . with the corporals and the privates."[27] They didn't.

Dwight Eisenhower defeated Democratic candidate Adlai Stevenson by a margin of 6 million votes in November 1952, and was reelected in 1956. He received substantial campaign support from the AMA, and aggressively denounced any nationalized health program as "socialized medicine."[28] Thus, with a president who opposed it, and most prominent national politicians having been intimidated into silence, the issue again returned to the political back-burner during the Eisenhower years.[29]

KENNEDY'S MODEST PROPOSAL

The election of 1960 marked a turning point for the politics of young and old in America. The Presidential campaign of John F. Kennedy, often noted for its youthful aspect, became the first to note the shifting demographics in the country and consciously target the "senior vote" as a discrete voting bloc. The Democratic party established "Senior Citizens for Kennedy," in order to attract older voters. The question of whether government had a legitimate role in promoting the welfare of such a large group had long since been resolved: Democrats now sought to exploit growing sentiment among seniors that government wasn't doing enough.

The organization had little impact on the senior vote, or on the outcome of the election.[30] But by focusing the attention of top political strategists on the political potential of the elderly, the group would be an important portent of things to come. Some 13 million Americans over the age of 65 had voted in the election, 79% of the 17 million eligible senior citizens. Political analysts recognized that the elderly had a higher voter turnout than any other age group in the country, and there were more and more of them. Furthermore, it was beginning to be noticed that the elderly could be appealed to as a single voting bloc. "Elderly votes," writes political gerontologist Henry Pratt, "could be appealed to, like the farm vote or the Negro vote, on the basis of their own separate identity and self-interest."[31]

The election of 1960 was a modest beginning. With the Democrats pursuing such a potentially important constituency, it was inevitable that in a short time the Republicans should join the effort. And with politicians courting them as a group sharing common political interests, senior citizens soon came to think of themselves in those same terms.

Partly as a component of its effort to attract older voters, Kennedy's New Frontier platform prominently featured a program of medical insurance for the elderly.

It was not an empty promise. Days after taking office, Kennedy called for a broad program of government health insurance for Americans over the age of 65. In a speech before Congress, he said that the work of providing genuine Social Security to elderly Americans was incomplete. There remained a gap in welfare protection: "the high cost of ill-health in old age."

Kennedy's plan drew heavily upon the Truman proposal. It emphasized free choice in the selection of medical services, and included an extension of Social Security benefits to encompass health care. This was to be financed by a 0.25% Social Security tax increase. Specifically, it provided for 90 days of hospital care (with deductibles of $10 per day for the first nine days); 180 days of in-home nursing care following hospitalization; out patient diagnostic services in excess of $20; and follow-up nursing services. These services would apply to all individuals eligible for Social Security or railroad retirement benefits. The increase in the Social Security tax by 0.25% and an increase in the maximum earnings base from $4,800 to $5,000 would be sufficient to cover all costs of the added program.

Aware of the controversy surrounding the first attempt at a national health plan, Kennedy assured the Congress that "this program is not a program of socialized medicine. It is a program of prepayment of health costs with absolute freedom of choice guaranteed. Every person will choose his own doctor and hospital." The program was, he assured skeptics, a "very modest proposal." The "unfinished business" of health care for older Americans must now be the top priority of the administration and Congress.[32]

Immediately, the usual array of organizations on both sides of the issue sprang into action, and as usual, the AMA dominated the debate. As part of "Operation Hometown" each local branch of the Association was sent a package of materials instructing how to help defeat the proposal for "socilized medicine." It included prepared speeches—and instructions on giving them: "look interested during the meeting," "radiate authority," and "be friendly, warm, humble, smile"—and pamphlets, to let every congressperson "know that Medicare is really 'Fedicare'—a costly concoction of bureaucracy, bad medicine, and an unbalanced budget."[33]

Even a strong Democratic party advantage of 263 to 174 in the House was inadequate to form a consistent, working legislative majority for Kennedy. In health care and in many other areas, it was a time of political gridlock. Given the power of the "conservative coalition," a combination of Republicans and conservative (mainly Southern) Democrats, 16 of the 25 members of the House Ways and Means Committee opposed the Medicare concept. They were able to easily tie up the measure in committee.

Pursuing an agenda of other high-priority issues, Kennedy was reluctant to go to the mat for a proposal that was doomed from the start. He accepted the bill's defeat in committee, but aggressively campaigned to influence public opinion on the issue.[34] His efforts must have had some impact: at the height of Kennedy's public campaign for Medicare, in the summer of 1961, polls showed that 67% of Americans supported the proposed policy.[35]

LYNDON JOHNSON: VICTORY AT LAST

More than any other event of the period, the assassination of John F. Kennedy on November 22, 1963, changed political discourse in the United States. Kennedy had been the first president to take a deep interest in developing ties with the elderly as a potential political constituency, including activities both at the White House and elsewhere. But he had been unable to achieve legislative success on the issue of health care for the elderly, and when it came time to set legislative priorities, this had not been at the top. Civil rights and economic issues were more pressing. For Lyndon Johnson, in the election of 1964, it was made a cornerstone of the Great Society agenda. By 1964, after years of advocacy for Medicare by proponents in and out of government, with an increasingly activist bloc of older voters pressing for its passage, and with greater than two-to-one support in the public at large, the program was the most popular issue the Democrats possessed.[36]

Having aggressively advocated passage of Medicare during the 1964 campaign, Johnson regarded his election as a national mandate for the program. In addition, Democrats had made substantial gains in the House of Representatives (from 258 to 290 seats), and now enjoyed a nearly two-to-one margin over Republicans, who had fallen to only 140 seats. The election meant a 44-seat gain for House supporters of the Medicare proposal.[37]

Perceiving the inevitable, and wishing to retain some influence over the outcome, House Ways and Means Committee Chairman Wilbur Mills, a conservative Democrat from Arkansas, took up the issue as the first item of committee business in 1965. After years of tying up the issue in committee, Mills now switched to support for Medicare.

Supporters of the bill, sensing the new popularity of their issue, put pressure on Congress to expand the proposed level of benefits. Congress, in no mood to put up a fight on the issue, went along. The resulting changes yielded huge additions to the program as it had first been conceived, and included the important physician payments (now Part B of the Medicare program).

A bidding war ensued. The House had wanted 60 days of hospital care with a $40 deductible. The Senate plan called for unlimited duration with $10 copayment for each day over 60. The final compromise included the House benefits as well as the Senate's $10 copayment addition for 30 days longer. Such "compromises," in which both sides were given what they wanted, resulted in adding provision for 100 days of posthospital care, 100 home health care visits, 20% copayment on outpatient diagnostic services, and 190 days of psyciatric services.[38] The House passed the Medicare bill on July 27, 1965, by a margin of 307-116. The Senate followed two days later, by a margin of 70-24.

The ceremonial signing of the bill was held at the Harry S. Truman Memorial Library in Independence, Missouri, so that Truman, himself now well into his "senior" years, could be present. It was an emotional day. Johnson signed Title 18 of the Social Security Act, referring to the "long years of struggle" which so many had put into passage of the legislation.

No longer will older Americans be denied the healing miracle of modern medicine. No longer will illness crush and destroy the savings that they have so carefully put away over a lifetime so that they might enjoy dignity in their later years. No longer will young families see their own incomes and their own hopes eaten away simply because they are carrying out their deep moral obligations to their parents and to their uncles and aunts. And no longer will this nation refuse the hand of justice to those who have given a lifetime of service and wisdom and labor to the progress of this progressive country.[39]

The ailing Truman expressed his satisfaction at the bill's passage in a brief speech. "These people are our prideful responsibility," he said, "and they are entitled, among other benefits, to the best medical protection available." He thanked Johnson for his "inspired leadership and responsiveness." "Mr. President, I'm glad to have lived this long and to witness today the signing of the Medicare bill, which puts the nation right where it needs to be."[40] A generation after the passage of the original Social Security Act, the agenda it had established was finally being fulfilled.

The powerful AMA had been defeated. In June, *Medical World News* declared, "After nearly two decades of struggle and controversy, million-dollar advertising drives, rallies, and political-action campaigns, the AMA's crusade has failed. And in the opinion of many knowledgeable people in Washington, the AMA's own strategy of uncompromising resistance contributed to the dimensions of the defeat."[41] The defeat of the AMA, though, was not primarily a victory by the elderly. They remained rather weak and incipient as a political force, with more potential than actual power. Throughout the period that Medicare was under consideration, public policy for the aged continued to be a matter of politics for the elderly rather than politics by the elderly. Political scientist Theodore Lowi observes that "the only surprise in the Medicare case was the difficulty of passage. But that was due to a contest not between liberalism and conservatism but between the unorganized and apathetic elderly and the intensely felt and highly organized trade union interests of the American Medical Association."[42]

The interests of the elderly would come into conflict again, in later years, with the AMA, and with other powerful, organized interests. Henceforth, however, seniors would be better armed. After a history without much organization or unity, the elderly now had substantial incentive for both. The process of coming together as a single political bloc had begun slowly after the passage of Social Security. In the wake of the struggle over Medicare, and its eventual passage, the process accelerated. These policies for the elderly, based upon the vulnerability of older Americans, provided the rationale of shared interests that would make them, in the view of many, the most powerful political group in the nation. The "gray lobby" now had abundant reason to coalesce, to defend its political gains, and to work for more. As it did, it would, in time, become as organizationally sophisticated and politically adept as those groups which had worked so hard against passage of the programs designed to assist older Americans.

5

The Programs That Ate the Government

It started out so well. Social Security and Medicare were funded by a rapidly growing economy and provided a vital security net for the most vulnerable Americans. They were, in addition, under control. Their payment obligations were strictly limited, and spending projections were moderate. Social Security, as originally created, barely covered a majority of working Americans, and its benefits were modest.[1] The Medicare budget, government economists said, would still be under $10 billion a year in 1990.[2] (They were off by over $100 billion). Surely a country with the vast economic resources of the United States, the world's unchallenged economic leader, could afford to spend that small sum to free the poorest of its elderly from poverty's grip.

Things changed. Benefits expanded. Life expectancy expanded. The number of elderly, and the proportion of elderly, grew rapidly. The proportion of the elderly who qualify for benefits expanded. The link between what one paid into the system, and what one was entitled to receive, diminished. And political control over the growth of the programs became negligible.

Now, the programs are in crisis. Trustees for the Social Security fund report that it will be bankrupt early in the twenty-first century. Medicare trustees warn that it will be bankrupt around the end of the 1990s. Bipartisan, non-partisan, and public interest committees have been formed to address the problem, and all have warned of the need to take immediate action in order to prevent future catastrophe. But the political system has done nothing, fearing the leviathan political clout of the elderly. Lifelong politicians have given up political careers and left Washington in frustration over the inability of the system to resolve, or even meaningfully address, what is now a problem, but will become a crisis if the present course is maintained.

In President Bill Clinton's address to the Bipartisan Commission on Entitlement and Tax Reform, established with high-ranking members of both parties to dissipate the political heat inevitably generated by any discussion of controlling what has come to be called "entitlement spending," he hinted at the politically incendiary nature of the subject: "Many may regard this as a thankless task," the president said. "It will not be thankless if it gives us a strong and secure and healthy American economy and society moving into the 21st century."[3] He was not exaggerating what was at stake.

Ultimately, the Commission concluded that if America was indeed to maintain a strong and secure economy into the next century, major reforms needed to be undertaken, starting immediately. It warned that current policies would lead to a situation, by 2012, in which "projected outlays for entitlements and interest on the national debt will consume all tax revenues collected by the Federal government."[4] The dramatic statement failed to create much of a stir in Washington, not because it was believed to be hyperbole, but because the facts regarding the entitlement crisis were already generally known. Politicians were already aware of the problem, and had already decided to avoid tackling it head-on. The Commission's recommendations were as a capsule shot off into space, containing signs of intelligent life on earth and waiting for a response from somewhere out there. As of yet, there has been none.

Why not? What is it about America's programs for the elderly that has transformed the nation's political life and national budget? How did Social Security and Medicare become programs that we cannot afford and cannot reduce? How did we get here from those (relatively) modest beginnings, and why are we stuck?

THE INSURANCE PRINCIPLE IN POLITICS

Suppose that you could vote to increase the value of your private pension fund, or raise the benefits of your private insurance program, far out of proportion to any increase in cost to yourself. Sound tempting? In private programs such manipulation of benefits is impossible, because there must be some connection between what we pay into the system and what we can receive. With public programs, however, such a linkage is not mandated. In both Social Security and Medicare, the individual retiree, like the beneficiary of a private health insurance program, has virtually no personal interest in controlling the costs of the system: no matter how great the benefits I receive, it will not materially affect my personal costs. Why not try, then, to get as much out of the system as I possibly can? Yet, when that logic is used by tens of millions, overall costs escalate out of control.

That fact, combined with the political benefit to be gained by politicians promising to increase benefits to the elderly, and then distributing the costs of those benefits broadly across the population, produced decades of incremental expansion of the programs. Yet even incremental growth starts to compound upon itself, and can eventually become something more enormous than anyone had envisioned, or that anyone can control.

The first major revision of Social Security occurred just a few years after its passage, and presaged what was to come. In 1939, Congress entirely abandoned the analogy of the private insurance program which had been necessary to sell the Social Security program to the public, and adopted the pay-as-you-go system that continues to arouse such emotion today.[5] Under the original plan, it was necessary for the system to be self-sustaining: that is, the benefits that individuals received could, on average, be no greater than their contributions into the system, with accumulated interest. But under the pay-as-you-go system, current expenditures are funded by taxes currently paid in, not by past investments of particular recipients. The effect was to remove the need for actuarial balance. The link between what one paid into the system and what one could receive disappeared.

What a worker now pays into the system is not being invested for his own retirement, but is being given to someone currently retired. When that worker, in turn, retires, his level of benefits will not depend strictly on how much he has paid into the system, but on the degree to which Congress is willing to tax those who are employed at the time.

Without the necessity for actuarial balance, the programs became subject to enormous political pressures. In promising future benefits, politicians need not be constrained by past contributions. If there are many workers contributing and few retirees covered, benefits may be distributed generously, because there is no need to invest the funds. What happens when those workers wish to retire is a question for future politicians to cope with.

Coverage was extended, and benefits did expand. In 1940, only 57.8% of workers were employed in fields covered by Social Security; today, less than 10% are not covered: less than a third of employees of state & local governments, civilian employees of the Federal government hired before 1984, and some "casual workers" such as babysitters and housekeepers.[6] In 1950, 15 years after the inception of the program, only a 25% of Americans over age 65 qualified to receive Old-Age Insurance pensions; by the 1980s, 95% did.[7]

When the economy was flourishing, politicians felt free to expand program obligations. Prosperity seemed easy and natural, and the federal government had a rapidly growing pie of resources to distribute. In the postwar boom of the early 1950s, benefit levels were increased 77%.[8] When Secretary of Health, Education and Welfare Wilbur Cohen came to the President Johnson requesting a 10% across-the-board hike in Social Security benefits, Johnson responded, "Come on, Wilbur, you can do better than that!"[9] Other benefit increases would follow, including a 20% increase in 1972. Times were good, and politicians could afford to be generous with benefits for their elderly constituents.

Just as important as raising benefit levels, though, was Congress' passage of a "cost-of-living-adjustment" (COLA) clause, also passed in 1972, that required automatic increases in benefits whenever the Consumer Price Index rose 3% or more.[10] After increasing Social Security benefits and coverage during years of plenty, Congress had surrendered control over future increases. Now, those increases would be automatic.

For Medicare, similarly, expansion was gradual, accelerating when the economy was booming, slowing when the economy slowed. And since coverage was quite generous from the outset, expansion of benefits was more modest. Growth of costs, as we shall see, was not.

Medicare Part A, which accounts for roughly two-thirds of total Medicare spending, is the part of the program in which participation is mandatory. Like Social Security, it is funded by payroll taxes—"contributions." In 1966, when the program went into effect, it provided health insurance benefits for all those covered by Social Security. Coverage primarily included 90 days of inpatient hospital services, such as a semiprivate room, operating costs, lab tests, and so on. Hospital diagnostic services and another 100 days of home medical visits were included, as was 190 days (during a lifetime) of inpatient care at a psychiatric hospital. Benefits added since the inception of the program include coverage for new treatments such as liver transplants, and unlimited home health care for those who qualify.[11]

Participation in Medicare B is voluntary. Those who participate pay monthly premiums in return for coverage of services not provided by Part A. These include physician services, rental of home medical equipment, outpatient medical care, and 100 days of in-home health care for those not covered by Part A. While politics has not greatly expanded the benefits for recipients in this area, costs have risen markedly. Medicare B, as crafted in 1966, was designed to be funded half by the monthly premiums paid by beneficiaries, and half by general tax revenues. Today, premiums account for only 28% of the program's costs. In ten years, they will account for only 17%. General tax revenues of the federal government fund the rest.[12]

THE DEMOGRAPHIC DILEMMA

Politics, clearly, has contributed to the costs of the entitlement programs for the elderly. But in the long run, the activity of politicians may seem marginal in comparison with inexorable demographic forces. For, while politics can tinker with benefit levels, it cannot control the twin demographic phenomena of the modern age: the remarkable extension of life expectancy, and the contraction of fertility. People are living longer, much longer than ever before in history; and they are having fewer children. The former increases the costs of our programs for the elderly, the latter magnifies the effects of those increases on workers. Either condition alone would dislocate a society's provisions for its elderly. Together, they will reshape society altogether.

AN AGING NATION

America is not a young country anymore. In 1900, life expectancy in the United States was 47 years. Today, it is 75 years, an increase of 28 years in the span of less than a century.[13] Put another way, life expectancy has advanced an average of one year during every three years of this century. It is unprecedented in human history (see Table 5.1[14]).

In 1935, when Social Security was established, life expectancy was 63 years. The retirement age was purposely set at 65, beyond average life expectancy, so that most Americans would not live long enough in their retirement years to impose much of a burden on the system. The likelihood of an individual worker living long beyond the period when one became eligible for benefits was actuarially small, and was offset by those who died before they became eligible. Put bluntly, most people did not live long enough to strain the system. In 1945, only 771,000 Americans received Social Security benefits. In 1995, over 35 million received them. By 2045, the Social Security Administration reports, 72 million will.[15]

Incremental increases in life expectancy can have dramatic consequences for the costs of government programs for the elderly, since the time added to life is tacked on entirely to the retirement years. Thus, between 1935 and 1995, life expectancy increased from 61.7 years to 76.3 years, less than a one-fifth increase in overall life expectancy. But, while life was prolonged by 20%, retirement was extended by more than 1000% during that period, having a huge impact on spending for those programs.

If the system were viewed as a private insurance program, in order to remain actuarially intact it would have been necessary to revise the benefits formula to compensate for advancing life expectancy. Other factors being constant, as life expectancy was extended, it would have been necessary to extend the retirement age, the time when one could start to receive benefits. What is economically utilitarian, of course, is not always politically plausible, or even socially desirable. But if the retirement age is not extended, some similarly substantial measure must be taken to account for increasing longevity. As longevity continues to advance, no such measure has been taken. The average 65-

Table 5.1
Life Expectancy at Birth

1900	47.3 years	1950	68.2 years
1905	48.7	1955	69.6
1910	50.0	1960	69.7
1915	54.5	1965	70.2
1920	54.1	1970	70.9
1925	59.0	1975	72.6
1930	59.7	1980	73.7
1935	61.7	1985	74.7
1940	62.9	1990	75.4
1945	65.9	1995	76.3

year-old who starts collecting Social Security in 1995 can expect to receive those benefits for 17 more years.[16] And, while life extension has been one of the great triumphs of the twentieth century, it has brought challenges, as the number of Americans who live 65 years and beyond has skyrocketed (Table 5.2[17]).

Increasing longevity is affecting one end of the age spectrum: there are more elderly than before. Another modern phenomenon is affecting the other end: we are having fewer children (Table 5.3[18]). More retirees at one end, fewer youngsters on the other. The result is an aging population, and a growing proportion of retirees (Table 5.4[19]).

The combination of declining fertility and advancing life expectancy magnifies the relative economic burden that each senior puts upon the system. There are fewer workers to support him, and he will spend more years in retirement than earlier generations. The shift in the composition of the population, with

Table 5.2
Number of Americans Age 65 and Older (in thousands)

Year	Number
1900	3,080
1910	3,949
1920	4,933
1930	6,634
1940	9,019
1950	12,269
1960	16,560
1970	19,980
1980	25,550
1990	31,079

Table 5.3
U.S. Fertility Rate

Year	Rate
1900	3.38
1910	3.42
1920	3.26
1930	2.53
1940	2.23
1950	3.03
1960	3.61
1970	2.43
1980	1.78
1990	1.81

Table 5.4
Percent of Americans 65 and Over

1900	4.0
1910	4.3
1920	4.7
1930	5.4
1940	6.8
1950	8.1
1960	9.2
1970	9.8
1980	11.3
1990	12.6

Table 5.5
Elderly Support Ratios (number of people 65 and older per 100 people age 18 to 24)

Year	65+
1900	7
1920	8
1940	11
1960	17
1980	19
1990	20

relatively fewer young people and more elderly, has altered the nature of the "support ratio": a rough estimate for the economic burden upon workers placed by the nonworkers in society (Table 5.5[20]). The ratio compares the number of those in the working-age population (age 18-64), with the number of those beyond typical working age. The result is an inexact but useful indication of the relative economic burden placed by retirees upon workers.

In 1900 there were only 7 Americans aged 65 and older for every 100 aged 18-65. When Social Security was created, there were ten workers for every retiree. By 1990 that figure had dropped by half: there were only five workers for every retiree. Even if the costs of aging had not changed between 1935 and 1990, the economic burden on the average worker would have doubled.

But the costs have increased, mainly because of developments in medical technology that have allowed us to live longer, but at enormous expense. Indeed, technological breakthroughs have made those over age 85 (those whom demographers refer to as the "oldest old"), the fastest-growing age segment in the population (Table 5.6[21]). Americans are not just living longer than 65 years, they are living a lot longer.

THE VERY HIGH COST OF LIVING

In the earlier years of life, medicine typically protects us from, and cures us of, less expensive diseases. It is as life progresses that the expensive diseases, such as cancers and cardiovascular disease, affect a larger portion of the population. They require more heroic—and more costly—measures to cure the disease and extend the life. And the cost of treatment increases progressively with age (Table 5.7[22]).

Table 5.6
Americans Age 85 and Over

Year	Thousands
1900	123
1910	167
1920	210
1930	272
1940	365
1950	577
1960	929
1970	1,409
1980	2,240
1990	3,254

Table 5.7
Personal Health Care
Expenditures, by Age, 1987

Age	Per Capita Amount
19-64	$1,286
65-69	3,728
70-74	4,424
75-79	5,455
80-84	6,717
85 and over	9,178

For every 100 Americans 65 and older, there are an average of 100 acute medical conditions per year, requiring an average of eight days per year of restricted activity.[23] Over 80% of older citizens suffer from at least one acute condition in a given year.[24]

Each year, nearly 85% of seniors interact with physicians or medical facilities,[25] and 37% are hospitalized, for an average stay of around nine days.[26] Older Americans are more likely to become ill, and that illness is likely to be more expensive to treat, than any other age group. Some 75% of all deaths among the elderly are related to heart disease, cancer, or stroke—illnesses which require the most intensive medical treatment for each increment of prolonged life.[27] It is expensive to stay alive.

The later years of life have been extended by modern medicine, and the quality of those years has been immensely enriched, but the costs of doing so have been substantial, and are rapidly rising. Medicine has advanced in cost as it has progressed in technological sophistication.

When escalating costs of medical technology are compounded with an expanding senior population, the result is a Medicare program with expenses rising out of control. In 1965, when Medicare was created, the program cost the federal government under $50 million dollars. By 1990, government estimates predicted, it would still cost less than $10 billion. In fact, in 1990 Medicare cost the government $110 billion.[28] The doctors' groups which fought so hard to prevent the government from becoming involved in insuring health care for the elderly need not have been so concerned: government involvement has been one of the main forces fueling rising medical costs. Where elderly individuals might otherwise have opted for less-expensive treatments, when medical costs are paid by someone else, the natural impulse has been, predictably, to utilize the latest technology, the most intensive treatment. The United States has eight times as many magnetic resonance imaging (MRI) machines and seven times as many radiation therapy units as Canada,[29] the country with the second-highest percentage of gross domestic product (GDP) going to health care. Although the proliferation of such expensive machinery is acknowledged by the medical profession to be redundant, every major hospital wants its own (Table 5.8[30]).

How is all this expensive technology paid for? Medicine is one of the few fields in which supply can create its own demand. Peter Peterson, Secretary of Commerce in the Nixon administration, sees the infatuation with technology as an important part of the reason for America's runaway health care costs:

Part of the explanation is that incentives in our medical marketplace don't reward efficiency, they reward providers who bill the most. And any hospital administrator knows that the way to generate the biggest bills is to buy expensive technologies like MRIs and CAT [computer axial tomography] scanners, then write off the cost by getting lots of patients to use them. Medical professionals are perhaps unique in their ability to do this, since in almost no other industry are the buyer and the seller of a service in effect the same person.[31]

Table 5.8
Rate Per 10,000 Elderly for Three Heart Operations

	1976	1980	1986	1993
Angioplasty			7.1	52.1
Bypass Surgery	5.3	15.0	42.9	79.2
Catheterization	15.2	32.6	94.7	148.0

If, in the midst of a painful and traumatic illness, your doctor tells you that you need an MRI, you do not argue in order to save money, particularly if it is someone else's money. "What no one anticipated" in 1965, Peterson explains, "was the way that perverse economic incentives embedded in these new benefit systems would themselves induce demand for health care."[32]

The result of the "perverse economic incentives" of American medicine is that costs have spiraled in the past 30 years—often at unsustainable double-digit annual rates. The United States spends more of its national wealth on health care than any other country in the world. In 1991 we spent 13.4% of our GDP on health care. Japan, by comparison, spent 6.6%,[33] and has a life expectancy three years longer than ours.[34] Not coincidentally, medical costs have risen disproportionately for the elderly in the United States, fueled by Medicare funding, and per capita spending for senior health care is more than twice as high in the United States as in any other nation.[35]

Medicare spending for the elderly, meanwhile, with its enormous stimulus effect on the medical industry, is seen as a key factor in the escalation of medical care generally. And costs have certainly been escalating. During the 1980s, for example, the consumer price index rose 63%. Federal expenditures for education increased 107%. Health care spending rose 193%.[36] Janice Castro writes:

There are two kinds of prices in America today, regular prices and health care prices. The first seems to follow some sensible laws of supply and demand. But America's medical bills are something else. They flow from a surreal world where science has lost connection with reality, where bureaucracy and paperwork have no limit, where a half-hour tonsilectomy costs what an average worker earns in three weeks.[37]

Spending more is, apparently, not the whole answer: Americans spend twice as much as other industrial nations on health care, and rank only fifteenth in life expectancy.[38]

We have said that the United States now spends over 13% of its entire economic output on health care. Only a decade ago, the figure was 9.4%. If trends persist, some estimates suggest that the United States will spend an impossible one-third of its entire national economic output on health care within 15 years.[39] That is money which, while providing the most expensive medical treatment in the world and maintaining a certain level of good health for most citizens, will build no roads or factories, educate no young people with the skills necessary to prosper in a competitive world. Governor Lawton Chiles of Florida, the state with the largest proportion of elderly citizens, warns, "Health care costs have created an American state of siege. It's going to break us."[40]

With the growing smorgasbord of expensive treatment options, Medicare costs per enrollee have increased rapidly since its inception. And, as life expectancy rises, the number of enrollees has exploded (Table 5.9[41]).

Table 5.9
Medicare Expenditures per Enrollee, 1966-1991 (in 1991 constant dollars)

Year	Expenditures Per Enrollee	Number of Enrollees (in millions) Part A*	Part B**
1966	$ 351		
1967	984	19.5	17.9
1968	1,138		
1969	1,238		
1970	1,244	20.4	19.6
1971	1,304		
1972	1,359		
1973	1,341		
1974	1,488		
1975	1,618	24.6	23.9
1976	1,792		
1977	1,888		
1978	2,017		
1979	2,079		
1980	2,211	28.1	27.4
1981	2,384		
1982	2,573		
1983	2,767		
1984	2,864		
1985	2,974	30.6	30.0
1986	3,037		
1987	3,111		
1988	3,204		
1989	3,405		
1990	3,421	33.7	32.6
1991	3,575		

*Hospital Insurance
**Supplementary Medical Insurance

By 1995 the number of elderly Americans receiving Medicare benefits had risen to 37 million.[42] As costs per enrollee have escalated, along with the number of enrollees, total Medicare spending has ballooned beyond even the most pessimistic estimates (Table 5.10[43]). It does not take a congressional Special Committee to detect a pattern—and, perhaps, trouble on the horizon.

SOCIAL SECURITY: THE BENEFITS OF OLD AGE

Medicare, then, has spiraled rapidly in both its spending per enrollee and the total number covered. Costs, as a result, have exploded. But it still has far to go before it approaches the cost of the grandfather of all entitlement programs, Social Security.

Once having been derailed from the concept of a pension-type system, where retirement benefits would have some correspondence with what one paid into the system during the years of employment, the benefit structure of Social Security became loosened from economics, and was driven instead by politics. Workers retiring in 1980 recovered the entire amount they and their employer paid into the system, plus interest that would have accrued under a private pension, in around 36 months.[44]

Such a fine return on investment might have been tenable when the system was initiated. At that time, after all, the average age of a Social Security beneficiary was only 68, and many died before being able to take anything out of the system.[45] But, today, when Social Security beneficiaries can expect to live an average of another 15 years after receiving their first Social Security check,[46] what was once economically sustainable no longer is.

Economics, however, is not driving this process. Indeed, far from controlling costs, politicians expanded benefits even as the number of beneficiaries began to explode. "Buoyed by ever-rosier views of the future," *The Economist* wrote, "the federal government made benefits increasingly generous during the 1960s and 1970s. . . . And although economic growth has since come back to earth, the benefits have not."[47] Monthly benefits have grown, therefore, nearly

Table 5.10
Total Medicare Expenditures (in millions)

1967	$ 4,737
1970	7,493
1975	16,316
1980	36,822
1985	72,294
1990	110,984*
1995	176,000 (approx.)

*Medical enrollees, 1991

Table 5.11
Average Monthly Social Security Benefits for Retired Workers
(in 1991 constant dollars)

1950	$ 241.93
1955	318.51
1960	342.62
1965	363.92
1970	409.20
1975	514.78
1980	545.53
1985	603.86
1990	621.02

as rapidly as the number of those receiving them (Table 5.11[48]). More benefici-aries. Rising benefits. As with medicare, the trajectory with Social Security is unmistakable. In 1995, the program spent $334 billion, or one-fourth of all revenues taken in by the federal government.[49]

A GOVERNMENT WITHOUT DISCRETION

For those who believe that government has a legitimate role, a responsibil-ity, to address social and economic inequalities, and to improve the general quality of life for American society, such statistics ought to be actuating. In the context of a system mandated by law to automatically devote an expanding share of public resources to support payments for the elderly, there is a diminishing share of "discretionary" funds available for the things we normally think of as what government does: preserve law and order; build and maintain roads, bridges, and airports; promote education; and fight poverty (including poverty among those under age 65). These activities of government give American soci-ety a fighting chance in an increasingly competitive global economy, and they promote social and political stability at home. But government will be forced to spend less and less on them, as the "mandatory" spending for the elderly con-sumes a growing share of all federal revenue, reducing the money left over for such "discretionary" spending as national defense and crime control. Because of legally mandated increases in spending, the government will be required to spend billions more on programs for the elderly each year, not because anyone voted on them, but because of laws that were enacted a generation ago. Of course, with more retirees each year, it would be reasonable to expect that total costs have increased. But, in fact, with cost-of-living-adjustment increases triggered automatically, even the increases in the amount of spending per retiree are out of the hands of politicians—or anyone. The Bipartisan Commission on Entitlement Reform has outlined the remarkable growth of mandatory spending

Table 5.12
Growth of Mandatory Spending

Year	Discre-tionary	Net Interest	Entitle-ments	Manda-tory
		(as share of all federal spending)		
1963	70.4%	6.9%	22.7%	29.6%
1973	55.0	7.0	38.0	45.0
1983	43.7	11.1	45.2	56.3
1993	38.6	14.1	47.3	61.4
2003*	28.0	13.8	58.2	72.0

*projected

(the combination of entitlements plus interest payments on the national debt) in the federal budget over the past 30 years (Table 5.12[50]).

While "entitlement spending" also includes food, housing, and welfare benefits for the nonelderly poor, these benefits have actually declined as a percent of GDP since the 1940s. Health care and retirement benefits for the elderly, meanwhile, have increased by 6.7% of GDP since the inception of Medicare. Once a small fraction of welfare spending for the poor, spending for the elderly now accounts for over three-fourths of all federal "entitlement" spending.[51] Indeed, we are already beginning to see real reductions in welfare spending for the poor, brought about by the new "economic realities" of a chronic national deficit and the necessity of diverting a growing share of federal resources to the elderly.

The federal government is often viewed as a transfer payment mechanism for redistributing wealth from the rich to the poor. It would be more apt to say that government is becoming a bureaucracy whose primary function is the transfer of payments from the young to the old. As mandatory expenditures drive out the discretion of government (and, thus, of politics), responsiveness to social and economic challenges will be diminished: the political system's hands will be tied. The Department of Health and Human Services reports that by 2030, expenses for supporting America's retirees will consume 56.3% of the federal budget. Once interest on the debt and national defense have been funded, that will leave only 4.4% of the budget to pay for everything else that government does.[52] Everything. The Bipartisan Commission concluded that by that time, unless changes are made in the existing system, federal spending for retirees "will consume all tax revenues collected by the Federal government. If all other Federal programs (except interest on the national debt) grow no faster than the economy, total Federal outlays would exceed 37% of the economy. Today, outlays are 22% of the economy and revenues are 19%."[53] Spending for needy children, job training, and other programs essential to preparing the nation for the future are already being reduced. "Sunrise" investments, those that will make America more competitive and prosperous in the decades ahead, are being reduced, as government funds are diverted to fund the mandated "sunset" requirements of retirees.

Government has vital functions in addition to its care for the elderly, but its ability to carry out those functions is already being eroded by the growing pressures of mandated entitlement spending. It will be eroded further in the years to come. Senator Bob Kerrey (D-NE), cochairman of the Bipartisan Commission, notes that government spending will be largely predetermined by mandate (read: out of control) long before 2030, when the youngest baby boomers begin to retire. By 2012, when the oldest boomers turn 65, the problem will have already become entrenched. "In 2012, when today's young children are just getting started in the labor force, there will not be one cent left over [after mandated spending] for education, children's programs, highways, national defense or any other discretionary program."[54] What government does nowadays, mainly, is provide resources to the elderly. Yet, even as government discretion in spending declines, the long-term stability of the programs remains uncertain.

Everyone involved acknowledges the problem. The Social Security Administration predicts bankruptcy within a generation. Trustees of Medicare put bankruptcy much sooner. Virtually everyone who has studied the question has concluded that entitlement spending for the elderly must be contained if some degree of fiscal sanity is to be restored to the federal budget process. Politicians know it. The agencies for the elderly know it. Most Americans know it. The crisis is almost universally acknowledged. And we know, further, that the longer the delay before taking action, the more painful the remedy. Yet we postpone the inevitable, like a smoker already suffering from emphysema, but waiting for the cancer before he quits.

Susan Dentzer has compared America's crisis of entitlement spending to conditions in the Soviet Union prior to the collapse of that system. She recounts a joke that circulated there about a dissident who went about the streets of Moscow hanging up blank posters as a protest against the corrupt regime. "The police nabbed him and roughed him up—then, curious, asked him why the posters carried no message. 'There's no need,' the dissident replied; 'the message is known to everybody.'" Dentzer believes that the message about Social Security and Medicare is known to most Americans. "Almost everyone knows that these programs' long-term financial footing is crumbling and that promised benefits probably won't be available for tomorrow's retirees. The question is whether painful measures will be taken to start shoring up the programs over time—or whether, like the Soviet empire, they will continue to deteriorate until they collapse."[55]

Everybody knows, yet nothing is done. Indeed, the problem is barely addressed. Why? Because politicians cannot solve the problem of runaway entitlement spending without the consent of the elderly, and the elderly have not consented.

6

Power

Times have changed. Within a single generation, the elderly have gone from being the poorest, most vulnerable age group in American society, to being the wealthiest, most politically potent one. The politics of government entitlement have made them economically secure, and the dynamics of demographic change have made them politically invulnerable. What began as comparatively modest social insurance programs have become the untouchable sacred cows of American politics. While programs for children in poverty are cut, few politicians dare to discuss the possibility of reducing entitlement benefits for retired millionaires. Roosevelt was right when he said that the elderly would feel entitled to their benefits, and that "No damn politician can ever scrap my Social Security program." Few have even dared try to control the program's spiraling costs. None have succeeded.

We might have seen it coming. In the early 1930s, when the elderly made up just 5% of the population,[1] they were already beginning to shake up American politics. In fact, the adoption of the Social Security plan was itself, in part, prompted by a desire to appease the growing political clout of older citizens, and to stave off a demand for more radical reform.

THE ELDERLY FIND A POLITICAL VOICE

Just months before the creation of Social Security in 1935, there had sprung up the first tentative beginnings of a genuine mass movement of the elderly. And, when Congress held its hearings on the proposed Social Security legislation in February of that year, they called upon the leader of this movement to come to Washington and testify. More than any other individual in the nation, Francis Townsend could claim to speak on behalf of the aged in America. When he traveled to Washington to support his own entitlement proposal, much more sweeping than any envisioned by Congress, he brought with him real political clout.

Just two years earlier, Francis Townsend had lost his job as a public health official in Long Beach, California. He was destitute and, at 67 years old, was unlikely to find employment. In the language of the day, he had been "super-annuated." In the midst of the Great Depression, men in their late 60s were not likely to find any sort of employment.

But Townsend did not go quietly. With his friend, realtor Robert Clements, Townsend established, in January 1934, Old Age Revolving Pensions, Ltd. The company was mainly a platform for the promotion of an agenda: greater government support for the elderly. Townsend had devised a plan to bring about economic recovery. Under the Townsend plan, the government would pay $200 monthly to every American over 60 years old. In return for the money, they would have two obligations: to retire, and to spend all the money they received each month. The former action would make room for younger workers to be employed, the latter would create a demand-side economic boom, generated by older Americans with plenty of money and plenty of time to spend it.

Townsend's vision was of a system where unemployment had been solved, workers' wages had risen, and the elderly were given generous sums of money each month which it was their civic duty to dispose of. The elderly, needless to say, were especially attracted to the program, and quickly became vigorous proponents of "the Townsend plan."

It was a historic development. The first mass movement by and for the elderly in the United States. What Old Age Revolving Pensions was selling was an idea. Millions were buying. Within a year, the two policy entrepreneurs had 100 employees, and there were over 1,000 "clubs" where the Townsend message of hope could be preached, and fellow believers could gather.

In fact, it was a kind of evangelism by which the gospel according to Francis Townsend was spread. At meetings of the believers, the tone was often explicitly religious in nature. Iniquities such as cigarettes and lipstick were decried. The Townsendites, as they came to be called, believed that when the elderly were spending their government subsidies, young people would be less likely to fall into sin, because they would be working, and would not have time to be tempted by such vices as sex and alcohol, which were seen as the conse-quences of excessive free time—among the young, anyway.

In addition to saving young people, the plan would have the added virtue of saving capitalism, by thwarting the encroaching socialism embodied in the expansive government programs of the new deal. The elderly, after all, would be free to spend their monthly government stipend wherever they chose, an essential attribute of the free market system to which they were committed.

The organization's publication, *The Townsend Weekly*, proclaimed that the "vision" of the plan had been "god-given." Its adoption by Congress would usher in a utopian age for America, and mankind.

Peace, good-will and universal brotherhood will be born in a day when the Townsend Plan, the plan of "live-and-let-live," becomes the law of the land. We believe Dr. Townsend's perception of such an idea is not an accident but rather an answer to the prayers of tens of millions of organized children of God lost in a wilderness of doubt.[2]

As with all dogmas, disbelievers and heretics were anathema. One report told of a Townsendite collecting signatures demanding that Congress enact the plan into law. When an elderly merchant declined to sign the petition, saying that he believed the plan was "unsound," the reaction suggested the zeal of a true believer:

"You don't [support the plan], eh?" George shouted at a pitch that arrested the attention of passers-by. "Well, you'll see the day when you wish you had." He noted the man's name on a list of opponents.

"See this? This goes on file at headquarters. Your name, and word that you're against us. Copies will be posted at every Townsend club in town and read at every meeting. You'll never see one of us in your store again.

"And you wait until the pension checks begin to come in. Six million dollars a month in this town and you'll never see a dime!"[3]

The merchant, of course, was correct in his concerns about the economic soundness of the plan. Townsend's pension program was to be funded by a 2% "transaction tax" on every business transaction. It was widely criticized by economists, social workers, politicians, and others who had recognized that Townsend's math did not add up. The program would have cost at least $24 billion at the outset, with costs escalating as the retirement age dropped to 50, as Townsend believed it eventually would. The cost would be offset, the Townsendites insisted, by the overall economic prosperity that would be generated by the stimulus effect of the plan. So much prosperity that the working population would not even be inconvenienced by the added cost.

In a sense, it was irrelevent that the plan was economically unsound. Through it, millions of older Americans had found a shared voice in national politics that they had never known before. In a matter of months, they had gone from being a disorganized mass to a "mass movement" with a clear agenda of demands upon government, and growing political muscle. More important than the economic viability of the plan was its political validity. Particularly in states with larger populations of elderly, as is often the case of such political equations, the math of economics was frequently subordinated to the more pressing calculus of election returns. When support for enactment of the Townsend plan was put up for a vote in the California state assembly, only one assemblyman out of 80 dared to oppose it. The governor supported the plan, and it was also passed in the state Senate.[4]

As the Townsend movement swept across the United States, *Harper's* magazine called it "the strongest pressure movement in the country."[5] The elderly were finally coming into their own as a potent political force. By 1935, membership in the Townsend movement was reported to be 5 million, with Townsend claiming to have "voting power" of 25 million. "The most conservative estimate," wrote *Harper's*, "by the most caustic critic of the plan, admits the Townsend organization has a minimum of ten million supporters, included in which are at least three million affiliated Townsend club members."[6]

The "Old People's Crusade," as some were calling it, was having an impact on Washington, pressuring for sweeping legislation on behalf of elderly Americans. By late 1934, the organization had moved its headquarters to the nation's capital, and turned its attention to calling for national enactment of the plan. Members of Congress introduced the Townsend plan in the House and Senate,[7] although most continued to keep their distance from the plan, recognizing its untenability. Nevertheless, the growing power of the Townsendites, and the radical, economically spurious program they proposed, ultimately provoked the Roosevelt administration into accelerating advocacy of its own Social Security plan, which was relatively modest by contrast.

By the time congressional committees were holding hearings for the Social Security plan, in early 1935, Townsend's movement had such an enormous popular following that Congress could not afford to ignore it, even though most snickered at the plan in private. Townsend was invited to testify before Congress on the proposed legislation, and when he did, the appearance attracted greater public and media attention than any other event during the several weeks of hearings. Hundreds of supporters packed the Committee room when Townsend testified before the House Ways and Means Committee on February 1.

Rather than addressing the Social Security proposal, Townsend called for enactment of his own program. He began by denouncing those politicians who had rejected his program: they were elitist, and out of touch with the people. Referring to Relief Administrator Harry Hopkins' description of his plan as "cock-eyed," Townsend displayed the knack for rhetorical appeal (some thought demagoguery) that had made him beloved by many, feared by others. To denounce the plan, Townsend argued, was to denounce the millions who fervently believed in it. "Surely a plan which has aroused the intense interest of ten million old people of this country, and their relatives, cannot be dismissed as cockeyed: not unless the utterer of that phrase wished to go on record as believing these millions of people and their relatives also to be 'cock-eyed.'"[8] Townsend decried the "elitists" in Washington who rejected his plan. If they continued to ignore the wishes of the people, there would be dire consequences for American society.

This is the last Congress of the United States that is going to uphold our old economic system or seek to solve the nation's ills through the application of outworn economic theory. I had hoped it would be the first to adopt the new system. It's going to be done.[9]

When Townsend was asked how he knew his plan was the "one and only" way to save the American economy, he answered: "I have twenty million people supporting this plan."

"Oh yes, but they only had the $200 a month dangled in front of their face; and anyhow, numbers are no sign of its soundness." "That inference," Townsend snapped back, "assumes the essential ignorance of the American people."[10]

Members of the Committee wanted more details on the operation of his plan. How would it be financed? What would be the economic ramifications? But Townsend, as always, spoke in general terms. Under his plan, he insisted, the country would become so prosperous that the typical workman would go to work "in a silk shirt."

Still pressed for more specifics, Townsend abruptly said that he had "left a hospital bed at Johns Hopkins this morning in order to be here. I had to pledge to the physicians there that I would return to Johns Hopkins within a few hours. I therefore beg to be excused from the wearing process of answering questions relative to the details of my plan."[11] Townsend left, without answering the questions of the skeptical congressmen.

Returning to testify before the Senate two weeks later, Townsend met an even chillier response. Some broke into derisive laughter as Townsend evangelized his plan. They grilled him for details on how his plan was to be financed: what of the estimates, one asked, that the plan would cost $24 billion a year, resulting in a federal deficit of at least $19 billion? Such expense, Townsend assured them, would be "a mere trifle," because the plan would promote such economic expansion that it would result in "an era of plenty." And anyway, he insisted, estimates for the early costs of the program were exaggerated, since it would take years to sign up all those eligible. In reply to which, one senator mockingly asked if there would be "much trouble drafting people to take these pensions?"

The subject then shifted to how the pensions would expand the economy. "Would shooting dice with half a dozen other fellows" count in the "goods and services?" Of course not. "What about buying the dice?"

What then, asked Senator Alben Barkley of Kentucky, would the pensioners purchase with their new bounty? "Why bless your soul," Townsend answered, "I should think anyone who had ever had that salary would know. They would buy a car, rebuild their home, refurnish it, travel, buy books, get things for their children."[12]

Townsend gained no new converts among the members of Congress. Those who already accepted the plan did not do so for its logical persuasiveness. But the attraction of the Townsend plan had never been among society's elites, or based upon its practical appeal. Instead, it was among the masses of American elderly, many of whom felt neglected and forgotten by American society, that Townsend's impassioned rhetoric resonated.

The effect of Townsend's appearance before Congress, wrote Edwin Witte, architect of Roosevelt's Social Security plan, was that the real issue became the Townsend Plan or the [Administration's] Economic Security Bill. Few members of Congress ever thought the Townsend Plan a practical possibility, and [Townsend's] testimony . . . did not strengthen his case with the Congressmen. His testimony, however, plus the thousands of letters in support of the Townsend Plan with which all Congressmen were deluged at this time, caused practically every other feature of the bill, and all other sources of opposition, to be forgotten.[13]

Ultimately, the anthem of the Townsend movement, "We are coming, father Townsend, 50 million strong, and 50 million Americans can't be wrong," was not translated into political reality. In 1935 the elderly in America still lacked the political clout that their counterparts in successive generations would wield. The Social Security Act, perhaps partly a response to the growing unrest of the elderly, was not all they had hoped for.

In memoirs not distinguished by self-effacement, Townsend expressed astonishment that the movement had not had more of a direct impact on the New Deal's social welfare legislation for the elderly. Like others before and since whose political ambitions have been unrealized, he attributed the failure to corruption within the system. "All thinking people recognized that [the Townsend movement] was a manifestation of power and determination on the part of the people to right the wrong that had afflicted them so long and so severely, and politicians became alarmed. It became whispered about Washington that this thing must be stopped before it completely upset the political cart."[14]

Townsend had not succeeded, but the Townsend movement had not failed. Older Americans had, for the first time ever, come together as a genuine national mass movement, and politicians across the country had genuflected. The seniors had, in addition, spurred the administration in its quest for a policy for the elderly. The fact that the movement was a reaction to quixotic, occasionally demagogic appeals was beside the point; as was the dissolution of the movement shortly following passage of the Social Security Act. What had been derided as "The Old People's Crusade" had shown that the elderly could come together as a single political force, and that, even at that early stage, could make their shared political voice heard. They would be back, and their voice would thunder.

SPLIT-PERSONALITY LEVIATHAN

The Townsend movement quickly evaporated when Social Security was enacted, but the importance of the elderly in society continued to grow. As Americans lived longer, senior citizens grew in number and influence. New organizations sprang up to address the new demands placed upon society by the burgeoning older population. In 1947, just over a decade after the Townsendites had pressed their failed movement, a new movement was taking root. And, like the Townsend organization, this one would also have its origins in California, fertile soil for so many of the nation's new political movements. It was the postwar period, and Social Security had been in existence for over a decade now. Dr. Ethel Percy Andrus, a retired teacher and activist for the rights of the elderly, established the National Retired Teachers Association (NRTA) to lobby for the political and economic rights of retired schoolteachers. Operating with funding from membership dues, the Association experienced modest success, building a membership of around 20,000 within a decade. But it would only be with the infusion of economic incentives that the Association would really boom.

In 1958 Dr. Andrus met Leonard Davis, an aggressive young New York City insurance salesman. Davis had succeeded in convincing his insurance company, Continental Casualty, to underwrite the health insurance of around 800 retired New York teachers. It was an unusual move at that time, because insurers generally believed that insuring the elderly as a group was a risky proposition. Andrus, who had been troubled by the lack of health insurance available to many retired teachers, asked Davis to do for the NRTA what he had done for the New York teachers. He did, and the rest is history.

Davis immediately recognized that he had a service which wasn't being offered elsewhere. One-fourth of the NRTA members signed up for the insurance offer on the first proposal. "And so evolved," as the organization's own literature explains it, "what seemed the strangest of collaborations—between a man of 32 and a woman of 72 who became totally absorbed in shaping the tenets of a new philosophy of aging."[15] On July 1, 1958, the American Association of Retired Persons (AARP) was established as a nonprofit corporation. But it had not been, of course, the search for a philosophy of aging that had brought the two together; it had been the desire to sell insurance to the elderly.

At first, Davis sold Continental Casualty's insurance to the new AARP members. But as he began to recognize the sheer economic potential of this exploding new market, Davis grew discontent, and within a few years he had left Continental to set out on his own. In 1965 Davis established Colonial Penn. It wasn't much of a risk: by this time, under his aggressive marketing direction, AARP already had built a membership of 750,000. Within a decade, Davis had amassed a personal net worth of over $160 million.[16] His retirement was announced in 1983, amid controversy and allegations of profiteering.

Since then, of course, AARP has grown exponentially. Membership is open to all Americans over age 50, and a great many of them have joined—33 million of them.

THE 800-POUND GORILLA OF CAPITOL HILL

However, while the numbers have changed, the emphasis remains the same: a split-personality organization, caught somewhere between the idealistic heritage of Andrus and the commercial impulse of Davis. Is AARP, then, a genuine advocacy group for the elderly, or a business which happens to cater to the elderly, and enjoys the benefits of nonprofit, tax-free status? It is both. It reflects the influence of both of its parents, Ethel Percy Andrus and Leonard Davis.

Travel and accommodation discounts are nice, but AARP can be regarded by its members as a powerful voice on behalf of many of the economic-political issues that are of critical importance to their daily lives. Its major emphasis in politics has been to protect existing programs from being cut, an increasingly vital activity during the recent years of ballooning federal deficits and effort to contain government spending. The Association's 1995 *Public Policy Agenda* outlines its political goals. Foremost among these is preservation of Social Security and Medicare.

The Association strongly supports a retirement income structure that maintains an adequate and equitable living standard for those no longer in the workforce. Social Security is the foundation on which retirement income security is built. It reflects the country's commitment to the economic security of retired and disabled workers and their families.[17]

Regarding Medicare, the Association calls for reforms of the health care system to provide universal access and cost containment. And, at a time of major cutbacks elsewhere in government spending, it seeks not merely to protect the existing level of Medicare benefits, but to expand them. Or, in its own words, to "improve" them. "Medicare pays only about 50% of beneficiaries' health bills," the *Agenda* laments. "The Association supports continued improvements to the Medicare program that would expand beneficiary access to high quality care. . . . AARP opposes a cap on entitlement spending."[18]

Other major policy goals include legislation that would eliminate age discrimination in employment,[19] support for federal action "to assist state and local agencies in preventing and combatting elder abuse,"[20] stronger protection for seniors from consumer fraud,[21] and income assistance for older Americans living in poverty.[22] Not exactly a controversial agenda. Aside from universal health care coverage, they are issues, in fact, on which most Americans, not only the elderly, agree. Any organization which hopes to attract and retain 33 million members cannot take many controversial or divisive policy positions.

It may be, as some critics charge, that the potential political vision of an interest group is dissipated by increasing its size to too gargantuan a level. But, by attracting so many members, what AARP gives up in the political zeal of a typical member, or the specificity of its agenda, it gains in the strength that comes from sheer size. If AARP lacks laser-beam focus, it possesses shotgun force; and that shotgun has protected the elderly's entitlement programs from would-be budget-cutters more effectively than any other interest group in the country. The Association is, says Washington lobbyist Marion Hopkins, "the 800-pound gorilla of Capitol Hill."[23]

Of course, there are numerous other groups out there representing the elderly. The National Council of Senior Citizens, with over 4 million members, was created by the AFL-CIO to promote the passage of Medicare. The National Alliance of Senior Citizens has about half that number.[24] The Gray Panthers, founded by activist Maggie Kuhn in 1970, takes a much more aggressive approach. With around 75,000 members,[25] it considers itself a revolutionary movement against discriminatory "ageism" in American society, just as activist blacks or Hispanics fight against racism. Indeed, Kuhn's rhetoric was revolutionary. "The old-order, acquisitive society, which values property more than people, is under attack. Leading the battle are young dissenters and other powerless ones—including certain militant elderly."[26]

Such groups provide an outlet for social and political expression for many older citizens, but when we talk of political clout for the elderly in Washington, we mean AARP. The several dozen other national organizations representing the elderly are lost in the shadow cast by the gargantuan Association. "There are other, smaller senior groups," observes Thomas Rosenstiel, "but the lobby that counts is AARP."[27]

AARP's influence is pervasive in Congress. Even when it remains silent, the organization's impact is felt. An aide to Florida Congressman Buddy McKay was fired after openly criticizing AARP for its strong-arm political tactics. Had the organization pressured McKay for the action? "I didn't tell McKay to fire Longman," said the legislative director. "I didn't have to."[28]

According to Philip Longman, the dismissed aide, AARP exercises an intimidating influence over congressional policymaking. "When AARP's lobbyist shows up, it's like Darth Vader at the door. He tells people how to vote."[29] For an elderly person intent on preserving Social Security or Medicare benefits intact, that may not sound like criticism.

AARP does not run a political action committee. Instead, it established, in 1985, a "voter education program" designed to increase the awareness of elderly voters of the issues important to them. It states the policy positions of the Association, and the degree of support for those issues among the various candidates. With 33 million members, 200,000 new recruits monthly, 350,000 activist volunteers, and a $400 million budget, AARP can command political resources that are the envy of other Washington lobbies. With a single announcement in its Newsletter, the Association can cause legislators to be flooded with more phone calls, cards, telegrams, and hand-written letters than any other organization in the country. Jack Carlson, the former executive director of the Association, sums up its leviathan clout: "The fear level of AARP in Congress is just incredible. There is no other group like it." Edward Roybal (D-CA), chairman of the House select Committee on Aging, puts the matter in more politic terms: "AARP is instrumental in bringing about change."[30]

A Political Action Committee, indeed, might be anticlimatic. The contribution of a few thousand dollars to a candidate pales in signicance when compared with the potential political might that the largest independent political organization in the country could bring to bear. With nearly one in four of all registered voters as members,[31] AARP does not have to lobby, but simply to make its will known. *Newsweek* sums up the Association's power: "It is hard to exaggerate the awe in which politicians hold the AARP."[32]

IN THE BUSINESS OF DOING GOOD

AARP's political muscle is excelled only by its commercial might. What are the benefits of membership? A subscription to *Modern Maturity,* the magazine with the highest circulation in the country, focusing on lifestyle issues relevant to retirees; a subscription to *AARP Bulletin,* the Association's newspaper, reporting the latest developments of concern to the elderly; and political representation of your interests in Washington. Not bad for $8 a year.

Then there are the commercial aspects of membership. Anyone who has traveled in the United States has seen the ubiquitous restraunt and hotel advertisements proclaiming "Discounts for AARP Members." Membership also brings more direct consumer opportunities. Along with one's membership card, a new member receives a notice: "Your new card brings you the many benefits of membership. Please refer to your membership number on the front whenever you write or call AARP. On the back of your card are important toll-free numbers for your convenience." What are these important services offered by the Association?

> Pharmacy service
> Motoring plan
> Mobile home insurance
> Life insurance
> Health insurance
> Auto insurance
> Homeowner insurance
> Credit cards
> Investment program
> Annuity program

To some, AARP seems more like a marketing empire which also has lobbyists than a political association which also offers commercial services. From the beginning, AARP's emphasis on marketing has raised questions about its status as a public interest group deserving of tax-exempt, nonprofit status. Part of the problem, as regards taking particular policy positions, is the organization's strength, its huge membership. With around 33 million members in 4,000 local chapters around the country, AARP has more members than any other organization in the United States except for the Catholic Church. It has a population the size of a medium-sized nation, and is as unlikely to have consensus among its members on controversial issues.

There will be no uniformity of opinion among any group of 33 million people—even of the same age. In this sense, AARP's enormous size can be a limitation as well as an advantage. With such a large portion of older Americans as members, its membership is inevitably more diverse, and more representative of the larger population than those of smaller, more narrowly focused organizations. The National Committee to Preserve Social Security and Medicare, for example, with fewer than 1 million members, is able to take more concrete and aggressive political positions. "I wouldn't be surprised if an extremely high ratio of retired doctors are members of AARP," said William Weaver, the National Committee's executive director. "AARP is in a tough position. They have a membership that is much more divided than our membership," and are thus not as capable of focusing exclusively on Social Security and Medicare issues.[33]

"What limits their power," according to one political consultant, "is that they are strictly nonpartisan."[34] In fact, AARP does not endorse candidates, undertake a scorecard of how politicians vote on seniors' issues, or maintain a Political Action Committee.

AARP does not claim to be a strictly political organization. It has not been such since its inception, nor was it meant to be. Take, for instance, its membership requirements: for the small sum of $8 per year, anyone can join. In the 1980s it lowered the age requirement to 50, adding millions of members, and further enriching its commercial enterprises, but also diluting its political focus. A 50-year-old member may have a very different political agenda than one 65 or older. The membership fee is so low that it is not an obstacle to the vast majority of older Americans, and one does receive a good deal in return: the magazines, the services, the discounts. Even in recruiting members, the emphasis is on commercial incentives rather than the political ones. Eric Schurenberg and Lani Luciano, analyzing the commercial offerings of the Association, refer to an AARP marketing line: "You can save the cost of membership many times over by using just one of the services AARP provides you." Schurenberg and Luciano write, "This is certainly persuasive bait, but it hooks bargain hunters, not political activists."[35]

One Association member explained to me why, like millions of other Americans, he had joined AARP as soon as he turned 50: "The membership is cheaper than the dickens. You get all that stuff in the mail that keeps you on top of what you need to know. And you get all those discounts." Senator Alan Simpson (R-WY) describes the Association's enormous membership as "thirty-three million people paying $8 dues, bound together by a common love of airline discounts and automobile discounts and pharmacy discounts." He says that members are attracted by the pecuniary advantages of membership, not political ones. "They haven't the slightest idea what the organization is asking for [politically]."[36]

Like Francis Townsend, AARP has done well by calling for the government to do good. A growing number of critics, some in government, most outside, are asking whether its political activities are merely diversionary; a needed rationale for its existence, a facade to conceal the real focus of the organization, making money.

If AARP has a population the size of some countries, it has a budget larger than some governments. Therein lies much of the trouble. Where does all that money come from, and what is it used for? Senator Simpson held hearings in 1995 to investigate the Association's business practices and, in particular, the tax-free benefits it receives from its status as a nonprofit organization. In 1994, AARP made $173 million in such commercial ventures as contracting with private firms the sole right to sell insurance, credit cards, and annuities. It made another $47 million selling them advertising space in its publications. Its own pharmacy brought in another $4 million.[37] For a nonprofit organization, the Association generates earnings that would make most tax-paying, profit-seeking corporations envious. It is the most profitable nonprofit organization in the world.

How can an organization be nonprofit, Senator Simpson and others wanted to know, when nearly 60% of its revenues come from commercial enterprises? If less than half its revenues come from membership dues, how can an organization be expected to truly reflect the interest of its members? "It is easily prone to represent the source of its money," said Simpson. "Which is business."[38] Congressional critics are not the only ones who are interested in that question. AARP's deals with insurance companies and other service providers have prompted investigations by the Internal Revenue Service, and a battle over taxes that has lasted, thus far, for seven years.[39]

The Association's status is further clouded by the federal grants it receives—$86 million in 1994.[40] Should an organization be able to lobby the government with money it receives from the government? In Senate hearings on the tax-exempt status of the AARP, Simpson said that he was considering introducing legislation to prevent tax-exempt organizations from receiving government grants.[41]

The charges against AARP, predictably, yielded no concrete political action. In Washington, Simpson was regarded as politically heroic—or reckless—for holding the two-hour hearings at all. AARP has its vocal critics, but few who hold elective office. Meanwhile, Allstate Insurance has attempted to copy AARP's successful pattern. It has established a subsidiary to target the senior market. Membership is inexpensive ($7.50), and comes with *Mature Outlook* magazine, and countless discounts on everything from insurance to eyewear to pharmaceuticals. With nearly 2 million members already, it is a duplicate of AARP's commercial operation in nearly every respect but one: it pays taxes.[42]

THE STRANGE CASE OF CATASTROPHIC CARE

The question for many critics, then, is whether AARP genuinely reflects the wishes of the elderly. Can any organization of 33 million members reflect the interests of all of them? Probably not. And, as with most political organizations, AARP's membership, and its policy orientation, is skewed away from lower-class participation, and disproportionately toward middle- and upper-class interests. According to one legislative aide, "what the organization likes to do is confuse members of Congress that the Association represents the interests of all the elderly, while in fact it does not represent the poor and those without an employment history."[43]

The Association has at times, however, had difficulty in identifying and representing the policy preferences even of those who are its members. The unusual political path of catastrophic care legislation, passed in 1986 and then quickly repealed, reveals much about the difficulties of representing the wishes of 33 million people.

When Ronald Reagan submitted his annual budget to Congress in February 1986, it contained deep cuts in social and other domestic spending, while continuing a vigorous military buildup. Reagan sought to mitigate the anticipated criticism by calling for a study of the possibility of providing the elderly with insurance against catastrophic illness. In his State of the Union address, given February 4, he told the Congress

After seeing how devastating illness can destroy the financial security of a family, I am directing the Secretary of Health and Human Services, Dr. Otis Bowen, to report to me by year-end with recommendations on how the private sector and government can work together to address the problems of affordable insurance for those whose life savings would otherwise be threatened when catastrophic illness strikes.[44]

There is no indication that Reagan expected, or wanted, the study to result in the creation of a new federal program. But that is what he got—for awhile.

For critics, the proposed study was a public relations ploy by the administration. Their doubts were bolstered when, in early July, documents leaked from the Department of Health and Human Services revealed that the administration was considering placing limits on Medicaid payments, the health assistance plan for the poor. The proposed new policy would require, among other things, that indigent recipients of health care pay for their own share of their medical bills before the government would pay its allotted portion. "The threat of hardship is essential," the document said, "in order to get people to pay their fair share."[45] Later in the year, the Office of Management and Budget proposed further cuts in Medicare and Medicaid of $90 billion over five years. All indicators coming from Washington did not seem to suggest an administration contemplating a major expansion of the federal commitment to public health care.

But Secretary Bowen took his assignment seriously. He held hearings. He consulted health care providers and economists and everyday citizens. And, in November, to the surprise of most observers and the chagrin of the administration, Bowen released a concrete proposal. The most important element of the plan was the proposed extension of Medicare to cover catastrophic illnesses, such as cancer, which could so often have devastating consequences for a family's resources. Catastrophic illness had, in innumerable cases, eaten away at a family's savings and investment until, having spent their way into poverty, they qualified for Medicaid. Bowen's plan called for a $2,000 annual limit on individual medical expenses for catastrophic diseases. It would be funded by a $59 yearly premium, to be charged to all beneficiaries of the new program. The plan would benefit around 800,000 elderly Americans whose annual health expenditures exceeded the $2,000 limit.[46]

The plan, like the initial study itself, seemed anomalous. It was out of place in an administration whose central policy orientation had been toward the retrenchment, not expansion, of government activity. Within weeks, White House officials were either criticizing Bowen's report, or keeping quiet. Beryl Sprinkel, chairman of the President's Council of Economic Advisors, declared that the plan was "inconsistent with the Administration's policies to strengthen competitive markets, to restrain the growth of Federal spending, to use private sector solutions whenever possible and to support the recently enacted tax reform."

The Democrats, on the other hand, were hailing the plan. "If the President and his advisors are listening," Senator Edward Kennedy (D-MA) said, "they will hear 28 million elderly Americans saying, 'Thank God for Doctor Bowen.'"[47]

The timing was critical. Bowen's report had been released just after the midterm elections of 1986. Republicans, who had held majority party status in the Senate, were now back in the minority. In the House of Representatives, the Democrats had increased their advantage to a margin of 258-177 over the Republicans. The Iran-Contra scandal was taking its toll on public approval of the administration. Democrats were moving back onto the political offensive for the first time during the Reagan years. The Bowen plan seemed made to order.

Few congressional leaders wanted to oppose Bowen's plan, which seemed to be popular among seniors. Moderate Republican Senator Dave Durenberger (MN) applauded Bowen, saying that he "deserves strong support for his leadership." Durenberger criticized those in the administration who "seem more concerned with superficial analogies and ideology than a careful examination of Secretary Bowen's report."[48] Catastrophic care was gaining a political momentum of its own.

With Bowen's plan co-opted by congressional Democrats, the administration saw that it had lost the political high ground on the issue, and risked alienating the elderly, probably the single most important political constituency in the country. Around the nation, supporters of expanded insurance benefits were holding rallies, conferences, and demanding action. Robert Ball, former commissioner of Social Security, announced that there were gaping "holes in the safety net" for the elderly, caused by the expense of catastrophic illness. Under the Reagan administration, Ball warned, the elderly were experiencing the "dimming of bright hopes," because of rising costs. Medicare covered only 40% of their health care costs.[49] In Congress, Democrats were even talking about financing the program through general Treasury revenues rather than by contributions from participants. The issue was definitely out of the administration's control.

In February, Reagan reacted by proposing a plan of his own. It would provide insurance coverage for "acute catastrophic illness" for Medicare beneficiaries who paid an additional premium of $4.42 a month. But, while the plan addressed catastrophic care, critics charged that it ignored the problem of long-term care, a distinction which included such potentially crippling expenses as protracted in-home nursing support. Still, Reagan, the great opponent of expanded government activity, had now proposed a major expansion of the federal role. Republicans in Congress who might have opposed the Democrat policy juggernaut found that they had no ideological refuge in their conservative president. Between the Democratic plan and that of the president, there was a difference of degree, but not of kind. The Heritage Foundation's Stuart Butler called the dual proposals a "political catastrophe" that would provoke a "bidding war" which the president was "bound to lose."[50] The *New York Times* noted the paradoxical nature of the president's sponsorship of the program: "Reagan, Apostle of Less, Assures Expanded Care for Elderly."[51]

Reagan had drifted into a no-win political situation. He was being criticized by conservatives for advancing any program at all, and by Democrats in Congress for not going far enough. Claude Pepper (D-FL), Congress' in-House spokesman for the elderly, expressed outrage that the president would "deceive the American people" by implying that his proposal reflected genuine comprehensive coverage for catastrophic illness. Excluding such expensive medical catastrophes as Alzheimer's disease and nursing-home care, it was, Pepper said, "the step of a dwarf."[52]

On May 7, the House Ways and Means Committee approved a bill which lowered the proposed monthly premiums to just $1.00, to be supplemented by taxing the insurance value of the new benefits. The new tax, though, would affect only the wealthiest one-third of seniors: 26% of beneficiaries would pay $265 a year in new taxes, and 8% would pay $495.[53] This alteration of Bowen's original proposal would ultimately spell defeat for the entire effort.

Sending the bill to the House floor for debate, Dan Rostenkowski (D-IL) acknowledged that the measure owed its existence to Reagan's State of the Union speech, but insisted that Congress had "improved the benefit package offered by the President, and financed it in a more equitable manner."[54] The Senate, meanwhile, was in the process of adopting a similar measure of its own. Members of both chambers were met by a full-court press of AARP lobbyists. The Association aggressively pressured Congress for passage of the bill, despite the fact that the sentiment of its members on the issue had never been gauged. Unlike political battles in earlier years, when seniors had been defeated by powerful medical and insurance lobbies, this time the elderly—or at least those claiming to speak for them—were having their way with Congress.

Members of the House, prodded by AARP's strenuous lobbying campaign, passed its version of the Catastrophic Care bill in late July 1987, by an overwhelming margin of 302 to 127. In October, the Senate passed its own version, by an even more lopsided margin of 86 to 11. Few dared to oppose the organized power of America's seniors.

By the spring of 1988, House and Senate negotiators had reached agreement on a compromise bill. The most salient difference in the new bill was the modification of its funding mechanism: Catastrophic Care insurance for America's elderly would be financed by (1) a uniform monthly premium of $4.00 (rising gradually to $10 by 1993); and (2) an additional premium, assessed to roughly the richest 40% of beneficiaries. This would be a 15% surtax, indexed to one's federal income tax, and paid directly to the Internal Revenue Service (IRS). The surtax would be capped at $800 in 1989, rising to $1,050 by 1993.

When the bill was passed in early summer, AARP lobbyists could barely contain their glee at the important political victory. The Association's director, Horace Deets, waxed poetic in his praise for the legislation. It marked, he said, a historical advance in public care for the health needs of the elderly. Their voices had been heard who had "repeatedly expressed concerns about their need for protection against high prescription drug costs, large doctor bills, and long hospital stays."[55] This was their triumph.

The Health Insurance Association of America admitted defeat. Geza Kadar, its Washington counsel, acknowledged that there was nothing else to do. "Now it's here and it's history," he said, "and we're going to live with it."[56]

One final question remained. Would Ronald Reagan sign the bill that he had earlier denounced as socialistic and dangerous to the very existence of Medicare itself? Or would he veto the bill, and risk alienating the elderly? On July 1, 1988, amid a deeply negative presidential election campaign between Vice-President George Bush and Democrat Michael Dukakis, Ronald Reagan took a hiatus from denouncing Dukakis as a friend of "big government" long enough to sign into law the largest expansion of the public welfare system since Medicare. The IRS was already at work designing a new tax form, to be mailed to millions of elderly taxpayers, assessing them as much as $1,600 per couple for their new benefits.

The problem was that most seniors who would be paying the new premiums were already receiving those benefits. Most older citizens, and nearly all of those in the wealthiest 40%, paid an average of $500 per year for "Medigap" insurance, to insure the gap between Medicare coverage and total medical costs.[57] The Catastrophic Care plan, it turned out, would be financed by those who were already covered under their own insurance plans, and who would not be its main beneficiaries.

At first, even after the bill's passage, most seniors were unfamiliar with the details of its funding provisions. Leonard Hansen, publisher of a senior-oriented newspaper, said that the funding mechanism would come as a surprise to the elderly community. "I think it's going to come as a massive, monumental shock to senior citizens. When it's really going to hit is in April, 1990, when a senior citizen sits down to fill out his or her 1040 [Federal tax form] and there will be a new requirement that says, 'If you're over 65, take 15% of your tax and add it on.'"[58]

Word spread quickly. And as seniors became more aware of the contents of the bill, particularly its progressive financing mechanism, opposition grew. Around 3.3 million elderly citizens already received "Medigap" coverage from their former employers; any new taxes they paid to fund the program would go to provide insurance to their less-fortunate counterparts. It was beginning to become apparent that not all seniors support the same policy agenda. The "gray lobby" is not so unitary a political bloc as many legislators had supposed. While virtually all support programs funded by broad public taxation, many oppose programs for the elderly if they are to be financed by the elderly—even those best able to afford them. And that group of the wealthiest elderly are also the most politically active. It was this richest half of seniors who were becoming increasingly vocal in their opposition to the new bill. They complained that their representatives, both in and out of government, were not reflecting their will or their interests.

As opposition grew by this segment of the elderly, members of Congress who had been largely silent on the Catastrophic Care bill were now joining in the growing chorus of criticism. Senator Phil Gramm (R-TX) charged that proponents of the bill, political elites and interest group representatives of the elderly, were out of touch with their constituencies. They were, he said, like a Boy Scout who is intent on helping a little old lady across the street "whether she wants to go or not."[59]

New organizations sprang up to take advantage of the growing outcry. United Seniors of America mailed requests to millions of seniors for $15 donations, "to help spread the word to get this unfair law changed." Existing organizations likewise jumped into the fray. Howard Phillips' Conservative Caucus, a direct-mail fund-raising machine, turned its attention to the issue, targeting seniors for contributions to help repeal the new law. "Your contribution is a good investment. It could keep millions of Americans (including you) from paying an extra $800 per year (and more) in taxes—year after year.[60]

For the wealthiest half of seniors, the appeals hit home. They had supported the new program until learning that they would be the ones paying for it. Now, they recoiled at having to subsidize the benefits of the poorer half of older Americans. Architects of the measure grew defensive. Congressman Pete Stark (R-CA), a key architect of the legislation on the Ways and Means Committee, bewailed that "some seniors just take the attitude that they should have these benefits and pay nothing."[61]

AARP officers likewise experienced growing criticism, and were forced to defend their actions. The Association's legislative director, John Rother, explained "The financing mechanism was not our proposal. There were compromises and negotiations. You do the best you can. We supported it at the end." In fact, of course, the Association had been a driving force for the legislation from the outset. And Rother's prediction that even wealthier seniors would come to support the legislation "once they understood the benefits and the reasoning behind it," was being proved wrong. By late 1988, opposition among wealthier seniors was increasing rather than eroding, as they learned more about the specifics of the new law.[62]

Opposition to the bill continued to gain momentum, and continued to be driven by grassroots concerns rather than by the organizational prowess of the interest group superpower, AARP. When 40 smaller senior advocacy groups met in Washington in January 1989 to discuss ways to repeal the bill, the most noted fact about the meeting was AARP's absence.

Politicians were feeling the heat. Discussions about modifying the financing mechanism began to be heard in the halls of Congress. In April, Senate Finance Committee chairman Lloyd Bentsen (D-TX), one of the chief proponents of the original bill, came out in support of reducing the surtax on the wealthy.

Newly elected President George Bush, meanwhile, desperately wanted to avoid any revision of the funding mechanism. He had won on a pledge of "No New Taxes," and any modification of the plan's funding mechanism would further burden an already strained federal Treasury. On April 24, he released a letter written to Ways and Means Chairman Dan Rostenkowski (D-IL), hoping to silence the proposals for reform of the new bill that were percolating in Congress. "It would be imprudent," Bush wrote, "to tinker with Medicare catastrophic insurance literally in its first few months of life."[63]

For his part, Rostenkowski stoically continued to support the plan, but others in Congress were retreating at full stride. In June, the Senate managed to defeat, by the narrowest of margins—51 to 49—a proposal to delay implementation of the new surtax. But the crescendo of phone calls, letters, and visits from angry elderly constituents was taking its toll on Congress. With an eye on the 1990 elections just around the corner (House elections are always just around the corner), Ways and Means leadership finally acceded to pressure from members, and agreed, on July 13, to examine ways to reduce the surtax.

It was not enough. Continued pressure from both constituents and House Democrats prompted Rostenkowski, on July 18, to propose deep cuts in the surtax. It would be reduced from 15% to 5%. Monthly premiums to be paid by all beneficiaries, though, would have to be increased to make up the difference: they would be nearly doubled, from $4.00 to $7.50.

It was not enough. Wealthy seniors, now sensing the momentum in their favor, demanded that the program be funded by the general public, from general revenues—not by its elderly beneficiaries. On July 25, the Ways and Means Committee approved a 50% reduction in the surtax.

It was not enough. As members of Congress returned to their home districts for the August recess, they felt the full wrath of the elderly opponents of the bill. One classic image of the period is that of Rostenkowski, trapped in his car outside a Chicago community center, beseiged by angry, placard-wielding seniors. "Rosty," the political veteran, lost his political judgment. Disconcerted by the shouting seniors, he stubbornly refused to speak with his elderly critics. "Liar!," "Impeach!," and "Recall!" they shouted angrily. He sat silently, locked in the car. One placard said, "Read Our Lips: Catastrophic Care Is a Catastrophe." It was not the type of media photo opportunity that politicians hope for.

Protesters blocked the car's exit. Finally, after a frustrated wait, chairman Rostenkowski bolted from the car and began to walk briskly up the street away from the chanting crowd. They followed. He still refused to speak to the seniors who chased him, and declined to answer questions from the press, except to say "I don't think they understand what's going on. That's too bad."[64]

Home for the summer recess, congresspersons across the country received similar treatment. They were stopped and grilled by angry elderly constituents, and inundated with phone calls and letters. No longer insulated by Washington's geographic and political distance, they were now feeling, many for the first time, the intensity of the opposition to the Catastrophic Care law. Representative Mike Synar (D-OK) summed up the political climate: "There's only one issue: Catastrophic." Senator Thomas Daschle (D-SD) found "unbelievable irritation" among seniors toward the system in place, and Representative David Skaggs (D-CO) reported that even such issues as crime and drugs had taken a backseat to catastrophic care. Senator Simpson of Wyoming, in his sardonic manner, simply reported, "We're getting lots of hell about catastrophic."[65]

By the time members returned to Washington from the summer recess, Congress was ready to act. And the small circle of those calling for repeal of the bill was by now a chorus, growing increasingly vocal in the knowledge that opinion among seniors supported their position. Immediately upon returning to Washington, members of the Senate Finance Committee held a closed-door meeting to discuss revising the bill in order to save it. "There's no question," acknowledged Committee Chairman Bentsen after the meeting, "that you're going to have a very serious effort to repeal [the measure]." By early fall, House Republican Whip Newt Gingrich (R-GA) could announce confidently, "Given the anger among seniors . . . I think it will be repealed before we end the session."[66]

The issue cut across partisan and ideological lines. Republican Senator Durenberger (MN), writing an Op-Ed piece in the *Washington Post,* maintained that the original financing mechanism was the fairest way to fund the plan. It was a position that politicians were increasingly unwilling to take, at least openly. Senator John Danforth (R-MO), a moderate Republican known in Congress for supporting many social welfare programs, replied in an opposing Op-Ed piece that reflected the sentiments of many congresspersons: "Scrap It," he wrote. Many politicians just wanted the whole thing to be over. "It is my strong suspicion," wrote Danforth, "that if we conduct a broad national debate on health care priorities, catastrophic care will not be the first choice of the elderly for national attention."[67]

Catastrophic care had been a policy issue driven largely by the announced spokespersons for the elderly, advocating the purported interests of the elderly. Many of those advocates, it was now clear, were out of touch. On October 4, 1989, House members voted to repeal the program. They voted to repeal the bill by an even larger margin than they had passed it: 360 to 66. Two days later, the Senate voted to save the bill, 73 to 26. But most senators wanted changes in the bill, and House and Senate conferees met in intense, often contentious negotiations to find a middle ground.

They could not. By this time the bill had been so pared down that it was unable to attract strong support from even its original backers. On the morning of November 19, 1989, the conferees gave up. They agreed to scrap the plan altogether.

Still, a few ardent supporters persisted. Among them now, ironically, were conservative Republicans, who feared being blamed for repeal of the bill, and still uncertain of where the elderly stood on the issue. Senate Republican leader Bob Dole (R-KS) warned that "There are going to be some very old, very poor and very sick senior citizens who are going to be hurt if we don't make some provision."[68] But now it was time for Christmas recess. Time to return to the home district, and many did not want the summer experience to be repeated.

In a last-ditch effort the save the plan, Chairman Bentsen asked House and Senate negotiators to return to the table. He hoped that the vote to repeal the bill might have served as "shock treatment" for many in Washinton, and that the backers of the original bill must surely want to save a modified plan rather than have no plan at all.

The shock treatment was not sufficient to revive the Catastrophic Care program. In the early hours of November 22, 1989, a beleagured Congress repealed the 1988 Catastrophic Care Act, just a year and four months after it had overwhelmingly passed the bill.

The Catastrophic Care measure had been the largest expansion of Medicare since its inception, and one of the most significant extensions of social welfare in American history. Its repeal was also historic: it marked the first time that a major piece of social welfare legislation had been repealed—and even before it had gone into effect. For some, it signified the triumph of older Americans over their interest group representatives and political officials, many of whom claimed to speak for the elderly without ever consulting them. For others, it was a triumph of prosperous seniors over needy seniors.

The issue dispelled the notion of a unified senior bloc which marched in lockstep on every policy question. Once the debate moves beyond preserving intact such major existing programs as Social Security and Medicare, senior solidarity begins to break down. The interests of wealthy retirees are very different from their poorer counterparts. Moreover, on issues where there is substantial division among them, the elderly may have no better luck politically than anyone else.

And the directionality of power was clarified, if clarification was needed. The elderly are not a feared political bloc because they have the technical political expertise of the AARP working on their behalf. Rather, AARP is feared because it speaks, or purports to speak, for the elderly. When it ceases to reflect their will, it ceases to be feared. Ultimately, though, that political clout is not a result of strategic political brilliance or shrewd lobbying tactics, but of millions and millions and millions of senior citizens who vote. The spectacle of AARP taking credit for political triumphs brings to mind Aesop's adage: "'What dust I raise!,' said the fly, sitting on the axle of the chariot."

But what the strange, circuitous fate of Catastrophic Care revealed most clearly was the magnitude of the political power of America's elderly. When Francis Townsend took his program to Capitol Hill, politicians could still afford to openly laugh at the spokesmen for the country's older citizens. No one is laughing any more. The concerted political power of the elderly is the most feared political force in Washington. By the end of the grueling Catastrophic Care imbroglio, some politicians had even taken to calling it, sarcastically, the "geezer lobby." But not in public.

Within the span of barely over a year, that "geezer lobby" had politicians jumping through a hoop, first one way, and then the other.

HEGEMON

A "hegemon" is defined as "the leader; that which is capable of command; that which is in power or authority." The United States is sometimes said to have experienced hegemony in international affairs during the period following the Second World War. We emerged from that conflict strong militarily and economically, while all other potential competitors were recovering from the devastation of total war fought on their soil. The United States, during the early postwar years, was powerful enough to dominate the world scene; and, although Americans were not unopposed in their policy aims, and did not achieve every goal they sought, when the United States was unified in focusing on an international objective as a national priority, there was no international force that could successfully oppose it. That is not to say that the United States could take on the world, but that it did not have to, and that it could defeat any adversary that did actively threaten its interests.

The elderly are of comparable predominance in American politics today. They are the superpower of domestic politics. Senior citizens are able to dominate domestic politics in much the same way that the United States was able to dominate international politics immediately following the war. As was true of America in the postwar world, being the hegemon of domestic politics does not mean that America's elderly are able to have anything they desire from the system. It means that they already have much, and that they have the power to protect what they have from potential encroachments. Indeed, opposition to their major interests is, at present, of negligible impact.

On the issues upon which the elderly are in general accord—namely, maintenance of their existing social insurance framework—such opposition as does exist has little prospect of making fundamental reductions in those programs. Two elements work in favor of the elderly in protecting their political bounty. The first, their political activism, makes their programs secure. The second,

Table 6.1
Reported Voting in National Elections, by Age Group
(percentage of eligible voters)

Age Group	1980	1984	1988	1992
18 to 20	35.7%	36.7%	33.2%	38.5%
21 to 24	43.1	43.5	38.3	45.7
25 to 34	54.6	54.5	48.0	53.2
35 to 44	64.4	63.5	61.3	63.6
45 to 64	69.3	69.8	67.9	70.0
65+	65.1	67.7	68.8	70.1

widespread public concurrence, makes their programs, in any practical sense, untouchable.

THE ELDERLY VOTE

Bemoaning the increasing diversion of federal funds from those that serve the needy young to those that serve the middle-class elderly, Senator Daniel Patrick Moynihan (D-NY) reiterated a theme that is heard more and more in Washington these days: "The elderly vote, and kids don't."[69] The Americans most likely to vote are those in the age groups just on the doorstep of retirement, and those already retired. It is a formidable coalition. For politicians, the demographic tide of older citizens has become an irresistible force: the elderly make up an increasing share of the population, and they are more likely to vote than any other age group in the country. Voting turnout increases with age. Or, in other words, the closer Americans get to retirement, the more likely they are to vote (Table 6.1[70]).

THE UNIVERSAL INTEREST GROUP
(or: Just Like You and Me, only Older)

Notwithstanding their broad political participation, if seniors were alone in support for their entitlement programs, concerted opposition might succeed in reversing some of the enormous gains of those programs in the past half century. What makes Social Security and Medicare invulnerable is not merely the political might of the elderly, but the general national consensus in support of those programs. Some 82% of Americans oppose any reductions in spending for Medicare, and 86% oppose reductions in Social Security.[71] In fact, as spending for the programs has grown, so has popular support for them. In 1936, at the outset of Social Security, only 68% of Americans supported the new program.[72]

Talk of a "generation war," then, may have sensational appeal for journalists and writers, but it distorts what is going on. Older Americans do not maintain their government benefits merely because they are able to impose their political agenda on an unwilling public, but because the vast majority of Americans, of all ages, share that agenda. No other federal programs enjoy levels of public support comparable to those of Social Security and Medicare. They are the most popular things that government does. In a 1995 survey asking Americans what federal programs should be cut as part of the ongoing effort to balance the budget, Social Security and Medicare were the last things on the list (Table 6.2[73]).

If this is a generation war, it is a one-sided conflict, with nearly everyone on the side of the elderly. But why is there such universal support for their programs? The answer to that question lies in the unique nature of the elderly as an interest group in society. America is divided into two groups: those who are old, and those who are becoming so. That fact has not made for great political conflict over programs for the elderly.

I know nothing about you, reader, but this: you are aging. It is, in political terms, the only thing that we all have in common. Whatever our race, income, education, religion, occupation, or party affiliation, we are all moving further away from youth, closer toward being "elderly," however that is defined.

Every other interest group in society is particular and exclusive. Interest groups set us apart from, and often put us in conflict with, other segments of the population. The interests of blue-collar workers frequently conflict with those of management; interests of the poor often clash with those of the rich; environmentalists contend with opponents of government regulation; advocates of welfare spending are opposed by would-be tax cutters. From the sugar farmer seeking subsidies to the college student seeking aid to the automaker seeking

Table 6.2
"In Order to Reduce the Federal Budget Deficit, Should the Government Cut Spending on . . . ?" (percent agreeing that programs should be cut)

Arts	65%
Welfare	64%
Defense	58%
Public TV & Radio	56%
Food Stamps	53%
Farm Subsidies	48%
Environment	44%
Medicaid	34%
Anti-Crime Programs	32%
Education	20%
Social Security	19%
Medicare	18%

protection from foreign competition, each request for public assistance pits one claim for benefits against other opposing claims.

In addition, our group affiliations change little over time. If you are black, you will never be white. If you are white-collar, you'll likely not become blue-collar. If you are an advocate of gun control, or of the environment, it is un-likely that your position will be much different ten years from now. And you will never, never, never be younger. But whether you are young or middle-aged you will become, with luck, old.

One group is different from all the rest. The elderly are the only interest group to which we all expect to belong someday. They are the only universal interest group. Most Americans will never be farmers, or auto manufacturers, or educators, or employers, or recipients of food stamps. Each of those pro-grams is selective: the benefits are narrow and exclusive. Those programs go to assist *them*, and most Americans will never be among *them*. But the interests of the elderly will one day be your interests and mine. Their political agenda is everyone's agenda. We are not all prospective members of the National Rifle Association, the United Auto Workers, the American Medical Association, or the National Education Association; but we are all prospective members of the AARP.

Attitudes toward the Social Security tax suggest an important phenomenon at work. When Americans are asked about the fairness of the Social Security tax, no age group describes it as the least fair of the taxes paid, and for most age groups it is seen as the most fair (Table 6.3[74]). Concerns about the fairness of the Social Security tax increase during midlife, but drop dramatically as one approaches one's own turn at the trough of entitlement benefits. By age 45, when one is just five years away from the AARP, support for the Social Secur-ity tax is practically at the same level as for retirees. This is where voting turn-out becomes important. Because older voters participate at higher levels, they

Table 6.3
"Which Do You Think Is the Worst Tax—That Is, the Least Fair—Including Social Security?" (1992)

Age	Federal Income Tax	Social Security Tax	State Income Tax	State Sales Tax	Local Property Tax	Don't Know
18-24	22%	7%	13%	22%	21%	15%
25-34	30	13	9	14	23	11
35-44	28	15	7	17	23	11
45-65	24	8	9	17	27	15
65+	25	7	9	8	28	29

Table 6.4
Reported Voter Turnout, 1992

Age Group	Voting Age Population (in millions)	Percent Who Voted	Total Turnout (in millions)
18-20	9.7	38.5%	3.73
21-24	14.6	45.7	6.67
25-34	41.6	53.2	22.13
35-44	39.7	63.6	25.25
45-64	49.1	70.0	34.37
65+	30.8	70.1	21.59

carry disproportionate weight at the polls, and thus wield disproportionate influence on lawmakers.

Table 6.4[75] shows the reported voter turnout in 1992, broken down for age groups. In 1992, of 105.6 million potential voters under age 45, only 57.78 million actually voted; of 79.9 million potential voters 45 and older, 55.96 million voted. Thus, although those older than 45 comprise a much smaller portion of the voting-age population than those younger, because of their greater voter turnout, they comprise around half of all those who vote. Although, as an age cohort, they do not have a numerical advantage on behalf of their entitlements, they do have an operational one, particularly given the general disunity among younger voters on the issue. As long as Americans continue to age, supporters of Social Security will continue to constitute a formidable political force on behalf of retirement entitlements.

The argument that Americans support the entitlements for the elderly out of our sheer national compassion and generosity is comforting, but not ultimately convincing. It would be more persuasive if we showed similar compassion and generosity toward the youngest Americans, those age 18 and under, who are more economically disadvantaged than the elderly, and certainly no less vulnerable. For, if there is as yet no generational war, nevertheless there are casualties of our generational policies, despite that their voices remain largely unheard, and that the costs that they bear will not be fully known for decades.

Rational self-interest is the better explanation, if not the more flattering one, for why most Americans oppose reductions in the federal entitlement programs for the elderly. Devoting resources to the young is a more selfless enterprise. Those benefits will not directly benefit us: we have already been there, and shall not pass that way again. But by supporting programs for the elderly, we are paving a road upon which we will someday travel; and the closer we are to taking that journey, the more agreeable is the collective expense.

The elderly, moreover, have a paramount tactical advantage: like a fortress in a military battle, government programs, once in existence, are more easily defended than assaulted. To capture a growing share of the nation's resources, the elderly need not struggle to capture new political territory, merely to defend that which is already theirs.

UNTOUCHABLES

Between the direct political power of America's elderly and the broad levels of popular support for their interests, their entitlement programs are effectively immune to fundamental retrenchment. When presidents want to avoid taking the political heat for difficult policy choices, they create commissions. When President Clinton, who was elected in part by warning seniors that George Bush would threaten their entitlements, created the Bipartisan Commission on Entitlement and Tax Reform in 1994, the aim was to make it possible for politicians to candidly address the long-term problems facing Social Security by establishing a broad consensus covering the entire political spectrum. The chairman was moderate Democratic Senator Bob Kerrey (NE), and the vice-chairman was moderate Republican John Danforth (MO). In addition, the Commission included a broad array of political perspectives ranging from Democrats Carol Moseley-Braun (IL), Kika de la Garza (TX), and Daniel Patrick Moynihan (NY), to Republicans Pete Domenici (NM), Alan Simpson (WY), and Bill Archer (TX). In addition, the Commission included members from outside of government, ranging from United Mine Workers President Richard Trumka, to Nixon administration Commerce Secretary Peter Peterson, to former New Jersey Governor Thomas Kean, a Republican. In all, the Commission contained 32 members, in and out of government.

The Commission members were able to agree that crisis looms ahead for Social Security and Medicare. That was the easy part. It reiterated what most observers already knew, and made no news. However, the Commission was unable to fulfill its assignment of recommending concrete reforms that would address the long-term viablity of the programs. That part was too politically sensitive, too divisive. Members of all political viewpoints recoiled at the prospect of going on record for specific solutions (read: specific reductions) for the elderly's entitlements programs.

Thus, in an August 4, 1994, memo, Kerrey and Danforth assured Commission members that the final draft would contain no mention of remedies for the troubled programs. "We have made many of the requested changes and believe we now have a true consensus document that reflects your input. We have deleted any language that suggested particular solutions."[76] The "consensus" included such blunt warnings as "the [Social Security] Trust Fund is projected to run out of money in 2029."[77] Commission members added that "a better future for America can be secured if the country embarks on the course of long-term reform."[78] But, like every other group that has tackled the problem, they left the first perilous steps of that course up to someone else.

Medicare's accelerating spending, far from being cut, cannot even be slowed down much. When Newt Gingrich and the Republican Congress presented a seven-year plan for a balanced budget in 1995, it included, necessarily, reductions in the growth rate of Medicare spending. Their plan proposed a reduction in the *rate of growth* of Medicare spending from 10% annually to over 5% a year for the next few years. The Republicans' "drastic cuts" consisted of expanding Medicare at twice the rate of inflation. It was decried by President Clinton and many Democrats as an "assault" on the elderly, and the Republicans, faced with plummeting approval ratings, began to back off of the issue. As long as it is politically profitable for one side to warn seniors that the other side is threatening their benefits, it will not be politically safe for any politician to discuss controlling spending; and it will be politically profitable for the foreseeable future. Social Security continues to be what former House Majority Leader Tip O'Neill once called "the Third Rail of American politics. Touch it and you die!"[79]

THE CANDOR OF FORMER POLITICIANS

Many congresspeople have given up trying to control the problem of entitlement spending, content to let the next generation solve the problem. Some are getting out of politics in frustration. Shortly before announcing his retirement from the Senate, Sam Nunn (D-GA), a seasoned Washington insider, complained that it was impossible for the government to achieve fiscal balance because seniors' entitlement programs were effectively off limits to economic policymakers, forcing politicians to try to find major savings in programs with comparatively modest budgets. "The way we go about trying to deal with the fiscal problem in the Congress is like Jesse James robbing parking meters."[80]

When Timothy Penney (D-MN) announced in 1993 that he would not seek reelection to a seventh term in the House of Representatives, a certain victory for the popular young politician, he expressed growing frustration over Congress' inability to come to terms with spiraling seniors' entitlements. Penney said of the budget agreement:

We left entitlements nearly untouched. Even with our so-called cuts, Medicare and Medicaid will be growing at 9% a year. . . . We're going to have to tamper with COLAs [cost of living allowances]. We have to tell people that COLAs are not a God-given right. We can't put the retirement programs on automatic pilot and expect to solve our budget problems.

We had an opportunity to have an income-based need test, and we didn't tackle that issue. We didn't tackle it because Democrats are the traditional champions of Social Security and Medicare, and Republicans are afraid to touch them. So no one wants to put them on the table. [But something must be done, Penney warned.] People are becoming more agitated with every year that goes by. They've figured out that we're on a danger-ous course.[81]

When Bill Bradley (D-NJ) announced his retirement from the Senate in 1995, he likewise declared that the system was "broken" and incapable of making the hard choices that must be made.

Political hopefuls, campaigning for office, often criticize "the system" as a means of being elected to it. But when successful politicians voluntarily leave office out of frustration in order to call attention to the "bankruptcy" of Ameri-can politics, that is news. When Senator Warren Rudman (R-NH) left profes-sional politics in 1992, it was not a case of a steward abandoning a sinking ship, leaving the passengers to their ruin. Rudman took the dramatic step precisely in order to wake up Americans to what he considered to be a crisis in the ship of state. The inability to address the crisis of entitlement spending would bring economic stresses in the near term, and crisis in the long term, he warned. Who was responsible? "Congress is not out of touch," he said of a frequently heard complaint. "It is too much in touch, so that most members are afraid to do what needs to be done."[82] That is, politicians are giving Americans what they want.

It is no coincidence, then, that the political bravery of a Rudman or Penney is the bravery of those on their way out of public office, not on their way in. No one gets elected by saying that too great a portion of the federal budget is being spent on senior entitlements. "The only advocates of specific entitlement cuts," laments *Business Week,* "seem to be former politicians."[83]

Until public opinion changes, the policies will not change, regardless of their negative long-term consequences. Peter Peterson has made the issue a per-sonal crusade, traveling across the country, making speeches, trying to change public opinion. In particular, he knows that if the elderly, the hegemon of domestic politics, continue to resist any effort to touch their "entitlements," those programs will continue to be off limits. Peterson's speeches are an effort to alter the views of seniors, and in them, he makes a patriotic appeal to the generation that won the Second World War.

I don't accept for one moment that this generation has forgotten the meaning of sacrifice or surrendered its sense of citizenship. I think there's one last challenge for this genera-tion—a challenge that takes its bearing not just from our rights, but from our responsibili-ties. I'm not here to put down the "greedy geezers"; I'm a geezer myself. But I hope we'll remember, our first loyalty is not to the AARP, but to our country and to our children.[84]

Peterson is in growing company with that sentiment. "What's going on down there in Washington constitutes reckless endangerment of the next genera-tion," laments Boston University economist Larry Kotlikoff.[85] Even as the senti-ment becomes increasingly widespread, though, the entitlements remain off limits.

Announcing Congress' "historic" effort to reduce government spending and balance the federal budget in 1995, House Majority Leader Newt Gingrich and the majority Republicans promised to make deep cuts in everything from food stamps for indigent legal immigrants, to tax breaks for the working poor, job training for the unemployed, and financial support for needy college students.[86] They promised to cut federal assistance for 847,000 poor children who are disabled or suffering from chronic illnesses.[87] And they promised to repeal the National School Lunch Act, which, since its inception at the end of the Second World War, has helped to provide nutritious meals for millions of disadvantaged schoolchildren who otherwise could not afford them.[88]

But before explaining what would be cut, Gingrich was careful to begin the process by explicitly promising what would not be touched: "Everything is on the table except Social Security," he said. "We cannot . . . cope with Social Security politically."[89]

Trading Places

What does one generation owe another? This has been the enduring question, as America has for centuries tried to come to terms with the challenge of intergenational fairness. How do we achieve justice between generations? Among reasonable and well-intentioned observers, there are disputes over that question, but there is little dispute over this: we are taking better care of the last generation than the next one.

"Old people vote." They are the richest segment of the American population. Children cannot vote. They are the poorest segment of the population. There is more than coincidence at work here. The elderly are winning the struggle for resources.

As recently as 1966, when Medicare was just getting underway, poverty among the elderly was the highest of any age group. In that year, just over 10% of those aged 18-64 lived below the poverty line. Around 29% of seniors did.[1] As the benefits of government entitlements have enriched the golden years, poverty among the elderly has steadily declined (Table 7.1[2]).

TRADING PLACES

America's elderly have done well over the past 30 years. Indeed, in economic terms, they have outperformed the nation. Today, 12.2% of seniors live in poverty; 15.1% of all Americans do.[3]

The shift between young and old has been even more dramatic. In the past 30 years, the relative proportions of federal spending on young and old have undergone a complete reversal, with steadily declining shares of federal spending going to the youngest Americans, and increasing shares going to the oldest. As more and more has been needed to fund senior entitlements, money has gradually been siphoned off from critical child-welfare programs. Federal spending

Table 7.1
Poverty Rates for Those Age 65+ and Under 18

	Poverty Rate	
Year	Seniors	Children
1966	28.5%	
1970	24.6	14.9%
1975	15.3	16.8
1980	15.7	17.9
1985	12.6	21.0
1990	12.4	19.9
1993	12.2	21.1

for each senior citizen, nearly $12,000, is over ten times the amount spent on each youngster under the age of 18, just over $1,000.[4] Local, state, and federal governments together spend three times more on each voter over age 65 than on each citizen under age 18.[5] As senior poverty has fallen below the national average, poverty among those under 18, at over 21%, is now the highest of any age group. In fact, the 1995 Luxembourg Income Study, an international comparison of the incomes of families with children, sponsored in part by the National Science Foundation, revealed that child poverty in the United States is higher than in any other Western democracy (Table 7.2[6]). In fact, says Dr. Sheila Kamerman, Columbia University professor of social policy and planning, because the study only included income wealth, and did not take into account other benefits such as the public medical and child care services available in most other countries, the plight of American children is actually understated. "If you were looking at in-kind benefits as well as cash benefits, the situation in the U.S. would look even worse."[7] As it is, the situation looks bleak enough.

Those abstract figures have concrete consequences. Americans' neglect of the rising generation is manifested throughout the entire spectrum of a child's life. Lee Smith writes that, in order to fund the growing economic burden of senior entitlements,

other worthy causes, most critically investment in children, increasingly get pushed aside. Head Start, despite its impressive track record, is budgeted to reach only about one-quarter of the 3- and 4-year-olds who live below the poverty line. That means 1.5 million kids will not be able to start school ready to learn. Vaccination funds are so short that only half the 2-year-olds in Hartford and New Haven, Connecticut have been inoculated against such diseases as measles, tetanus, and tuberculosis, a much smaller percentage than in Algeria or Uganda.[8]

Table 7.2
Poverty Rates Among Those Under Age 18

United States	21.5%	Netherlands	6.2
Australia	14.0	Norway	4.6
Canada	13.5	Luxembourg	4.1
Ireland	12.0	Belgium	3.8
Israel	11.1	Denmark	3.3
United Kingdom	9.9	Switzerland	3.3
Italy	9.6	Sweden	2.7
Germany	6.8	Finland	2.5
France	6.5		

Infant mortality in the United States, around 10 deaths per 1,000 births, is highest in the industrialized world. Many Third World nations do better.[9] America also leads the industrialized world in the death rate of children under age 5, with 12 deaths per 1,000 births.[10] Communicable childhood diseases such as whooping cough and rubella, easy and inexpensive to prevent, are a major factor in the disparate death rates. "Communicable diseases have become more common among this nation's children," concluded the Carnegie Task Force on Meeting the Needs of Small Children. "The reason for this is clear: far too few 2-year-olds are being immunized in the United States."[11]

As poverty among the elderly has plummetted in recent years, poverty among those in their most crucial developmental years has skyrocketed. Between 1971 and 1991, while there was less than a 10% increase in the number of children under age 6, there was more than a 60% increase in the number of those children living in poverty. One-fourth of all American children under age 3 now live in poverty.[12] Nearly one-fourth of all those under age 18 do.

CHILDREN FREEZE BEFORE THEY STARVE

"Our nation is suffering and will continue to suffer from our comparative neglect of our children," writes Harold E. Fey, former editor of *The Christian Century.*

Reasons for the disparate treatment of the old and the young include the simple fact that the elderly vote and children do not. Entitlements for the elderly have become the sacred cow of American politics. Officeholders and candidates threaten entitlements at their own peril.[13]

The phrase has become ubiquitous in modern politics: "The elderly vote and children do not." Alan Pifer, chairman of the Aging Society Project, sees the shift in the distribution of political resources as a reflection of broader national priorities: children do not occupy the same place of prominence and esteem in the national consciousness that they once did.

Today, fewer than 38% of households nationwide contain anyone under 18 years of age, compared with nearly 50% in 1960. In a situation where so few adults feel any direct personal stake in the quality, or even availability, of essential services for children, it is all too easy for those sevices to atrophy and decline.[14]

A recent study by the Council on Adolescent Development on the status of adolescents in America found that they were more likely to be raised in broken homes, neglected by parents, subjected to violence, suffer poor physical and emoptional health, and be inadequately educated than prior generations. They suffered from inadequate health care, inadequate school-related services, inadequate preparation for adulthood. They were, in short, inadequately nurtured. The Council concluded:

The social and economic costs of adverse circumstances that distort adolescent development are unacceptable. They encompass not only personal tragedies, but also widespread disease and disability, ignorance and incompetence, crime and violence, alienation and hatred. Such tragedies are not confined in any tidy way to certain geographic areas or specific groups. Like a toxin, they poison the environment and do wide-ranging harm throughout the nation.[15]

Perhaps the starkest measure of neglect is the incidence of hunger and malnutrition among American children. Here, too, the United States lags far behind other advanced industrial countries, and makes many Third World nations look good by contrast. According to a recent study sponsored by the nonprofit Food Research and Action Center, hunger affects the lives of more than 5 million American children.[16] This is particularly troubling, because children lacking adequate nutrition do more poorly in school, are less prepared for the demands of adulthood, and are more likely to become involved in criminal activities.[17]

The health effects of malnutrition are more predictable, and no less devastating. Children who live in poverty are two to three times more likely to have stunted growth than those who do not.[18] According to the Carnegie Task Force study,

children growing up in poverty suffer from higher rates of malnutrition and anemia than other children. In one urban hospital, low-income 2-year-olds were 40% more likely than other toddlers to be severely underweight and clinically malnourished. They were 60% more likely to suffer malnutrition in the winter months, when, researchers speculated, families diverted their limited funds from food to fuel.

During those first two years of life, receiving adequate nutrition is especially critical. Inadequate nutrition during this period, the Task Force notes, "has much more devastating consequences than at any other time, inhibiting normal growth and development."[19] The conclusion about malnutrition during the winter months is supported by other research. A three-year study conducted by Boston City Hospital found a 30% increase in emergency-room visits by underweight children during the coldest months. Dr. Deborah Frank, director of Boston City Hospital's Failure to Thrive Clinic, attributed the increase to a "heat-or-eat" dilemma faced by poor families. "Parents well know that children freeze before they starve, and in winter some families have to divert their already-inadequate food budget to buy fuel to keep the children warm."[20] It is not just that current policies are creating a future promising harder times awaiting today's children when they are older: millions of America's children are getting a taste of those hard times now.

If questions of generational justice do not play upon the nation's sensibilities, surely those of simple pragmatism should. For, even setting aside ethical considerations, from a strictly utilitarian standpoint programs dealing with childhood hunger would seem to be among the best investments a society can make. By adequately nourishing children, you enable them to learn better, and to better contribute to society when they are grown. Inadequate nutrition stymies both normal physical and cognitive development. By doing something as simple as assuring that all children are adequately fed, we assure a more productive, less violent future for American society. In our care, or neglect, of the young, we are planting the seeds that will determine the nation's destiny in years to come.

Children who live in poverty are:

- Two times more likely to die from birth defects.
- Three times more likely to die from all causes.
- Five times more likely to die from infectious diseases and parasites.
- Six times more likely to die from other diseases.[21]
- Two to three times more likely to be partly or completely deaf.
- 1.2 to 1.8 times more likely to be blind.
- More likely to be mildly mentally retarded.
- Three to four times more likely to suffer iron deficiency.

And in terms of educational performance, children raised in poverty:

- Have IQ scores an average of 9 points lower at age 5.
- Have average achievement scores 11 to 25 percentiles lower.
- Are two-thirds as likely to enroll in college.
- Are half as likely to finish college.
- Are between two and eleven times more likely to drop out of school.[22]

We are sowing the seeds of crisis. The rising generation we now neglect are those who will be called on, as adult workers, to shoulder an unprecedented social and economic burden, supporting the retirement of the enormous baby boom generation. But they are being deprived of the opportunities for development that prior generations enjoyed. "A work force cheated of protein when it is young won't have the muscle required when it matures to keep the economy rolling," Lee Smith writes. "That's especially worrisome because today's youngsters will have to feed and nurse an unparalleled army of oldsters—the 76 million baby-boomers born between 1946 and 1964."[23] Numerous studies confirm what common sense suggests, that being raised in poverty reduces a child's ability to contribute to the social and economic welfare of society when grown.[24] Neglecting the development of today's children is not merely immoral, it is imprudent.

EAT THE YOUNG

Yet we are neglecting them. Why? Describing Congress' promise, in February 1995, to spare the Meals-on-Wheels program for the elderly while it slashed government funding for programs providing food for needy children (programs such as school breakfasts, school lunches, and food stamps), Thomas Rosenstiel recurs to the mantra of modern American politics: "The reason was politics-as-usual: the elderly vote and children don't."[25] When budgets are to be cut, children don't rally, don't threaten political defeat, don't contribute to campaigns. They make easy targets. Jonathan Kozol asks, "How much tougher can we get with children who already have so little?"[26]

WIC (Women, Infants, and Children), the program created to assure adequate nutrition for mothers and very young children, is another case in point. The program provides nutritious staples such as milk and cheese to pregnant women and breast-feeding mothers, and to children under 5. What could be a more prudent expenditure of public funds than to feed developing infants? The National Commission on Children has calculated that, by taking part in the program, an expectant mother who is in a high-risk category (poor, uneducated, or minority) reduces her chances of giving birth to an underweight or premature baby by up to 25%.[27] Even leaving aside moral considerations, in strictly economic terms the program is a good investment. For each dollar spent on the program's preventative nutrition, several dollars are saved in reduced health costs later on. The Carnegie Task Force noted that "the average cost of providing WIC services to a woman throughout her pregnancy is estimated to be less than $250; the costs of sustaining a low-birthweight baby in a neonatal intensive care unit for one day are many times that amount."[28] Yet democratic politics is not particularly good at taking into account long-term benefits when distributing short-term resources. WIC works, but we need that money to fund Social Security and Medicare. The elderly vote, and all that. "Despite its demonstrated success, WIC has never been fully funded. It currently serves some 4 million women and children, out of an eligible population of 7 million."[29]

Even as the economic gap between children and the elderly grows wider, Congress continues to shave away at children's support programs while stoutly refusing to touch senior entitlements. Those, they say, provide security for the vulnerable. The pattern of impoverishment that has characterized much of

American—and world—history, has been turned on its head. The United States, says Senator Moynihan, "is the first society in history in which the poorest group in the population are the children, not the aged. A person six years of younger has a seven times greater likelihood of being poor than a person 65 or older."[30]

As federal spending becomes more constrained, programs for children are reduced in order to sustain funding for middle-class seniors, after the manner of certain reptiles which, under conditions of scarce resources, will consume their young in order to nourish themselves. "Children are getting poorer as the nation gets richer," says Marian Wright Edelman, president of the Children's Defense Fund. "It's unconscionable."[31]

In 1720, English satirist Jonathan Swift noted that an undue share of the nation's attention and resources were being diverted to the needs of poor children. Ireland, Swift complained, was becoming "crowded with beggars of the female sex, followed by three, four, or six children, all in rags, and importuning every passenger for alms."[32] Swift's classic solution was "A Modest Proposal for Preventing the Children of Poor People in Ireland from Being a Burden to their Parents or Country, and for Making Them Beneficial to the Public." The modest proposal: eat the children before they could become an economic hardship. "I have been assured by a very knowing American of my acquaintance in London, that a young healthy child well nursed is at a year old a most delicious, nourishing, and wholesome food, whether stewed, baked, or boiled."[33] Devouring the children of a nation has a twofold benefit: it provides an inexpensive source of nourishment for older generations now, and diminishes the need to expend scarce resources caring for the children later. It is the ultimate form of consumption for a consumption-driven society.

Earlier in the twentieth century, the cry of revolutionaries was "Eat the rich!" Today, public policy has turned that on its head: government aid for children living in poverty is being reduced so that wealthy retirees can continue to receive their annual cost-of-living-adjustments, partially tax-free. Policy analysts Subrata Chakravarty and Katherine Weisman, studying the intergenerational distribution of resources within American society, found that the United States is, for the first time in its history, "witnessing a massive transfer of income and wealth from the younger generations to the older." This transfer of wealth has resulted in diminished upward mobility for the rising generations. As more and more of the nation's resources are diverted to support the elderly, younger Americans are less likely to own homes and less likely to experience rising real wages than their parents did. They will be the first generation in American history not to live as well as their parents. "Simply put," Chakravarty and Weisman write, "in economic terms we are consuming our children."[34]

In research sponsored by the Department of Education, Laurence Kotlikoff and Jagdeesh Gokhale analyzed the flow of government benefits to different generations, compared with the relative lifetime tax burdens of those generations. Their conclusion: older Americans today receive far more in government benefits than they ever paid in taxes. Moving down the generational ladder, however, the pattern shifts. The younger you are, the more taxes that government is likely to take from you over your lifetime, and the less, proportionally, you can expect to receive in return. "Is it fair that today's children may have to hand upwards of 40% of their lifetime income over to the government while their grandparents will end up paying just over a quarter of their income?" they ask.[35] "If society's notion of generational equity entails extracting an equal proportional sacrifice from each generation, these numbers are highly discomforting. They reveal a U.S. generational policy that will burden today's children much more than today's adults. Tomorrow's children, meanwhile, are likely to be burdened even more."[36]

TREADMILL

Young people in America today are more likely to experience childhood poverty, malnutrition, violence, and thwarted life prospects than the generation whose retirement years they will be expected to support. Compared to the preceding generation, they will be more neglected in their youth and more taxed in their working years. Indeed, their primary economic inheritance from the prior generation will be a multi-trillion-dollar national debt they will be expected to pay. That debt, furthermore, represents money that was not spent on them—relative spending on children has declined—but on the retirement expenses of their parents and grandparents.

The generation that will be required to do more is given less support in its own development. That is the conclusion reached by economists Kotlikoff and Gokhale: "A significant body of evidence points to a deterioration in the living standard of children relative to that of adults. . . . It is undeniable that the cost of the U.S. government's kind treatment of today's elderly will be borne on the backs of tomorrow's children."[37]

In addition to a national debt and higher tax burdens, they will inherit an employment marketplace in which prospects for upward advancement are diminished compared with those of prior generations. Workers in the United States today are finding that they are having to work longer hours than their parents and grandparents did, simply to make ends meet. According to a recent study, Americans work an average of 163 more hours per year than they did 20 years ago—the equivalent of an extra month on the job.[38] While leisure time expands for older Americans, it is contracting for nearly everyone else.

An increasing proportion of women, moreover, are entering the workforce, not primarily in hopes of self-fulfillment, but in order to help balance the family budget. Studies show that the majority of women with young children would prefer to be at home with them, but for most of these, this has ceased to be an option. In the 1960s, about one-fourth of women with children worked outside the home; by 1990, two-thirds did.[39]

With people working more, and with more people working, we might expect the American family to have experienced a tremendous economic boom during the past generation. It hasn't. The problem is that real wages have been stagnant during the past 20 years. According to the Census Bureau, median family income in 1990 was $35,353, only $2,000 more, when adjusted for inflation, than in 1970.[40] But workers today are working more hours than they were then, and the mother is more likely to be out of the home, working as well. The 1995 *Economic Report of the President* noted, "The dimensions of the family income problem are compelling. The real median family income in 1993 was virtually unchanged from what it had been in 1973, despite the fact that during the intervening 20 years real output had increased by 57%."[41]

If national output increased so dramatically, and the average worker did not benefit, where did all that added wealth go? Much of it went to the richest Americans. According to the Congressional Budget Office, 60% of the increase in after-tax income between 1977 and 1989 went to the richest 1% of American families, those earning at least $310,000.[42] Between 1977 and 1988, real family income increased substantially only for the richest 10% of the population (Table 7.3[43]). The other 90% have been working longer in order to stay in place, and many haven't even done that.

Nationally, incomes have remained stagnant over the past generation. The president's *Economic Report* continues:

The stagnation of real median family income has been accompanied by an equally disturbing trend of increasing income inequality. In contrast to the years from 1950 to 1973, when average real family incomes increased across the entire income distribution, between 1973 and 1993 the share of total family income declined for the lower 80% of the income distribution.[44]

Table 7.3
Changes in Average Family Income, 1977-1988
(in 1987 constant dollars)

Income Decile	Percent Change
Poorest 10%	-14.8
2nd	-8.0
3rd	-6.2
4th	-6.6
5th	-6.3
6th	-5.4
7th	-4.3
8th	-1.8
9th	1.0
Richest 10%	16.5

Thus, although after-tax real incomes for the richest few percent have increased dramatically, incomes for most American workers have actually declined.[45] "This is the first generation I can identify," says Dr. Frank Cassell, professor emeritus of Industrial Policy at Northwestern University, "that's likely not to do as well as the previous one."[46] It is a startling contrast: the incomes of middle-age, middle-income families have declined over the past generation, as the incomes of the elderly, whom they are supporting with their payroll taxes, have risen dramatically. And, let us be clear, it is those "median income" workers, those who are struggling to stay in place, that fund the senior entitlement programs. They are the ones affected by each increase in the Federal Insurance Contributors Act (FICA) tax. Wealthy Americans, who have experienced rising incomes, actually pay a smaller portion of their incomes to the FICA taxes, those which go to support Social Security and Medicare, than those whose real incomes have declined over the past 20 years.

There is another paradox here: 75% of all workers, and 90% of workers age 18-34, pay more in FICA taxes than they pay in federal income taxes. "Ironically," says Alden Levy, National Planning Director of Thirteenth Generation, a group representing the interests of younger Americans, "because of these high taxes, many young people are forced to go without their own health care."[47]

Census bureau statistics confirm Levy's claim. According to the 1995 *Population Profile of the United States,* "Persons 18 to 29 years old made up only 17.4% of the total U.S. population, but accounted for 29.2% of all uninsured persons. About one-fourth (26.8%) of persons in this age group were without health insurance."[48] Young children are in a similarly precarious situation. The Carnegie Task Force found that "8.4 million children lacked access to health care services because they had no insurance."[49] The report concluded that "the United States lags far behind other nations in providing health care services to children. Except for South Africa, the United States is alone among industrialized nations in failing to provide health insurance for children . . . nearly 13% of America's children do not have access to the health care services they need to grow up healthy."[50] By contrast, according to the Census Bureau, "only 1.2% of persons 65 years old and over were without coverage."[51]

The final insult: after being neglected in their youth, and paying more in taxes during their working years, the rising generation should not expect to receive a positive return on their payroll taxes, in great contrast to the retirees they are now working to support. The Concord Coalition reports that

workers with average earnings who retired in 1980 got back their employee-employer retirement taxes in less than three years (including retirement COLAs and 2.3% imputed interest on payroll taxes). When average-wage workers who are in their late 20s today retire in 2030, they will need more than 18 years to recover their employee-employer taxes—two years longer than men's projected life expectancy for that year.[52]

Peter Drucker, the noted management expert, has an explanation for the growing gap between the well-being of young and old in America. "We [the elderly] are the greediest class in human history," he says bluntly.[53]

EMPIRE OF THE "VULNERABLE"

The arguments against reducing senior entitlements are emotionally powerful. The elderly have worked hard to contribute to society's prosperity, and now, when they are economically disadvantaged, they deserve society's protection, even if it means a much greater return than what they paid into Social Security when they were working.

Government spending for seniors is defended as sacrosanct, immune from cuts when all else is being cut, because the elderly are "vulnerable." It is the anthem of AARP lobbyists, and of politicians explaining why Social Security alone should be immune to budget cuts. The vulnerability of the elderly is the magic shield in the political arsenal of seniors, and practically cuts off further discussion of the issue. The elderly are vulnerable, and to reduce their benefits would be to leave them exposed to the harsh social and economic conditions that necessitated Social Security in the first place.

But it is not so. The view that all elderly are economically vulnerable, simply by virtue of being older, is based on an archaic conception of what it means to grow old. In 1935, it was a view that was grounded in the reality of the times. When Social Security was created, the question of need was not taken into account when considering one's benefits, because to be old was, by definition, to be needy. According to gerontologist Robert Binstock, of the Case Western Reserve Medical School, "'Old,' 'poor,' 'frail,' and 'deserving' used to be synonymous. So when the New Deal created the old age welfare state, we exempted the elderly from screenings based on need."[54]

Time has altered the material conditions associated with aging, but not the policies designed to address it. Aggregate statistics tell us that it is no more accurate to speak of the elderly as "needy" than it is to speak of, say, all Irish-Americans, or all single mothers, or all immigrants as being needy simply by virtue of belonging to that category. Some are needy, some are not.

Millions of older Americans are as healthy, and more economically secure, than millions of middle-class couples struggling to raise families in an economy where real median wages have been stagnant for a generation. Who is more vulnerable, the wealthy retiree with a paid house (or two) and few major expenses, or the young worker one paycheck away from poverty? Yet the wealthy retiree pays a lower tax rate on his Social Security income than the worker pays on her wages; the retiree is safe from political encroachments, secure behind the shield of vulnerability claimed, not due to any physical or economic condition, but due to the simple statistical fact of his age. For those interested in fighting "ageism," artificial distinctions and discrimination based on one's chronological years, the policy of taxing working-class young to support wealthy elderly might be a good place to start.

The Concord Coalition puts the problem of generational fairness in these terms: "Imagine two American couples with $30,000 in income, filing joint tax returns. One couple consists of two 25-year-olds with one child; the other consists of two 70-year-old retirees with no children. Who pays how much in total federal taxes?"

The answer: "The 25-year-old couple pays $7,103, eight times as much as the 70-year-olds, who pay $855."[55] "No other country tilts the tax code towards the elderly," says former Commerce Secretary Peterson, "and very few gouge the young as we do."[56]

The elderly are potentially vulnerable, children are absolutely so. The unemployed are vulnerable. The disabled are vulnerable. Yet poor children, the unemployed, and the disabled have all undergone reductions of public appropriations in recent years. Only older Americans have been immune. Well over half a million millionaires currently receive monthly Social Security checks, partly tax-free.[57] Put another way, for every elderly millionaire receiving a Social Security COLA this year, there are half a dozen poor children who are not receiving the nutritional support of the WIC program because the program has been underfunded. The seniors' shield of vulnerability leaves them largely immune to political assault on their benefits. Or, in other words, invulnerable. And thus we devote more public resources to seniors who are not needy than to children who are.

But it is not only the richest seniors who are better off than average Americans. Wherever you travel in America, wherever you drive or vacation, you cannot avoid the ubiquitous announcements of special services and discounts for older customers. It is not just that most seniors have more time: they have more money also. In fact, seniors have more discretionary income, more money left over after expenses, than any other group in the population (Table 7.4[58]).

In the past generation, consumption among seniors has spiraled relative to that of younger Americans. For every dollar that a 30 year old spends today, the average 80 year old spends $1.16. As recently as the early 1960s, for every dollar that the 30 year old spent, the 80 year old only spent 65 cents.[59] In addition to having more money to spend, seniors typically have greater net worth than other age groups, even when excluding the accumulated equity in their homes (Table 7.5[60]).

More free time, more money. Basic expenses such as housing and transportation dramatically reduced.[61] No wonder that Americans over 60 express higher levels of life satisfaction than any other age group in America. Whereas only half of those between the ages of 18 and 49 say that they are "quite pleased with the way things are going" in their lives, fully two-thirds of those over 65 say so.[62] Yet, despite having greater accumulated wealth, and more disposable income, the elderly are the only Americans presumed to be needy, as a group, by government policy. Much more so, for example, than the young, a group for

Table 7.4
Discretionary Income Per Capita

Age Group	Discretionary Income
25-29	$3,306
30-34	3,713
35-39	4,195
40-44	4,679
45-49	4,572
50-54	4,899
55-59	5,759
60-64	6,188
65-69	6,280
70+	6,073

Table 7.5
Median Net Worth of Households, 1988

Age of Householder	Total Net Worth	Excluding Home Equity
Under 35	$6,078	$3,258
35-44	33,183	8,993
45-54	57,466	15,542
55-64	80,032	26,396
65-69	83,478	27,482
70-74	82,111	28,172
75+	61,491	18,819

whom such a classification might be more appropriate. Poverty among the elderly is much lower than for the population as a whole, and when noncash benefits, such as Medicare and housing subsidies are included, estimates put their poverty rate as low as 5%,[63] or even 3%.[64] America's senior entitlements are, to some extent, a security net for those who are already secure; welfare for the well-off. In 1990, Social Security paid out $8 billion in benefits to families with incomes of over $100,000.[65]

THE TRULY NEEDY

Having suggested that being older is not synonymous with being needy, we must quickly indicate that for millions and millions of seniors, Social Security means the difference between sufficiency and impoverishment, between receiving vital medical care and being unable to afford it. Indeed, although the poverty rate for seniors is below that of the general population, 26.3% of Americans over 65 live near poverty (within 150% of the poverty line), compared with 22.2% of the overall population.[66] For a great many elderly, Social Security is a lifeline keeping them just out of poverty, the economic safety net intended by its creators (Table 7.6[67]).

As intended, Social Security keeps millions of older Americans out of poverty. But it is a peculiar security net which gives less to those who need more, and more to those who need less. Since benefits are not distributed according to need, those who depend most on the monthly Social Security check typically receive much smaller benefits than those who don't need them at all. Monthly Social Security checks going to those with incomes over $100,000 are, on average, twice the size of the checks going to those with incomes under $10,000.[68]

Table 7.6
Share of Income from Social Security Among Those 65 and Over

Lowest 20%	79%
Second	76%
Third	58%
Fourth	41%
Highest 20%	18%

In 1991, Social Security and Medicare paid $74 billion in benefits, one-fifth of all expenditures, to households with incomes over $50,000.[69] Those who advocate Social Security as a means for insuring the security of vulnerable older Americans might reasonably support political efforts to control benefits going to the more affluent, thus freeing scarce resources for those who more urgently need them.

SUNRISE, SUNSET

Spending for the elderly acknowledges past contributions, spending for the young enables future ones. A prudent society will search for a balance between the two, between the moral imperatives of caring for the past generation and the pragmatic need to care for the next. Our national inheritance is a good one, and we owe a debt to the generation who created it; the future, however, is uncertain, and we owe it to prudence to prepare those who will create it. Public spending, though, is increasingly devoted to the former, at the expense of the latter. We are taking better care of the last generation than the next one.

Economists refer to investment in the development of children as "sunrise investment," since it prepares the young to make contributions to the social health and material welfare of society. That investment will be returned, in the form of greater productivity, year after year, for 50, 60, or 70 years to come. It is the ultimate form of public investment because a small amount spent now can yield returns for decades to come. It is an investment in human infrastructure, like building roads, bridges, and communications systems that will generate greater prosperity far into the future.

"Sunset spending," by contrast, is the allocation of resources to those in their later years. This does not suggest that such spending is necessarily any less important or essential, but it does allude to the impolitic fact that it is, indeed, less economically profitable. Because the elderly are largely removed from economic productivity, and have fewer remaining years, the positive economic effects of spending on the elderly are generally more narrow in scope and more limited in duration than many other types of public spending.

To elucidate the distinction between "sunrise" versus "sunset" spending, we will assert an extremely unpleasant economic reality: when an older person is neglected by society, the material effects of that neglect, while terrible, are borne primarily by the elderly individual himself. But when a child is neglected, the effects of that neglect may persist for a generation, and permeate not only the life of the individual, but of her future family, employment, and the broader society for many years to come. Each year that the current level of childhood poverty is maintained costs the U.S. economy between $36 and $177 billion in lost future economic output alone.[70]

Of course, public spending is not, and should not be, a purely utilitarian calculus. Expected cost-benefit return cannot be the only consideration when evaluating the merit of government expenditure. But in times of severe budgetary constraints, we must at least begin to acknowledge the existence of an opportunity cost in the distribution of public resources. We must acknowledge that trade-offs exist, that choices are being made, if only implicitly: the greater the share that senior entitlements command, the smaller the portion remaining for other vital public needs. We must at least begin to acknowledge that there are costs to our public generosity toward the elderly.

Dr. Daniel Callahan, Director of the Hastings Center, a think tank focusing on the ethical challenges of scientific progress, puts the trade-off in its starkest terms: how much should society be willing to spend in order to keep elderly patients alive? $10,000? $50,000? $200,000?

A patient in her mid-70s receives a liver transplant. Her life is extended by, perhaps, a few years. The operation costs $200,000. It is covered by Medicare. Her extended longevity is indebted to advances in technology and expansions of public benefits. Dr. Callahan asks: Can we afford such progress?[71] Can we afford, as a society, to spend any amount of money necessary in order to gain that next increment of longevity, attained by that next technological breakthrough? Will Medicare pay for every new technology that comes along? Callahan points to projections that, by the year 2040, "the elderly will represent 21% of the population and consume 45% of all health-care expenditures." He asks, "How can costs of that magnitude be borne?"[72]

The $200,000 cost of that liver transplant might go to inoculate hundreds of poor children against disease, or to help feed them. What about heart transplants for 70 year olds? Ought we to support any medical procedure that will prolong life?

Where will the money come from? From further cuts in spending for the young? Organ transplants for 70 year olds are a form of public consumption, not investment. In Japan and Europe, they are not done at all. Vaccinating a 2 year old is a form of public investment. Spending on Head Start, on quality child care, on quality education, are forms of public investment. We may choose, as a society, to subsidize organ transplants, but we ought to do so after a public dialogue, and with the explicit public awareness that it involves giving up other public goods: that choices are being made, and priorities established. Where resources are limited, difficult choices must be made.

Terrible choices lie ahead. America is a rich country, but no country will ever be rich enough to afford every medical service that might extend life an increment. Within just 20 years, most hospital beds in the United States will be occupied by those 65 and older—those on Medicare. As technology progresses, costs rise. The patient, instinctively intent upon self-preservation, does not ask what it costs. The doctor, intent upon saving lives, does not ask what it costs. Somebody must ask what it costs.

Those who advocate setting limits on health care spending, as with other forms of support for the elderly, are called heartless and uncaring, as Dr. Callahan has been. The victims of those policies are here, now: the elderly patient unable to receive a federally funded liver transplant will make for sensational, touching television interviews. But those whose policies leave social insurance emaciated for future generations are not called heartless or uncaring, because the victims of those policies will not be as discernible for years. There are no simple answers to the ethical dilemmas of what a nation can or should spend on the old or the young, but we, as a society, have not yet even begun to acknowledge that choices are being made. The choices ahead only get harder.

WHAT GENERATION WAR?

Political analysts and pundits have been predicting it for years: the young, recognizing that the elderly are living well at their expense, will rise up in united opposition, and American politics will become a battleground between generations. "If I were under 30," says Senator Kerrey, "I would be angry at beneficiaries' unwillingness to make some changes."[73]

"When our children learn about where Social Security and Medicare are heading, ignorance and apathy will turn to anger," says Peter Peterson.[74] "I believe the young eventually will rebel against tax and other burdens," writes Nobel prize-winning economist Gary Becker. "They will demand restraints on transfers to the elderly and, possibly, even major modifications in age-discrimination and retirement legislation."[75]

Former Senator Paul Tsongas (D-MA), a vocal advocate of Social Security reform, sounds a similar warning: "This country is headed for generational warfare. Politicians running for future office won't be cast as Democrats or Republicans. They'll either be pro-worker candidates or pro-retiree candidates."[76] The drumbeats of impending generation war seem to be getting louder.

In some ways, the times seem suited for such a backlash. Young people now believe that they are paying more into Social Security than they will receive back. More young Americans believe in UFOs than believe that Social Security will be financially sound when they retire.[77] Joe Edelheit, age 21, a former field coordinator for 1992 presidential candidate Paul Tsongas, sums up the view of many young people, "The AARP has the power to mortgage our future. Our generation is under attack."[78]

"We don't believe in Social Security, the way it is now constituted, any more than we believe in the tooth fairy or Santa Claus," says Deroy Murdock, cofounder of Third Millennium, an activist group representing members of "generation X," the post-baby boom generation.[79] Murdock's resentment has not yet translated into action of any political consequence. His group has attracted around 1,000 dues-paying members,[80] barely even symbolic opposition to AARP. Rob Nelson and Jon Cowan, cofounders of Lead or Leave, another advocacy group for young voters, have likewise tried to rally members of their generation to political activism.

If each of us wrote Congress calling for Social Security reform, participated in a rally, or even talked to our grandparents about the need to fix the system (perhaps asking them to renounce their AARP membership), we'd make Washington feel the heat and actually start revamping the Social Security system to be fair to all generations. . . . Given the problems we have inherited, we can't start too soon."[81]

Nelson and Cowan call their plan "Revolution X." It is a call to put pressure on the political system, to force changes in a retirement system which all analysts acknowledge will treat future retirees less generously than present ones.

They gave a revolution, but nobody came. Like the term "generation war" itself, their pronouncements carried a certain dramatic appeal. They sold some books, and made the rounds of the talk shows, but the impact of their revolution on politics has been as the sound of a tiny pebble dropped into a great canyon.

There are a couple of reasons why the revolt of the young has not been, and may not be, as dramatic as many predicted. First, younger Americans still participate at much lower levels than any other age group. Even if there were a general consensus among the young on any issue, including Social Security, their influence would be muted due to their continued political apathy. In fact, of course, there is no such consensus. "Young voters rarely have the cohesion or the interest to become a political force," says American Enterprise Institute scholar William Schneider.[82]

More important, though, is the status of the elderly as a unique interest in American society. They are the universal interest group. Prophets of a generation war presume that the interests of the young, particularly as regarding existing Social Security policies, will be uniformly opposed to the interests of the elderly. This shared set of interests will then be the basis of political conflict between young and old. But because of the complexity of the elderly as an interest, that uniformity of interest among the young does not exist. Even among young people who do not believe that Social Security will give them a positive return on their monthly payroll contributions, millions have parents or grandparents who would be affected by any diminution of benefits. If a family member requires Social Security benefits to remain independent, it is not only in their interest that those benefits continue. All members of the family, young and old, are affected when a parent or grandparent loses his or her independence.

Indeed, younger Americans are more likely to support increased spending for senior entitlements than the elderly are themselves.[83] And, as we have seen, only a small portion of young people view the Social Security payroll tax as unfair. They are almost as likely as retirees themselves to report that the payroll tax is fair, even though most of them pay more in payroll taxes than in federal income taxes.[84] These are not the seeds of revolution.

Unless the elderly themselves support efforts to reduce their entitlements, it seems unlikely, in the foreseeable future, that the political system will succeed in substantially controlling costs. But, at present, there are no signs of such a willingness, even among those who do not really need the benefits. The commitment of America to the welfare of its elderly has not been matched, in the view of many, by the commitment of its elderly to the welfare of America. Earlier in this century the elderly needed the protection of society from economic adversity; now, a growing chorus of critics asks, who will protect society from the political demands of the elderly? If seniors do not consent, politicians are unlikely to take the political risks involved in curbing entitlement spending. In 1935, when the "Old People's Crusade" was pushing the Townsend plan, many politicians voted for the plan notwithstanding its obvious destructive effects upon the economy. Today, there are three times more seniors, and politicians are not three times more courageous.

To level the playing field, Paul Peterson, director of Harvard University's Center for American Studies, suggests "an immodest proposal," playing off Swift's essay. Dr. Peterson notes the growing imbalance in federal welfare benefits between young and old, and the resulting impact on living standards. Poverty among children has been rising as rapidly as poverty among the elderly has declined. The young are getting poorer and poorer, while seniors are getting richer and richer. "One need only compare the welfare of children with that of the elderly to see both the extent of the sacrifice being exacted of children and the importance of the ability to vote."[85]

Paul Peterson's immodest solution: "Let's give children the vote." After all, with twice as many children as seniors (65 million vs. 32 million), politicians would have to take account of their interests, and children would enjoy some of the political clout now reserved for seniors: "If children were enfranchised, fundamental policy changes would certainly follow. Groups representing children would immediately acquire status and power, they would frighten politicians with organized letter-writing campaigns, they would demand a bigger share of the welfare pie, and they would insist that programs for children be redesigned."[86] Extreme conditions call for extreme responses, he says. "What is alarming is the current imbalance [between young and old] in the structure of the current American welfare state and the nation's political incapacity to do anything about it."[87]

"Given the country's propensity to eat its future," writes Peterson, "it may be possible to avoid actions tantamount to Swift's own proposal only by giving children the right to vote."[88] His radical proposal is meant to highlight the radical disparity in America's treatment of its young and old.

The term "generation war" is, as noted, inappropriate at present, since war requires combattants on opposing sides, and at the moment there is not sufficient organized political opposition to the interests of the elderly to signify that level of conflict. Many contend that "plunder" would be more apt, since resources are being seized in the absence of their rightful owners, or without their ability to respond.

With the alluring power to vote benefits for yourself, democracy is a wonderful thing for present generations, but makes uncertain provision for future ones. Politicians react to political power more than justice, and the elderly have power on their side. In addition, democracy is short-sighted: an election or two in the future is the furthest horizon a politician can afford. The question for the candidate is: What must I promise voters today to retain office in this election? The short-term horizons of American politics have, thus far, been inadequate to address the long-term challenges ahead.

8

The Gray Years Ahead

"It's a great time to be silver!," the ad slogan goes. It has never been truer. It may not be so true in years to come. America has chronically put off making the critical political and economic choices necessary to accommodate one of the most dramatic demographic transitions in human history. In 1900, 1 in 25 Americans were over the age of 65; today, about 1 in 8 are; by the year 2030, 1 in 5 will be.[1] We are not prepared.

The year 2030 appears prominently in age projections for a good reason. In that year, the tail end of the baby boom will turn 65 and enter the ranks of senior citizens. Some 76 million children were born between 1946 and 1964 (roughly one-third of the entire population). For a number of reasons, including a hopeful economic outlook following the end of the Second World War, and the reuniting of soldiers long-separated from those they loved, a spike in the birthrate occurred in virtually all industrialized nations, although it persisted unusually long in the United States. The resulting "boomer" generation has transformed politics, culture, economic and commercial life, religion, and virtually every other aspect of American public and private life.

Demographer Ken Dychtwald has studied the effects of this enormous generation, a "pig moving through a python," and found an unprecedented influence:

When the boomers arrived, the diaper industry prospered. When they took their first steps, the shoe and photo industries skyrocketed. The baby-food industry, which had moved 270 million jars in 1940, ladled out enough strained meals to fill 1.5 billion jars a year by 1953. . . .

When the boomers hit school age in the early to mid-1950s, many schools went into double sessions. More elementary schools were built in America in 1957 than in any year before or since. There was a boom not only in teachers' colleges and in school-building, but also in the market for Hula Hoops, skateboards, Slinkees, and Frisbees. Television shows for and about kids became central to the television industry. We had become a child-centered nation.[2]

The impact on the American psyche of the interests and values of this single generation has persisted as the baby boom has aged. As they became teenagers, more high schools were built than ever before. Then there was an explosion in university admissions. When they took up marijuana smoking, profits from Zig Zag roll-your-own cigarette papers increased by 25% every year for a decade.

The shift in America's attention during the 1970s was toward the needs of young adulthood: books based on earning a living, self-esteem, and interpersonal relationships were popular. When the boomers were in their 30s, *Thirtysomething* became the hit television show of the 1980s. The *Wall Street Journal* became the bestselling newspaper, and books on business success were popular. Instead of "hippies" there were now "yuppies."[3] In the nineties came middle-age concerns, and the first boomer president, Bill Clinton. Whatever the future brings, we can be sure that it will be heavily impacted by the baby boom generation.

As of 1996, the first boomers were eligible for membership in the AARP. From now on, a baby boomer will turn 50 every seven seconds for the next two decades. Inevitably, in a few years the hit television show will be *Fiftysomething,* or the same show with another name.

In the January 1996 edition of its monthly *Bulletin*, the AARP was already honing its message in preparation for this huge new potential constituency. "Boomers Will Find AARP a Resource in the Future," the headline says. Horace Deets, the Association's executive director writes, "It is not the size of this group or their chronological age that matter most. It is their needs and interests that are important." Deets assures baby boomers facing the challenges of aging that the Association "stands ready to help."[4] The generation with the slogan "Don't trust anyone over 30" is now being recruited by the AARP.

"I hope I die before I get old," the boomers once sang. But the boomers did not die. They are, despite their best efforts, getting old. And will grow much older still. Older, in fact, than any generation before them in history. And, as with every prior stage in the their life-cycle journey, as the boomers grow older, America will follow. As the boomers reached middle age, a pharmaceutical firm had developed and begun to market a moderately effective remedy against baldness, something for which men had searched in vain throughout all the preceding millenia of human history. A large market of image-conscious boomer men had provided the economic incentive for drug companies to invest millions in developing the product. The baby boomers have already transformed American society, but the past is only prologue for what is to come. In the grocery store, meanwhile, Paul Simon's "Fifty Ways to Leave Your Lover" is playing to the soothing strains of Muzak.

BOOM AND BUST

The dramatic demographic changes of the past century have been only a few gusts in the forefront of a whirlwind that is yet to arrive. In the political stresses induced by efforts to control entitlement spending in the 1990s, Americans have felt the harbinger portending what is to come, but have not yet felt the real impact. The demographic storm on the horizon will alter much of the landscape of American politics and society forever. Where, in the past, some Americans have lived beyond 65, many will, in the future, live well beyond 85. Where the balance of young to old has shifted, it will shift further. Where the costs of supporting the elderly have been high, they will become much higher still.

We have seen how changes in the number and proportion of older citizens during the past 50 years have pushed costs of government programs for the elderly to levels that are already straining government budgets. An examination of where those demographic trends are headed in the next 50 years suggests the magnitude of the challenges facing the United States (Table 8.1[5]). Even the Census Bureau's moderate forecasts depict a nation, not too distant in the future, that resembles contemporary Florida, only older.

The only age group growing at a faster rate than the over-65 segment of the population will be the "oldest old," those 85 and older, the costliest group in the population to support (Table 8.2[6]).

Many have compared government programs for the elderly to a giant "Ponzi scheme," a wealth transfer that can function as long as there are a growing number of those paying into the system relative to those taking benefits from it. In 1967, at the height of America's postwar economic boom, Nobel prize-winning

Table 8.1
Actual and Projected Growth of the Older Population, 1960-2050
Americans 65 and Older

Year	Number 65+ (millions)	Percent of Total Population
1960	16.56	9.2
1970	19.98	9.8
1980	25.55	11.3
1990	31.56	12.6
2000	34.88	13.0
2010	39.36	13.9
2020	52.07	17.7
2030	65.60	21.8
2040	68.11	22.6
2050	68.53	22.9

Table 8.2
Actual and Projected Growth of Americans Over 85, 1960-2050

Year	Number 85+ (millions)	Percent of Total Population
1960	.929	.5
1970	1.41	.7
1980	2.24	1.0
1990	3.25	1.3
2000	4.62	1.7
2010	6.12	2.2
2020	6.65	2.3
2030	8.13	2.7
2040	12.25	4.1
2050	15.29	5.1

economist Paul Samuelson defended Social Security on precisely those terms. There was no need for benefits to correspond to what an individual, or a generation, paid into the system, he argued, because there would always be a fresh supply of younger workers with larger incomes supporting the retirees. "The beauty about social insurance," Samuelson wrote,

is that it is actuarially unsound. Everyone who reaches retirement age is given benefit privileges that far exceed anything he has paid in. And exceed his payments by more than ten times as much (or five times, counting employer contributions). How is this possible? . . . There are always more youths than old folks in a growing population. More important, with real incomes growing at some 3% per year, the taxable base upon which benefits rest in any period are much greater than the taxes paid historically by the generation now retired. . . . A growing nation is the greatest Ponzi game ever contrived.[7]

Logic like that produced the enormous benefit expansions of the 1960s and 1970s. But in the generation since Samuelson wrote, both of the foundations upon which he supported the pay-as-you-go funding mechanism for Social Security have been confuted: real incomes, far from increasing at 3% annually, have remained stagnant[8] and, despite a growing population, the proportion of workers to retirees has steadily declined. In fact, between 2020 and 2030, the number of Americans over 65 will grow by a remarkable 2.6% each year; the number of Americans under 65, meanwhile, will decline by .2% annually.[9]

Even the best-operated Ponzi schemes operate on questionable economic premises. In every such scheme, there is invariably someone at the tail end who will wind up taking out less than was paid in. *The Economist* sums up the problem:

As long as incomes and workforce are growing, each generation can give its predecessors a secure retirement, and expect to enjoy still greater comforts when its turn comes along. But if wages and population growth stagnate—or if beneficiaries become greedy—the virtuous cycle becomes vicious. This unhappy circumstance has now arrived.[10]

Like Samuelson, those who forecast an endless summer for the elderly's retirements shared a vision of a Ponzi scheme that would never wear down. For most of American—and world—history it would have been a reasonable forecast: they based their predictions on deeply rooted, age-old demographic trends. Since time immemorial, societies' populations had expanded, and there had always been a lopsided imbalance between the young and old. But those analyses were based on what had happened over the last several thousand years, not what would happen in the next several decades. During the century between 1850 and 1950, the U.S. population grew at the astonishing rate of 20.1% per decade.[11] In 1960, the median age of Americans was still only 29.[12] The United States has always been a young country, with a rapidly expanding population.

No longer. We are living at the moment in history when some timeless demographic trends are reaching their end. Following the Second World War and throughout the 1950s, the birth rate in the United States exceeded 25 births per 1,000 population,[13] a fertility spike which produced the baby boom. But both technology and cultural values underwent a dramatic transformation in a remarkably brief span of time. Social norms changed, so that many women delayed marriage and childbirth in order to enter the workforce, couples had fewer children, divorce rates spiraled, and the number of women who never married doubled, rising to around 10%.

Most important, a growing number of Americans report greater concerns about their own material welfare, causing them to delay or abandon having children altogether.[14] As recently as 1970, fewer than 9% of women between the ages of 30 and 34 had not had a child; by 1995, over 26% had not.[15] The net effect of these historical social changes was a birth rate that fell to 18 births per 1,000 in the 1960s, and fell again, to below 15 per 1,000 during the 1970s.[16] Social researcher Ben Wattenberg refers to this phenomenon as the "birth dearth." Whatever you call it, the baby boom generation was followed by a deceleration of population growth, which may ultimately wind up in a halt of growth altogether.

The World Bank has forecast population growth for the United States, using both the existing fertility rate of 1.815 births per woman, and the lower rate of 1.63, the level to which many demographers expect fertility to decline in coming years (Table 8.3[17]). World Bank projections reveal a population which not only fails to keep up with past rates of growth, but actually undergoes reversal, and begins to experience decline in absolute population figures.

For a retirement system that has been described as a giant Ponzi scheme, such forecasts are not auspicious. In a society which fails to reproduce itself, the

Table 8.3
Percent Change in U.S. Population

Decade	At Fertility Rate of 1.815	At Fertility Rate of 1.63
1990-2000	+6.1% per decade	+5.2% per decade
2000-2010	+5.1	+3.9
2010-2020	+4.1	+2.4
2020-2030	+1.5	-0.5
2030-2040	-0.6	-2.7
2040-2050	-1.4	-3.8
2050-2060	-1.4	-4.1
2060-2070	-1.9	-4.6

traditional pyramid of a larger number of workers supporting a smaller number of those unable to work (children and the elderly) is reversed, so that, over time, a diminishing number of workers are forced to support a growing number of nonworkers. At precisely the time when there will be the greatest need for workers, paying payroll taxes to support an exploding aging population, the number of American workers will be stagnant, or actually in decline. If a growing nation with a young population is "the greatest Ponzi scheme ever contrived," what is a contracting nation with an aging population?

Because of the altered demographic patterns, those in the workforce will face greatly increased tax burdens. Furthermore, the composition of those they will be supporting, the "dependent" population (typically comprised of those age 18 and younger, and those 65 and older), has not been stable either. Increasing longevity is not the only thing that is adding years to the nation's median age. As Americans have fewer children, seniors comprise a growing share of the dependent population, children a diminishing share. While America is growing more old, it is also becoming less young. In 1970, for example, there were 12 children under 5 years of age for every senior over 85. In 1995 there were 5. By 2040 there will be about 1.[18]

The "support ratio" provides a rough estimate of what portion of the population is in their (inaptly labeled) "productive years," compared with those who are "dependent." It compares the number of those under 18 and over 65, for every 100 in the population between the ages of 18 and 64 (Tble 8.4[19]). By 2050, every 100 Americans between age 18 and 64 will be supporting 75 Americans outside the workforce. In one sense, this figure is not so alarming. A support ratio in the 70s does not differ substantially from what it has been during most of this century. In 1920, for example, the support ratio was 76.[20]

When we look more deeply, however, we see that there is no cause for complacency. It is not just the gradually increasing dependency ratio that concerns

Table 8.4
Young, Elderly, and Total Support Ratios, 1990-2050
(number of people of specified age per 100 people age 18 to 64)

Year	65+	Under 18	Total
1990	20	41	62
2000	21	39	60
2010	22	35	57
2020	29	35	64
2030	38	36	74
2040	39	35	74
2050	40	35	75

demographers, it is the composition of that dependent population. In 1920, of the 76 dependents per 100 workers, 68 were children; only 8 were older citizens. By 2030, for the first time ever, there will be more seniors than children. The elderly, moreover, pose much greater costs for taxpayers than children. The Bipartisan Commission found, for example, that "even if the extraordinary increases in health care costs were eliminated after 1999," and health costs were held to the general rate of inflation (an extremely optimistic speculation, given recent history), Medicare spending will still double as a percent of GDP by 2030.[21] Even the optimistic forecasts are pessimistic. And, according to government forecasts, the number of workers supporting that expanding retirement population will drop precipitiously in the coming decades (Table 8.5[22]).

Table 8.5
Number of Workers to Support Each Retiree's Benefits, 1980-2030

1980	5.1
1985	5.0
1990	4.8
1995	4.7
2000	4.8
2005	4.9
2010	4.8
2015	4.2
2020	3.7
2025	3.1
2030	2.8
2040	2.0

A diminishing number of workers supporting a growing number of retirees: it would be enough of a challenge for any socio-political system to deal with. But there is more. For, as the generation of baby boomers lives into retirement and old age, they will incur much greater costs than present retirees. Living long, we have seen, is expensive, and the baby boomers will live longer than any generation in history. By 2040, men who live to be 65 can expect to live another 20 years, to age 85. Women can expect to live to be 88, up from 85 at the present.[23] That reflects an average increase of four years over current life expectancy, and those will be an expensive four years, requiring the most intensive—and costly—medical treatment. Americans will live to be older, and with fewer young people in the population, America will get older. Whereas the median age was 29 in 1960, by 2030 it will have skyrocketed to 42, and still rising.[24] There has never been anything like it.

Fewer children being born and more seniors, living longer; fewer workers supporting more retirees: the inevitable consequence—and it is inevitable—is that public benefits for the elderly cannot possibly be sustained at present levels without dramatic increases in payroll taxes. Future workers (those children now being neglected by the political system) will be called on to make greater sacrifices than present workers simply in order to keep the system going, and will ultimately be informed that the present boom in benefits, which they will help pay for, must be reduced when their own turn comes for retirement. This will be the real baby bust: when a generation becomes aware that it will receive back substantially less than it was required to contribute.

Baby boomer Christopher Byron has a dream. Or, perhaps, a nightmare. In his dream he is living in the "Time of Dying" when in a five-year period, nearly 10 million elderly boomers die. They're not dying quickly enough, though to keep from being a burden upon an unprepared society. A national political battle ensues, and the battle lines are generational.

On one side are the kids—the Generation X-ers—now middle-aged and muttering about "personal choice" and "individual rights." On the other side are my friends and I, the boomers, croaking back that the hidden agenda of our children is all too obvious: to get us out of the way before the task of keeping us alive bankrupts the nation. Which is more or less when I wake up, only to realize that this is really just a slightly out-of-focus glimpse of the future itself.[25]

LIVING LIKE THERE'S NO TOMORROW

Concerns like that are being increasingly heard from baby boomers, warily eyeing the gray years ahead. Many analysts believe that such concerns are justified. Perhaps buoyed by the expectation that government entitlement programs will provide for them when they grow old, and feeling less personal responsibility for their own economic welfare at retirement, boomers are borrowing more and saving less than their parents did.[26] "I don't think the nation as a whole understands the immensity of the situation that's going to unfold at the beginning of the 21st century," says the head of IBM's retirement program, Don Sauvigne.[27] By all measures, Americans in general, and baby boomers in particular, are ill-prepared for what is to come.

The consulting firm of Arthur D. Little estimates that, at current rates of saving, the average U.S. household will have saved only 33.8% of what it will need for a comfortable retirement.[28] Merrill Lynch, the investment firm, has a "Baby Boom Retirement Index," a measure of how well baby boomers are financially preparing for their retirement years. According to its index, boomers are saving at only one-third the rate required to be financially prepared for retirement.[29] John Steffens, an executive vice-president at Merrill Lynch, says, "We think there's a very large problem, and its going to get worse."[30]

There is a certain unrealism—or irresponsibility—which characterizes the approach of many boomers toward their later years. Two-fifths saved less than $1,000 for retirement in 1994, and one-third saved nothing at all. Yet an astonishing two-thirds of boomers expect—unreasonably—to live as well or better than they do today.[31] Joseph Seymour, head of retirement planning at Quest For Value, a mutual fund company, says that the boomers are in "a classic state of denial" in their retirement preparation.[32] To be prepared for retirement, say economists, boomers must increase their retirement savings threefold.[33]

The neglect of personal retirement savings is taking place, moreover, at a time when private firms are backing away from traditional defined-benefit pension plans, and moving toward defined-contribution plans,[34] making individual workers more responsible than ever for retirement preparations.

Workers with any sort of company pension plan are the fortunate ones, though: most American workers, over 55%, are not covered by any private pension plan at all.[35] Other than Social Security, they are on their own.

Americans are aware of the demographic bust ahead, the shrinking number of workers supporting an exploding number of retirees. But they are not preparing for it, either in private or public spending. Half of all baby boomers are near "negative equity" positions, which occurs when the value of one's assets is less than the amount of debt accumulated. Indeed, far from moving toward greater financial preparedness for the years ahead, the imbalance between production and consumption is moving in the opposite direction, and it is widening. While the imbalance between government income and expenditures is trumpeted daily, personal expenditures are no better balanced. Americans are on a spending spree. Sylvia Nasar, writing in the *New York Times,* sums up the findings of several recent research studies on the pattern of declining savings in the United States: "Americans drawing near retirement age today are saving less than their parents did at the same point in their lives. Moreover, Americans who are already retired—beneficiaries of relatively generous Social Security payments, pensions and health care protection—are consuming considerably more than previous generations consumed."[36]

Table 8.6
Credit Card Debt as a Percent of Disposable Income

1950	7.3%
1970	14.7
1980	15.5
1987	18.8

Between 1980 and 1986, disposable income rose 17.6%, but personal spending grew 21%.[37] Consumer installment debt (mainly credit card debt) similarly has spiraled out of control (Table 8.6[38]).

Baby boomers, moreover, are at the forefront of the borrowing binge. "They are far and away the heaviest users of credit cards and loans," says Geoffrey Meredith, president of Lifestage Matrix Marketing. "They're ending up paying more in interest than anyone else."[39] Consumer installment debt now exceeds $750 billion.[40] As with other cultural changes, boomers have led the way in the accumulation of consumption-oriented debt. It is a cultural trait they may bemoan in years ahead. Carter Beese, Jr., commissioner of the Securities and Exchange Commission, warns of dire economic consequences for the nation when an unprepared baby boom generation hits retirement age. It could be, says Beese, "as huge as the federal budget and potentially as devastating as the health care crisis."[41]

The generation that once sang "I hope I die before I get old" is living as though they were going to. During the 1980s, production increased by $950 per worker, but consumption increased by $3,100 per worker. The $2,150 difference represents accumulated debt.[42] According to the Census Bureau, only one-fourth of those between 35 and 45 have even started an IRA or Keough retirement savings account. Among the minority who do have one, the average total savings is a paltry $8,634.[43] One consequence of America's culture of consumption is the reluctance to put money away for the future when there are so many tantalizing things out there to buy right now. The United States, with income levels among the highest in the industrialized world, has savings rates which are the lowest (Table 8.7[44]). We are, moreover, moving in the wrong direction. After a low per capita savings rate averaging around 9% from the 1950s through the 1970s, savings declined even further in the 1980s, falling below 5%. In the 1990s they have dropped even further, to a minuscule 3%.[45]

The national saving rate declined substantially in the 1980s; it has dropped even more in the early 1990s, falling further below the levels of other industrial countries and raising concerns among policymakers and analysts [the Congressional Budget Office (CBO) warns]. National saving, along with the inflow of savings from other countries, is the main source of funds for machinery, buildings, and other investments that sustain economic growth. . . . The reduced rate of saving is worrisome because new challenges

Table 8.7
Net National Saving Rate
(national saving as a percentage of GDP)

	1960-1969	1970-1979	1980-1989
U.S.A.	9.8	8.2	3.6
Canada	9.8	11.4	8.4
U.K.	10.5	7.5	4.8
France	17.7	15.3	7.8
Germany	18.0	13.6	10.2
Japan	21.9	22.3	18.2

lie ahead. The pending retirement of the baby boom generation early in the 21st century is one such challenge. The retirement of the boomers will increase the ratio of dependent persons to working people and require that a given amount of national income be spread among more people.[46]

As the CBO indicates, investment is the other side of the coin in the national productivity equation. Without savings, there can be no investment, and without investment, new factories are not built, new products are not developed, workers do not become more efficient, the economy does not grow. Here, too, America is failing to prepare for the economic demands that the future holds.

Worker productivity, which is highly dependent upon investment, is a strict arbiter of permissible worker income and, ultimately, of national prosperity. Workers creating $9.00 an hour worth of value cannot be paid $10.00 an hour. Unionized workers trying to insist otherwise have priced themselves out of jobs. Although one may consume more in the short run than one produces, in the long run individuals cannot consume more wealth than they generate by their productivity.

Likewise a nation. If average per capita productivity yields $10.00 an hour worth of value, the average wage cannot be $15.00 an hour. Worker productivity is economic destiny, and that destiny cannot be altered by political or monetary tricks, only by raising productivity. Productivity requires investment, and, as with saving, Americans are laggards in investment. The statistics suggest that a culture of consumption is ill-disposed to make the sacrifices necessary to prepare for the future.

The Congressional Budget Office, studying the declining rates of saving and investment, states the problem explicity:

In order to achieve a higher standard of living in the future, individuals must be willing to reduce their current consumption because both saving and investment compete with consumption in the use of current income and production. . . . Thus, individuals must be willing to postpone consuming some of their current income if they want to increase their assets through domestic and foreign investment, and thereby increase future living standards.[47]

Thus far, Americans have been unwilling to postpone present consumption in order to prepare for what the future holds. Economist Van Doorn Ooms, formerly the chief economist for the U.S. House of Representatives Budget Committee, and at present the senior vice president of the Committee for Economic Development, writes that the trends in both public policy and private behavior indicate "a greatly increased priority given to the present at the expense of the future."[48] A *New York Times*/CBS poll taken in 1995 revealed that a majority of working Americans had not begun to save for their retirement at all.[49]

   "A comfortable retirement is one thing, but a nicely prepared filet mignon is something entirely different," writes *American Demographics* in an editorial. Citing a 1995 study by the Employee Benefit Research Institute, it warns that middle-class Americans are living it up in the present, at the neglect of the future: they "aren't willing to sacrifice middle-class pleasures to help ensure a comfortable retirement."[50]

   When we invest in technologically advanced equipment, the workers using that equipment produce more value in the same amount of time, and can be paid a higher wage (Table 8.8[51]). The economy grows. Government is able to supply more public goods, such as Social Security. Richard Suzman, a demographer at the National Institute on Aging, suggests that economic growth is critical in meeting the needs of an aging population: "The growth rate of the economy is a far more important variable than the simple age of the population," he says.[52] Even this is not particularly reassuring, though, because when investment lags, as America's does, productivity and economic growth also lag (Table 8.9[53]).

   Such disparities seem modest, but sustained over several decades they distinguish the world's rich nations from the poor. And they distinguish those

Table 8.8
Percent of GDP Spent on Productive Investment

Japan	30.6	Austria	23.5	Sweden	19.7
Norway	28.8	Spain	22.5	U.K.	19.2
Portugal	26.8	Canada	22.0	Iceland	18.5
Switzerland	26.6	Netherlands	21.4	Denmark	18.0
Australia	24.8	France	20.0	Belgium	17.8
Finland	24.8	Germany	19.9	Greece	17.4
Luxembourg	24.2	Italy	19.9	U.S.A.	17.1
Turkey	24.1	New Zealand	19.8	Ireland	17.0

Table 8.9
Average Annual Growth Rates of Per Capita GDP, 1969-1989

Japan	4.09%	Germany	2.50	Netherlands	1.83
Greece	3.16	France	2.46	U.S.A.	1.76
Canada	2.91	U.K.	2.18	Switzerland	1.50
Italy	2.91	Sweden	2.06		
Belgium	2.75	Australia	1.85		

societies able to provide generous public welfare services from those that are not. As productivity goes, so goes income, and during the past generation, productivity and income in the United States have not gone well. Writing in the journal *Science,* George Hatsopoulos, Paul Krugman, and Lawrence Summers note that the real income of American families "peaked in 1973." They write, "It is no exaggeration to speak of the United States in the past 15 years as passing through a 'quiet depression' in which the income of families has stagnated or declined."[54] That is not an auspicious starting point for a nation on the precipice of a retirement boom; a nation whose fastest growing profession during the next decade will be in-home health care for shut-in seniors,[55] and whose major growth industry may be, within 20 years, nursing homes.

A DEFICIT OF NATIONAL WILL

In oligarchy, the few may live at the expense of the many. In democracy, the present generation may live at the expense of the next. The same prodigality that Americans practice in their private finances they decry in their government. Yet the policies that have produced a $5 trillion national debt are simply a political manifestation of cultural values which, in their private manifestation, have produced plunging savings and escalating consumer debt.

The federal deficit is the amount of money that the federal government spends in a year more than it has taken in. The national debt is the accumulation of all those annual deficits. Each year, another year's deficit spending is added to the total debt. That deficit spending accelerated rapidly over the 1980s and early 1990s: for those turning 22 in 1994, 86% of the national debt was accumulated during their lifetime.[56] The money, we have seen, wasn't lavished on them. Each family owns over $50,000 worth of national debt. This represents money that must be paid back in the future for goods and services that were purchased in the past.

Why do we ever have to pay back the national debt at all? Why not simply let it ride from year to year, making interest payments? For one thing, interest payments on the debt represent federal money spent that yields nothing in return: no new schools built, no children immunized, no Social Security checks paid.

Interest payments on the debt now consume 16% of the entire federal budget, and 40% of all income tax revenues. Also, in order to make interest payments, the government must borrow funds, thus competing with private industry for capital that is already scarce because of Americans' low savings rates. That drives up interest rates, which raises the overall cost of doing business, which impairs the competitiveness of American firms. A quarter-century ago, government borrowing consumed 2% of total private-sector savings. By 1992, estimates put that borrowing as high as 71%.[57] One consequence of government borrowing has been rising interest rates, making it more difficult for middle-class Americans to afford that staple of the American dream, their own home. Another consequence of rising interest rates, according to Federal Reserve Chairman Alan Greenspan, is to weaken the value of the U.S. dollar against overseas currencies.[58]

There is, of course, a noneconomic argument against running a multi-trillion-dollar debt. It has to do with the ethical and moral propriety of one generation leaving a legacy of debt to the next; of one generation living well now, and leaving the bill to those who follow. After all, the consoling maxim often used to rationalize public debt, "we're only borrowing it from ourselves," is not precisely accurate. We're borrowing it from our children. "The earth belongs to the living," wrote Thomas Jefferson, who worried about the potential of democratic societies to accumulate debts which they would pass on to succeeding generations.[59] He hinted that a generation which inherited such a debt would have the right to repudiate it: "What is to hinder [government] from creating a perpetual debt? The laws of nature, I answer. The will and the power of man expire with his life, by nature's law."[60] And again, "The principle of spending money to be paid by posterity is but swindling futurity on a grand scale."[61] It is no right of one generation to live at the expense of another. Yet, with a national debt of $5 trillion, each new baby born in America inherits $20,000 worth of debt accumulated by his parents' generation before he was born.

Who ever heard of parents who left their children a negative inheritance? In order to assuage their consciences, many have consoled themselves with the belief that the American system is out of their control, dominated by "special interests," or even more sinister conspiracies. The title of William Greider's bestselling book captures the spirit of the times: *Who Will Tell the People?* The average citizen is no longer heard in Washington, Greider writes, because only large organizations and special interests with plenty of money to buy research and rent congresspeople are able to participate effectively. This "exclusion of most Americans from the debate," he explains, has come about "during the last generation" as a result of the "New Politics"; meaning big money, special interest politics.[62]

Every candidate for every office from City Council to the White House now belabors the "special interest domination/corrupt government" motif. Everyone is an outsider. "The people are good. It's the government that's corrupt," declaimed billionaire Ross Perot, running for president in 1992. "We need a government that's as good as the people," joined in candidate Clinton. Yet that may be what we have, and that may be the problem. Aristotle's observation on political virtue, over two millenia old, continues to hold deep meaning today: "That government is better which is exercised over better citizens."

Politicians lie to voters, pretending they can have low taxes and high spending, and voters lie to themselves, pretending to believe them. "We won't endure small hurts today to avoid larger hurts tomorrow, and we know it," writes economist Robert Samuelson. "Self-deception has become a way of life. . . . There's a conspiracy against candor. It's a charade in which all the actors demean themselves."[63]

There are, make no mistake, subtle and even conspiratorial manipulations of public power for private purpose in the United States. They accompany any large concentration of power, and are probably as infrequent in America, with its elaborate system of public and private checks and oversight, as anywhere else in the world. They are also probably about as infrequent as we can prudently expect them to be, given the leviathan scope of government. By and large, the escalating federal debt is the result of a conspiracy of the majority, not of any secret cabal. When Americans condemn "special interests," we mean those interests in which we have no special interest, whether farm subsidies, tax breaks for homebuilders, defense spending, welfare for single mothers, tariff protections, or senior entitlements. One's own interests, on the other hand, are not special interests, but the national good.

"In America," wrote Alexis de Tocqueville, "there are factions but no conspiracies." The insight is as true today as it was a century and a half ago. There is nothing secretive in the scramble for resources that is American politics. Interest groups (factions) compete for public money openly, aggressively, often with moral indignation, as though they had a civil right to it. Every representative promises to acquire "our fair share" of government spending for voters in his or her district. If the national debt is any indication, Americans have been getting their fair share, and then some.

In a $1.5 trillion government economy, there will be a scandal from time to time. Weapons systems will be boondoggled, officials will be bought, pork barrels will flow. That is a comment upon human nature, not upon the nature of a system of government. But the great shifts of wealth, whether under Franklin Roosevelt or Ronald Reagan, were not originated in back rooms and sprung upon unsuspecting publics. They followed intense, prolonged public debate, and were ratified in subsequent elections. As for the notion that some conspiratorial elite has twisted government to their own ends, an examination of the spending of the federal government in the $1.6 trillion budget reveals that the main conspirators in using government for their own ends are the American people (Table 8.10[64]).

As conspiracies go, whatever cabal it is that is "diverting politics" for its own purposes, it is barely holding its own against We the People. The bulk of

Table 8.10
Federal Spending, 1996

Direct Benefit Payments for Individuals (primarily Social Security and Medicare)	48%
Interest on National Debt	16%
Military Spending	15%
Grants to States and Localities	15%
Other Federal Operations	5%
Deposit Insurance	1%

government expenditures consist of three main categories: (1) entitlements for the elderly, (2) national defense, and (3) interest on the debt.

Before 2000, these three categories alone will account for nearly eight out of every ten dollars spent by the federal government. Other than interest on the debt, public expenditures are mainly transfer payments from the middle class to itself, mainly from the young to the old. Excluding payments on the national debt, by 1995, Social Security and Medicare consumed more than four out of every ten dollars in a $1.6 trillion budget.[65] Within 20 more years, they will constitute most federal spending.[66]

Those programs were not the result of a group of secret conspirators. They were born in the political light of day, and have grown like Topsy, not because Americans do not "speak the language of politics," or because they have been deceived and are unaware of what is happening with those programs, but because comfortable, middle-class Americans are fluent in the language of benefits, and will not allow their benefits to be cut.

Ooms points out that government spending does not go mainly to the needy, but overwhelmingly to those who are already doing well. Less than 20% of government spending is based on financial need. Social Security and Medicare, by contrast, which together comprise nearly half the budget, "in the aggregate, go predominantly to high- and middle-income rather than poor beneficiaries."[67] In other words, they are comfort for the comfortable; merely another form of aggregate consumption, albeit in the guise of political rather than private spending. .

An astronomical national debt and soaring consumer debt are two sides of the same coin. Americans want to consume more than they produce. Our rate of consumer debt is the highest in the world, and higher than at any time in American history.[68] In combination, public and private prodigality are limiting the economy's potential, and thus its future capacity to care for the boom in retiring baby boomers. "When the future comes to judge us, they're going to judge us based on whether we in fact make the transition from being a high-consumption society to being a high-investment society,"[69] says MIT economist

Lester Thurow. There is no sign that we are making that transition, or even contemplating it. Indeed, in terms of aggregate consumption versus production, we are heading in the wrong direction. Within less than a generation, America has gone from being the world's largest creditor nation to the world's largest debtor.

"The recent reduction in national saving and investment is likely to significantly reduce economic growth," Ooms warns. "This threat to future living standards is greatly increased by the inevitable retirement bulge of the baby boomers, beginning about 2010. . . . If labor productivity and incomes are not raised significantly, the squeeze on living standards of both workers and retirees could produce intergenerational political and social conflict."[70] If the United States is to be prepared for the graying years ahead, we must begin to make sacrifices now: sacrifices more demanding than balancing a budget during a time of peace, economic prosperity, and more taxpayers per retiree than we will have for at least the next century. Who will tell the people that?

Neither individuals, firms, nor government seem very well prepared for what is to come. Better hope those public Trust Funds are in good shape.

The Trust Funds Nobody Trusts

Less than 10% of the boomer generation believe that they will receive the same level of government retirement benefits as current retirees. Some 30% believe they won't receive any.[71] Among members of generation X, those fated to follow the baby boomers, pessimism is even deeper. And most Americans, of all ages, do not believe the current system will survive.[72]

"The Case for Killing Social Security," screams the headline of *Time* magazine. Regarding generation Xers' views on UFOs and Social Security, it says, "Whatever the merits of their judgement on extraterrestrials, on Social Security the new workers have it exactly right."[73]

The trustees of Social Security and Medicare themselves do not seem completely confident of the programs' long-term actuarial soundness. Even if efforts to control medical costs succeded beyond any reformers' wildest expectations, and health care costs are held to the same rate of expansion as the economy (something no policy analyst expects), federal Medicare expenses will double by 2030. But Medicare itself will be bankrupt long before that—by 2001, according to its own trustees. If reform efforts succeed precisely as envisioned (something that has not happened in several prior efforts at reform), the bankruptcy would be delayed by only seven years.

Social Security, according to its trustees, will begin to spend more than it takes in by around 2013. At that time, it will begin spending its "reserves," funds it is building up now while the ratio of workers to retirees is more favorable. Those reserves will be exhausted, and Social Security bankrupt, by 2029.[74]

Upon leaving her post as commissioner of the Social Security Administration in the 1980s, Dorcas Hardy wrote a book entitled *Social Insecurity,* warning of a crisis facing the system as the boomer generation retires, and urging readers to aggressively pursue private investments.[75] "It's unclear," says Gerard Anderson, director of the Johns Hopkins Center for Hospital Finance and Management, "whether Medicare and the Social Security programs will have any money to cover [their costs] in 2010 or 2020."[76] Sylvester Schieber, noted retirement analyst and member of Social Security's Advisory Council, states flatly, "The Social Security system cannot survive as it's currently legislated."[77]

Why is the fate of the Social Security Trust Funds so widely in doubt? The answer partly has to do with the way that the Funds invest individuals' contributions: they don't. Writer Paul Magnusson summarizes the process in a letter attempting to "tell the truth about Social Security" to a 7-year-old daughter.

I'm very sorry, but there's no money in your Social Security account and never will be. That's because no one has her own Social Security account. Instead, people send 7.6% of their pay to Washington, their bosses match it, and it's spent right away paying Social Security and Medicare benefits to older folks. And what's left over is spent on other important things, such as aircraft carriers, national parks, and foreign travel for members of Congress.[78]

In other words, Social Security is operated on a pay-as-you-go basis. Current revenues pay current expenses. It is not a pension plan, as it was originally sold to the American public, and as millions of Americans still believe it to be. "I know of no greater triumph of imaginative packaging and Madison Avenue advertising," says Nobel prize-winning economist Milton Friedman.[79] "The mythology of Social Security is so deeply embedded in our culture that it is very hard to get people to accept that it is merely an accounting artifice," says a former chairman of the Federal Advisory Council on Social Security.[80]

Nevertheless, the rhetoric comparing Social Security to private pension plans enables even wealthy retirees to defend their benefits as entitlements which they have earned through their payroll taxes. Joseph A. Arrighi, an elderly Social Security recipient, characterizes this perspective. Arrighi writes to the *New York Times,* describing Social Security as "an insurance policy," and therefore off limits to those wishing to control the growth of the federal budget. "Hands Off My Social Security," he warns politicians, speaking for millions of other seniors.[81] It is not his fault, Arrighi explains, that he lived long enough to receive more in benefits than he paid in payroll taxes. The problem for the Social Security system is that, because of extending life expectancy, most recipients are on the "much more" side of the benefits equation. As Susan Dentzer points out, "An average-wage couple retiring today at 65 can expect to receive almost $500,000 in Medicare and Social Security benefits—and you can bet that all the money didn't come out of their paychecks, even with interest."[82] Arrighi's argument, made by millions of retirees, carries tremendous force. Indeed, if Social Security were a pension plan, the argument "you owe this to us" would be compelling.

But Social Security is not a pension plan. It is not an investment fund wherein workers save for their retirement years. Even the Supreme Court says so. In *Flemming v. Nestor* (1960), a man being deported for activity in the Communist party sued the government for depriving him of property rights. He had been paying into the Social Security system since its inception, and argued that he was owed those benefits. If there was any doubt concerning the issue before *Flemming*, there was none after: Social Security is simply another tax. You pay it because the law says so, not because the government guarantees you a return on your money. "To engraft upon the Social Security system a concept of accrued property rights would deprive it of the flexibility and boldness in adjusting to ever-changing conditions, which it demands."[83] In other words, government will pay beneficiaries whatever benefits it deems appropriate at a given time. Beneficiaries are owed nothing, whatever their payroll taxes.

Notwithstanding the language of investment which is often associated with Social Security, it is in fact simply a redistributive tax, little different from the income tax. And like the income tax, the government spends the money as it comes in. In exchange, the federal Treasury gives the Social Security Administration IOUs, to be redeemed later. "Try a financing scheme like this for a private pension," quips former Commerce Secretary Peterson, "and you'd be sent to jail."[84] Today's workers, strictly speaking, are not investing for their own retirement, they are funding someone else's. In that light, the argument that "you owe this to us" makes less sense. For a wealthy retiree to demand of the struggling worker, trying to raise a family, "you owe this to me," carries no economic or legal weight, although it carries political weight. Politicians, in any event, are listening.

At present, the Social Security Trust Fund is accumulating a "reserve," because the large number of baby boomers currently in the workforce (and paying payroll FICA taxes) are more than sufficient to fund the benefits of current retirees. When those boomers retire, and there are fewer workers supporting more retirees, it will be necessary to cash in those reserves. When that happens, the Trust Fund will in fact only be cashing in the IOUs which are now accumulating. Those IOUs, of course, do not represent real money actually invested somewhere: they are simply government commitments to pay the benefits, either by taxing workers or by borrowing the money.

As the trustees have warned, however, even those theoretical "reserves" will run out long before the baby boom does. Yet retiring boomers will expect to continue receiving benefits, whether or not the resources are set aside. If the Social Security were run as a genuine pension system, it would be presumed to have sufficient resources invested to fund those retirees. But it is not, and it does not. The system is accumulating enormous "unfunded liabilities," the amount of money that today's workers will expect to receive in Social Security benefits when they retire, for which the system has neither capital "reserves" (government IOUs), nor taxes in place.

By sometime in the 2020s, Social Security will have spent all of the money accumulated in its "reserves." With a static number of workers and an exploding retirement population, the Trust Fund will quickly go into deficit, spending vastly more than it takes in. The gap between the income from payroll taxes and the expense of funding the boomers' retirement will quickly explode into an enormous annual operating deficit. According to the most optimistic economic projections, by 2030 the Social Security system will spend $250 billion (in 1993 constant dollars) more than it collects; ten years later, the annual operating deficit will be $650 billion,[85] making the current deficit crisis seem modest by comparison. Estimates of the system's current "unfunded liabilities" range from $6.7 trillion to $14 trillion, depending on whether one includes Medicare liabilities.[86] And you were concerned about the national debt.

PAYROLLS, TAXES, AND CONTRIBUTIONS

If the boomer generation has not paid sufficient payroll taxes to finance their retirement benefits, who will finance them? Who will fund all those unfunded entitlements? There are two principle options to address the gap between the revenues that will be coming in and the benefits the retiring boomers will expect to receive: reduce benefits, or raise payroll taxes.

How will retiring boomers respond to the prospect of reduced benefits? For one thing, compared with prior generations, financial stresses will not be mitigated by stable home environments. In their cover story on the baby boomers, the editors of *Time* found that they were more self-absorbed and had fewer strong social ties and commitments than members of earlier generations:

Long-absorbed in themselves, the baby boomers are a generation that has avoided or postponed commitments to others. Many have little loyalty to their employers and less to political leaders or ideas. Partly because of the economic squeeze, they get married later and have children later. They also divorce more than their parents did. Quite a few, it seems, are destined for an awfully old age.[87]

According to Harry Moody, deputy director of Hunter College's Center on Aging, "It's a generation not too concerned about what it owes other people. . . . It's a rather worrisome trend."[88] This isolation may make boomers more economically vulnerable when retirement comes. According to Dr. Douglas Wolf, a Syracuse University demographer, "[the boomers] will reach old age with an unprecedentedly high percentage childless. Who are these people going to turn to? Something has got to give."[89]

In a 1989 survey of 500 professional actuaries by the American Academy of Actuaries, 72% of those surveyed reported that, even with the assistance of Social Security, most Americans who reach age 65 between the years 2010 and 2028 will be unable to afford to comfortably retire.[90]

Financially unprepared for retirement themselves, the boomer generation will be economically dependent upon government benefits. They do not seem culturally disposed to consenting to a reduction of those needed benefits for the benefit of some broader public good. Boomers, moreover, are the first American generation to grow up from childhood in a political environment in which government programs supporting the elderly are universally considered to be "entitlements," something which government owes us. To a generation that has seen their grandparents, and then their parents, retire on Social Security, those benefits are regarded as "rights."

Like the present generation of seniors, baby boomers will use their enormous political power to preserve their level of benefits against what will be mounting political efforts to reduce them, regardless of the stresses those benefits may have on the larger social or economic system. Given the national demographics at the time of their retirement, they will pose a formidable political force, wielding even more clout than today's retirees. By 2030, when retiring boomers will already have placed enormous strains upon the system, one in five Americans will be over age 65. As important, one in three will be over 55.[91] The political power of the elderly is immense now, and will only increase in the next several decades as the baby boom ages. Aging boomers will use their unprecedented political power to maintain the current generous level of benefits, derived from the payroll taxes of the less-numerous, less-politically-powerful baby bust generation. It is here that the much-anticipated "generation war" may erupt openly. Members of the baby bust generation, politically apathetic in their youth, may become more activist when they enter their peak earning years and face stifling, unprecedented payroll tax rates. For, if current benefits are to be sustained into the boomers' retirement years, the payroll taxes paid by members of generation X will have to be increased dramatically. It does not take a government economist to recognize that if the number of workers supporting each retiree declines by nearly half of current levels, to only two workers per Social Security recipient in 2030, the existing financing structure will be wholly inadequate to meet the demands placed upon it as the population ages (Table 8.11[92]).

Payroll taxes have already risen to keep pace with an expanding population of retirees. In 1985, the maximum amount of Social Security tax that could be withheld from a worker's paycheck was $2,791; a decade later, it had risen 68%, to $4,681. The Consumer Price Index rose only 42% during that time.[93] Nevertheless, the real retirement boom has yet to arrive. Every politician who has looked at the numbers is aware of what is ahead, but most will not say: young workers now beginning to pay into Social Security to fund retirees for the next 40 years will receive nowhere near the same level of benefits when they retire. The demographics simply will not allow it.

For the first 15 years, Social Security taxes on employers and employees combined were 2% on the first $3,000 of income, rising to 3% by 1950, to nearly 10% of the first $7,800 by 1970 (with the addition of the new Medicare tax), and to over 15% of the first $48,600 by 1990.[94] The past is only prologue, however, for what is to come. Peter Francese, publisher of *American Demographics,* warns that "if present population trends continue, Social Security and

Table 8.11
Federal Pension and Health Programs as a Percentage
of GNP and the Federal Budget, 1995-2040

Year	% of GNP	% of Budget
2000	9.8%	40.8%
2005	10.0	41.7
2010	10.7	44.6
2015	11.0	45.8
2020	11.9	49.6
2025	12.9	53.9
2030	13.5	56.3
2035	14.1	58.8
2040	14.5	60.4

Medicare could take half of the average American's paycheck by 2040."[95] Former Commerce Secretary Peterson calculates that the payroll tax could range from 35% to 55% of every employee's paycheck.[96] The most modest projection, made by the public trustees of Social Security and Medicare themselves, suggests that payroll taxes would have to be raised to one-quarter of all payroll in the American economy in order to sustain the current level of benefits.[97]

Of course, after payroll taxes are taken, the income tax remains to be paid. Even in the next century, government will do things in addition to supporting retirees. It is the sum of the total taxes that must be considered—the overall tax bite. For, although Social Security and Medicare taxes are euphemistically called "contributions," just as the Trust Funds are not really trust funds, the employee and employer "contributions" are not really contributions.

On television there are sometimes advertisements asking viewers to send in donations of money that will be used to assist poor children in foreign lands, or some other good cause. One may decide not to make that contribution, with no negative repercussions whatever. Social Security contributions are not that type of contribution. Contributions made to Social Security and Medicare are of the kind that if you do not make them, you can go to jail. A tax is a tax is a tax. According to economists Kotlikoff and Gokhale, Americans who retired in the 1960s paid, on average, about one-fifth of their lifetime incomes to government. Those born in the next few years are, overall, "likely to pay well over half of their lifetime net incomes to the government."[98] Children born in the 1990s are apt to pay 50% more in total lifetime taxes than the retirees currently receiving Social Security benefits.[99]

Because of escalating payroll taxes, however, by the time that members of the baby bust generation retire, having funded the retirement of the boomers, they will have paid so much in payroll taxes that they may not even fully recover their contributions when it is their own turn to receive benefits, let alone receive a positive return on their pension "investment." According to Congressional Research Service calculations, those retiring in 1940 recovered all of the money they paid in Social Security payroll taxes within six months after retirement. Those who retired in 1980 were still able to recoup their taxes in fairly short order, within three years. Those who retire in 2030 will take more than 21 years to recover their payroll tax contributions, longer than average life expectancy,[100] yielding a negative real return on payroll taxes invested. Even in a very, very slow economy, one has a right to expect a return on investment greater than zero.

Lawrence Lindsey, a member of the Board of Governors of the Federal Reserve System, argues that, although Social Security "paid off nicely for the generation that set it up," giving each retiring worker of that generation a net wealth transfer of tens of thousands of dollars, those born after 1960 will suffer an average net wealth loss of tens of thousands of dollars. "If [Social Security] forces the young to put in more than they can ever hope to take out," Lindsey writes, "its fairness becomes debatable."[101]

Pete DuPont, former governor of Delaware and an advocate of Social Security reform, puts it this way: "Suppose your uncle put this proposition to you: 'Give $250 out of your earnings every month for the rest of your working life, and when you retire I'll return 90% of all you paid me. OK?' A 90% return on contributions is what 25-year-olds can expect."[102] University of Nebraska economist Karl Borden agrees that Social Security is a poor way for today's workers to prepare for retirement. "It's a sucker bet for most of the population," he says.[103]

One can understand, then, the growing frustration of many young people today. They pay much higher Social Security taxes than did the retirees they support, and are likely to pay much higher rates yet during their working years. They will face much higher overall tax rates. In return, they have been slighted by government spending in their youth, and in their own retirement are sure to receive fewer benefits than either the current generation of retirees or the baby boomers who will follow, both of which groups will have paid less in overall taxes than themselves.

It is not entirely unreasonable, then, for the twentysomething, earning twentysomething thousand and expecting little, if any, positive return on his own payroll tax "contributions," to resent paying escalating Social Security taxes to fund the leisure of a prosperous, healthy senior citizen who has retired at age 62.

RETIREMENT: A SUPERANNUATED CONCEPT

Retirement, the removal of an individual from the economic sphere solely because of age, is principally a product of industrialization, and the accompanying urbanization, which transformed American society in the latter half of the nineteenth and first part of the twentieth centuries. Younger workers were better able to keep pace with the high speeds of the factory machinery;[104] and in any case the growing concentration of labor in the cities made a supply of newer, younger workers constantly available. Thus, workers were employed (or used up) until they could no longer keep up, and were then replaced by younger substitutes, who would be replaced in their turn. Retirement was what happened once an individual became "superannuated," no longer useful. Franklin Roosevelt and his advisors knew that Americans, aware of the countless human tragedies of factory workers (often in their 40s or 50s) being left jobless and destitute after having been rendered superannuated by factory work, might support a welfare program for the elderly where they opposed it for the general population, because older people were viewed as being, as a group, largely unable to provide for their own needs.

Mainly, modern retirement is not a consequence of physical limitations, or of economics. It is a cultural phenomenon, rooted in outdated perceptions and expectations about the aging. In *A History of Retirement,* William Graebner describes a watershed in American public discourse about the place of the elderly in the workforce. The year was 1905, and the setting was Johns Hopkins University, where the world-renowned doctor, William Osler, was retiring. In his widely publicized valedictory speech, Osler warned that universities were threatened, as were many kinds of institutions, by all of the workforce "growing old at the same time." "The effective, vitalizing work of the world," Osler said, "is done between the ages of twenty-five and forty—these fifteen golden years of plenty, the anabolic or constructive period, in which there is always a balance in the mental bank and the credit is still good." The stinger: not only were older workers not as intellectually vibrant, or physically capable as younger men, they were a positive hindrance to productivity. "My second fixed idea," Osler continued, "is the uselessness of men above 60 years of age, and the incalculable benefit it would be in commercial, political, and in professional life if, as a matter of course, men stopped work at this age."[105]

Osler's remarks were incendiary at a time of growing public concern about the relatively new discovery of mass "unemployment," another effect of industrialism. Widely publicized by the media, the speech stimulated national discussion about efficiency, productivity, and human utility. Nevertheless, Osler's comments did not create new concerns, but brought to the surface those which had been percolating slowly since the dawn of industrialism, the move to the cities, and the growth of factory life. His statements about the inefficiency of the elderly would have made little social impact if not for the growing perception, already incipient, that the elderly were ill-suited to productive activity in the new industrial age: that aging was a growing social problem to be coped with. Graebner writes, "Osler only confirmed the values and fears of the larger culture."[106]

Of course, some younger workers saw the new attitude toward aging, embodied in Osler's speech, as "the harbinger of a new age of opportunity."[107]

Older, less productive workers ought to be cleared out to make room for newer, fresher, more efficient replacements. Mandatory retirement, they argued, served the larger good.

Others fought against the stereotyped attitude toward aging implicit in the concept of mandatory retirement. Aging did not, they contended, automatically make individuals unproductive. Newspapers ran articles on the achievements of men over 40.

Furthermore, critics of retirement warned, to force individuals out of productive activity due only to age was to relinquish them to a kind of social limbo in which they no longer had any meaningful place in the life of society. Retire to do what?, the *Saturday Review* asked. "Men shrink from voluntarily committing themselves to an act which simulates the forced inactivity of death."[108] And in any case, the *Brooklyn Eagle* commented, such a notion of retirement would require a massive redistribution of wealth from workers toward the elderly.[109] It was meant to be a criticism, not a prediction.

By 1935, when the New Dealers were looking for ways to boost employment, ideas about the declining economic usefulness of the elderly, already permeating the culture by the turn of the century, were now pervasive. What better way to gain support for a controversial public welfare program than by aiming it at the elderly, the one group widely believed to be incapable of productive participation in the economy? That perception of the elderly gave the United States a welfare system based on age rather than need. In 1935, to be older was, by definition, to be needy.

If that view was ever true (and to some degree it was), it no longer is. Dr. Lydia Bronte, director of the Aging Society Project, in an intensive study of the lives of older Americans, found that, far from being a time of diminished creativity and productivity, later life can be the period of greatest achievement and contribution—if individuals are given the opportunity. Furthermore, as increased longevity has added a "second middle age," between the ages of 50 and 75, Bronte suggests, older Americans are in an unprecedented position to contribute to society. Yet, public attitudes, still rooted in the realities of half a century ago, often inhibit those contributions. Both the individual and the larger society suffer from those outdated stereotypes.[110] For example, a Harris poll conducted for the National Council on Aging found that 40% of older Americans believed that frail health was in general a problem for the elderly, although only 20% had ever actually been affected by it themselves.[111] Bronte writes, "The negative image is shared by young and old alike, and it persists among older people despite their own experience to the contrary."[112]

The social perceptions of aging have not kept pace with the physiological facts. The American retirement system of the twenty-first century continues to be based on the gerontological assumptions of 1935, but 1935 is a world away from the realities of aging in the 1990s. Whereas in 1935 it was probably true that a 60-year-old man was ill-equipped to compete for most industrial jobs, both the physical condition of the individual and the nature of the workplace have undergone revolutionary changes during the past half-century. Americans are not only living longer than ever before, but are also healthier while they are alive. Recent studies have indicated that, even as the senior population ages, disability among the elderly is actually declining,[113] as is the number of those requiring personal assistance.[114] Today, 70% of all Americans over age 65 view their health as good, very good, or excellent;[115] and 80% of all those over 65 have no mobility or self-care limitations.[116] The sterotype that aging inevitably brings with it chronic physical disability is losing whatever validity it may have once had. "Demography ain't necessarily destiny," says Dr. Richard Suzman, director of Demographic Studies at the National Institutes of Health.[117]

The enactment of Social Security was politically possible in large part because of the social traumas associated with individuals being exluded from productive activity because of age. Until its inception, men worked until they could no longer work, and were then forced, along with their spouses, to depend on the beneficence of their families and community, often quickly sliding into poverty. In great measure, Social Security was successful in ending the economic terror of growing old, a historic accomplishment.

But the policy which intended to create a safety net under those no longer able to be economically productive has become, with gradual expansions of benefits, an incentive to abandon productive economic activity altogether. The unforeseen consequence of effectively extracting all individuals over a certain age from the workplace is that, with each increment that is added to life expectancy, an increment is likewise added to the economic burden that the elderly pose. "In addition to the costs of public and private pensions and health insurance, there's the lost output of a potentially productive worker who has withdrawn from the workplace," University of Massachussetts economist Harold Wolozin bluntly points out. "Output is produced only by working people. If we become a nation with a growing number of nonworkers, and a shrinking number of workers, living standards will decline."[118]

The concept of retirement, in its present form, makes aging a burden, not a boon, to the community. Society cannot afford both to continue to extend the length of life, and to preserve every added year beyond age 62 as a period of life free from the expectation that one continue to contribute economically. At the very least, it would seem reasonable that, as life expectancy is lengthened, the "retirement age," the time at which one leaves economic productivity, be likewise extended. Not only has that not been the case, but, as the "silver years" have become increasingly comfortable, Americans have been moving in the opposite direction, toward earlier and earlier retirement. Everyone wants to live longer, no one wants to work longer.

"The average age of retirement has precipitously dropped in recent years," writes Gina Kolata, "and no one knows why."[119] Increased financial independence of the postwar generation seems to be an important factor. Susan Dentzer explains, "Today's trend to retire at 65 or sooner took off after World War II, when economic and social forces aroused seniors' appetites for leisure. Social

Security benefits and private pensions vastly increased oldsters' wherewithal, leaving the elderly as a group substantially better off today than the rest of the U.S. population."[120]

Economic disincentives also drive some seniors out of the workplace. The Social Security "earnings test" reduces one's monthly Social Security check by one dollar for every three dollars earned in the workplace above a few thousand dollars. Peter Peterson criticizes the test as "a costly, demoralizing, and unnecessary tax on the economic contributions of older people." The earnings test, says Peterson, is "counterproductive in a society that must begin encouraging more Americans in their sixties to remain (or re-enter) the labor force."[121]

In addition to government, private industry has assisted older Americans' flight from the workplace, promoting early retirement as a means of downsizing, reducing the workforce to achieve greater efficiency.[122] By and large, though, the receding retirement age is not a result of downsizing employers. Certainly, mandated retirement at any age should be illegal: ability, not chronology, ought to decide. Yet, while legislation prohibiting age discrimination in employment is needed to protect those seniors who, going against entrenched social norms, want to remain in the workplace, most older Americans are leaving the workplace, eagerly and early, on their own; they are not being pushed out the door by cost-cutting management. Recently, corporations offering early retirement packages for employees have been confronted with a "rush to the doors" by early retirees, and are having to cope with more retirees than they had expected or wanted.[123] Retirement—early retirement—has become part of the culture. Some 70% of Americans view retirement as a basic part of the American dream, and 61% believe a comfortable retirement to be a civil right.[124]

Today, individuals can begin receiving Social Security benefits any time after they turn 62 (although retirement at 62 rather than 65 results in monthly checks averaging 20% smaller than if one waits until 65).[125] The most common age at which Americans retire is, predictably, 62.[126] Most, however, do not wait until the full-benefits age to retire. Today three-fourths of men and four-fifths of women begin collecting benefits before 65.[127] When Social Security was created, and life expectancy was 63 years, a retirement age set at 65 made some sense. Today, when life expectancy is 75, a retirement age of 62 makes no sense.

Can retirement age remain static as life expectancy—and the median age of the nation—continue to move upward? Barely a generation ago, in 1950, when life expectancy was 68 years, 46% of all men over the age of 65 were still working. By 1989 life expectancy had risen by a decade, to 75 years; but just 17% of men over 65 were working.[128] It seems that the longer Americans live, the sooner we want to retire. Will people still be retiring in their 60s when life expectancy is 85? Can we afford to have individuals removed from economic productivity, or subsidized by government old-age pension programs, for one-third or more of their productive lives?

Nobody wants a return to a world where an individual works until he drops dead; or until, no longer able to work, he is forced out of his job and into poverty. But a growing number of critics are asking whether an aging nation can afford to ignore the potential contributions of its older citizens. "I don't think it improper to ask most people to work five additional years if they're living thirteen years longer than their ancestors did two generations ago," says Richard Thau, executive director of Third Millennium.[129]

With a rapidly increasing portion of the population living well beyond 65, many possessing valuable skills and experience, both the individual and society suffer when age becomes a basis for exclusion. With luck, perhaps the notion of retirement at a preset age will be, within the span of a single century, a vision of aging that became prevalent, then prescriptive, then passé.

Reforms are already under way. Firms are adding semiretirement, part-time employment, split time (where two or more individuals jointly share a single full-time position), reduced responsibilities, and other options in order to attract (or retain) older workers, who are often seen as more mature, responsible, and experienced.

The trend among the elderly, however, is the other way. While some seniors are going back to the workplace, they are swimming against an intensifying current: in 1948, over 90% of men between the ages of 55 and 64 were in the workforce (either working or actively seeking a job); by 1989, just over 60% were.[130] The average retirement age has declined from 67 in 1950 to 63 in 1995.[131]

For those who see retirement as an artificial limitation on the personal development and public contribution of seniors, there is some good news: millions of baby boomers won't be able to afford to retire, even with help from Social Security. One recent government study found that, among those between the ages of 51 and 61, the group closest to retirement, 40% expect to have no income in retirement other than Social Security.[132] One in five have no real assets.[133]

"While the current generation of near-retirees will most likely be spared the impoverished old age that their inadequate private savings would otherwise guarantee, baby boomers won't be so lucky," *Fortune* warns. "On its present trajectory, Social Security will be unable to sustain today's benefit levels by the time the boomers shuffle off to shuffleboard."[134]

Most boomers report that they would like to retire by age 60, but many have not prepared, perhaps expecting government programs to be sufficient.[135] Four in ten currently save less than $1,000 annually for retirement. Steven Vernon, retirement practice director of the benefits consulting firm Watson Wyatt Worldwide, puts the matter bluntly: "If you're saving less than $1,000 and you ask the question at what age you'll be able to retire, the answer will probably be well beyond death."[136]

HARD CHOICES AHEAD

Among younger Americans, there is growing restlessness. Many doubt that Social Security will even exist when they retire,[137] and most do not believe that they will receive a positive return on their Social Security payroll taxes when their own turn comes to receive benefits.[138] Because of the shifting demographic context, with fewer workers supporting each retiree, they are probably right. What is undeniable is that young workers today will receive a far lower level of benefits when they retire than the retirees they are currently funding, or those due to retire in the next couple of decades. In order to support the exploding number of seniors, living longer than ever before, benefits will likely have to be gradually reduced, and payroll taxes gradually raised. That places those at the tail end of the baby boom, and the members of generation X, in the disagreeable position of paying a higher and higher portion of their income in taxes, with the expectation of receiving lower benefits upon their own retirement. Advocates of Social Security who, a generation ago, blithely described it as a Ponzi scheme, might have been more accurate than they knew: today's younger workers will pay more than the retirees they support, and receive less.

In American politics there is seldom agreement on any topic, but there is universal agreement on this: the existing public structure for the elderly cannot survive the aging of the boomer generation unaltered. By all accounts, there are difficult choices ahead. Yet most politicians, fearing the political power of the elderly, are reluctant to go on record supporting specific changes. While the trustees of Social Security and Medicare forecast crisis ahead for those programs unless reforms are made, substantial reforms always seem to be an election and a half away.

When politicians do propose reforms, they tend to be modest ones. Senators Alan Simpson (R-WY) and Bob Kerrey (D-NE), both of whom served on the President's Bipartisan Commission on Entitlement and Tax Reform, called for a reduction of Social Security taxes by 2%, with that money going into individual investment plans for retirement.[139] The proposal was designed to assuage concerns that current payments to Social Security are not likely to yield a decent investment return for today's young workers. A 2% reduction in payroll taxes to that end was a modest beginning, but was met with a storm of criticism from seniors' groups. The proposal got nowhere. Simpson, after his service on the Commission, charged AARP with distorting reform efforts in order to scare its members into conformity with its policy positions. Regarding the political courage of his fellow congresspeople in dealing with the gray lobby, Simpson said sardonically, "Our colleagues are solidly in back of us. Way, way back."[140] Shortly thereafter, he announced his retirement from politics.

Among those outside of elective politics, meanwhile, there has been a proliferation of reform proposals, ranging from mild to radical. The AFL-CIO, opposing reforms of the existing structure, acknowledges that changes must be made in order for Social Security to be viable in another generation. Its solution:

"The trust fund depletion could be solved with a gradual payroll tax increase, preferably accompanied by an expansion of the wage base."[141] A solution which raises payroll taxes and increases the amount of income subject to those taxes would only further guarantee that today's younger workers do not receive a positive return on their retirement investment in Social Security.

The "gray lobby" likewise acknowledges the problem facing the system, and likewise places the burden of salvaging it on the shoulders of the—politically vulnerable—young. Testifying before the Social Security Subcommittee of the Senate Finance Committee in June 1995, a spokesperson for AARP insisted that "Social Security's long-term solvency can be restored by increasing revenue [read: payroll taxes], reducing benefits, or some combination of the two."[142] Since any such reduction in benefits would be implemented very gradually, the prescription would mean that younger workers would pay higher taxes today in order to receive lower benefits tomorrow. Along with the fact that Social Security already provides fewer benefits to the truly needy elderly (by as much as half) than to the rich, such "solutions" fuel criticisms that American public policy caters to the political power of middle- and upper-class elderly at the expense of younger Americans.

Furthermore, many analysts believe that the modest, incremental adjustments advocated by AARP will simply not be adequate to cope with the momentous changes ahead. "Traditional tinkering with taxes and benefits just won't be satisfactory," says Carolyn Weaver, an economist and member of Social Security's Advisory Council. She suggests that the problem "stems from this pay-as-you-go system where we're promising a level of benefits and then trying to come up with a means of financing it. That's quite elusive in the face of the demographics we have."[143]

Some advocates of reform propose taxing Social Security benefits the same way that other income is taxed.[144] At present, 85% of Social Security income is taxed, but only for couples earning over $44,000 and singles earning over $34,000; most other beneficiaries are taxed on 50% of benefits. Couples earning under $32,000, and singles earning under $25,000 are not taxed on benefits at all.

Economists Kotlikoff and Gokhale suggest capping Medicare spending increases from 1993 to 2004,[145] a recommendation that looks Quixotic in the face of recent efforts to simply control the rate at which Medicare costs are escalating.

Former Senators Paul Tsongas (D-MA) and Warren Rudman (R-NH), founders of the Concord Coalition, propose comprehensive means testing for all entitlements. Social Security benefits would be based on need, not age.[146]

Many young people, believing that the current retirement system is fatally flawed, feel that it can be saved only if radical changes are made, starting soon. "Short of some ghastly plague that wipes out the senior population, or the unexpected arrival of tens of millions of tax-paying young immigrants, the entitlements pyramid we have come to know since the New Deal will topple over," says Richard Thau.[147]

"Today's Social Security system is unfair and headed for collapse," write Rob Nelson and Jon Cowan, cofounders of the twentysomething political organization Lead or Leave, and authors of *Revolution X*. "While [Social Security] worked for older generations, it is certain to penalize most in our generation (we'll be lucky to get any return on what we pay in)." Their solution: "Take only what you need, not what you want or think you deserve." They propose an "affluence test," similar to the Concord Coalition's means test, whereby all personal income over $40,000 would reduce Social Security benefits accordingly.[148]

Even the affluence test, though, would only be a "stopgap measure," something to save Social Security in the short term. In the long run, Nelson and Cowan argue, the system will have to be privatized. Rather than having money withdrawn from one's check in the form of payroll taxes, individuals would be required to invest those funds privately, in an individual retirement account (IRA), for their own retirement. Those elderly who did remain in poverty would be eligible for federal welfare benefits, just like members of every other age group.[149] (Advocates of the reform maintain that, at present, Social Security largely goes to benefit middle-class seniors, to the neglect of the truly needy.) The arguments are finding an audience. Third Millennium cites polls showing that as much as 82% of young Americans favor privatizing Social Security.[150]

Young people, concerned about the viability of Social Security, are not the only ones supporting that radical proposal. Former Delaware Governor Pete DuPont has advocated privatizing Social Security, arguing that workers today could receive a much higher return on their retirement savings by investing it themselves, rather than turning their money over to the federal government.[151]

Economist Karl Borden suggests that all workers below a certain age, perhaps 47 or so, could be allowed to opt out of the current Social Security system, which Borden sees as comparable to opting off of a sinking ship. Rather than have their taxes deducted, they would be required to invest that money for themselves. Borden believes that most young workers, given their lack of confidence in Social Security, would take up the private option.[152] Chile has already privatized its retirement program, requiring citizens to put 10% of their income, tax-free, into IRAs. One consequence of the private pension approach is to boost private savings: Chile's rate has risen to over 20% of GDP, compared with the U.S. rate of around 3%.[153]

At a time when it is politically risky to discuss fully taxing the Social Security benefits of wealthy recipients, most of the more radical proposals have slim prospects of enactment, or even of making their way into serious policy discussion. Today, we are arguing over how fast Medicare spending will be increased, and whether Social Security's cost-of-living allowances should be tied to the Consumer Price Index or some other measure by which to automatically increase seniors' benefits each year. Such grandiose prescriptions for reform as the twentysomethings' vision of a retirement program where seniors will "take only what you need, not what you want or think you deserve," seem almost comically out of place in a political milieu where even modest proposals for change make little headway.

When modest reform efforts are made, they invariably reveal much about the intractible nature of the political and demographic problems that must be addressed. When the 11 commissioners of Social Security met in 1980 to offer recommendations to sustain the actuarial integrity of the system, they rejected the idea of raising the retirement age. Although life expectancy had spiraled since 1935, the commissioners insisted, Americans have become accustomed to the idea of retirement at 65, and to raise the retirement age would be unfair.[154] Finally, in 1983, in a pique of political courage, and on the recommendation of yet another commission, Congress raised the age at which one can receive full benefits by two years (from 65 to 67). Life expectancy had increased by over a decade since the inception of Social Security, but it was considered a political triumph to raise the age at which one can receive full benefits by two years. (Most beneficiaries then, as now, will retire earlier.) The clincher: the age hike would be implemented very, very gradually, raising the full-benefits age to 66 by 2008 and to 67 by 2025. The age increase, then, far from addressing the dramatic extensions of life expectancy of the past century, may not even keep pace with the expansion of longevity that occurs during the decades it will take to go into effect. Nevertheless, it was, as things go in the incendiary policy world of old age, politically safe: the change will not go into effect until long after the politicians who voted for it—and their middle-aged constituents—are safely retired.

For many, such efforts are too little, too late. Pete Peterson has proposed hiking the retirement age to 67 by 2006. "It is wrong, to ask today's twenty-year-olds to retire at older ages when today's fifty-year-olds could just as easily do the same thing."[155] Senator John Danforth (R-MO), with the courage of a politician on his way out of office, goes even further. He would hike the retirement age to 70 by 2025.[156]

Among those currently in office, and who wish to remain there, however, the prevailing sentiment favors postponing difficult policy choices.

WAITING FOR THE CRISIS

In a sense, we can not really know what the gray years ahead hold for America, for history has never been down this demographic path before. So many people have never lived so long. This is all new. Yet, although the precise projections vary, there are a few things that we know for certain about the years ahead:

1. There will be fewer workers supporting each retiree.
2. Costs for each retiree (especially medical costs) will be greater.

3. The average American will live longer after retirement.
4. We are not prepared.

On our present course, for the next 20 years the political challenges of an aging population will be a national problem. After that, they will be a national crisis. In the early decades of the twenty-first century, the United States will confront a problem it has never confronted before. At that time, there will be an enormous, and growing, portion of the population that is old, not working, and dependent upon society for their support. Unprepared for retirement, and unwilling to forego it, the tidal wave of aging boomers will place unprecedented burdens on America's programs for the elderly. Just as the crest of baby boomers hits retirement, the Trust Fund's surplus will be depleted. Social Security will be bankrupt. The extraordinary economic stresses upon the members of the baby bust generation, forced to support an exploding number of retirees, will produce political pressures to constrain Social Security spending. But the political pressures from the powerful boomers, the "me generation," will be at their greatest, working to prevent any political efforts to reduce benefits. At that point, generational conflict may become acute.

It is troubling that Americans have been unable to come to terms with the choices available thus far, because the choices ahead are likely to get much harder. There are many difficult choices ahead, and some intractible ones, but we haven't yet even started making the fairly easy ones that are at hand. Those approaching retirement are less financially prepared than earlier generations: although incomes have been stagnant, consumption has escalated; savings rates have plummeted; investment has fallen; debt has spiraled. By one estimate, three-fourths of all those over age 20 will have less than half of what they will need to retire comfortably.[157]

The choices made in the public sphere replicate those of the private. Despite warnings by Social Security trustees to get the nation's economic house in order, the national debt surpasses $5 trillion; unfunded entitlement obligations add trillions more. Public efforts, not to reduce entitlement benefits, but merely to control the rate at which costs escalate, continue to be politically fatal. The possibility of actually capping, even on a per capita basis, increases in spending, is not even on the table. Demographically speaking, things will not start to get really difficult for another 30 years; but, on their present course, Social Security and Medicare will be bankrupt well before then. America, whose population will, in 25 years, be older than Florida's is today, is living as though it were going to be forever young.

Who is responsible? Shall we blame AARP, for its political bullying? AARP, a growing chorus of critics believes, does not truly represent the interests of all older Americans, as its name suggests. Rather, it represents only those who happen to be elderly at the present time. Seniors are, after all, the universal interest group. There will be elderly people in America in 30 years from now, and another 30, and another. What of their interests? In protecting today's retirees from sharing any of the burden of the choices that inevitably must come, we are insuring a less secure retirement for those yet to retire.

Or shall we blame timorous politicians, for their inaction? Or young people, for their apathy? *Congressional Quarterly* notes that there are 65 million members of generation X, "making them, potentially, one of the most potent forces in American politics. But they're not." Despite the fact that they "will be most profoundly affected by the mounting costs of Social Security," being compelled to support the retirement costs of the baby boomers "through payroll taxes that could go as high as 30% of their pay," they are politically disengaged. Only half of them are even registered to vote.[158]

Perhaps who is to blame is not so important as who gains, and who loses, from further delay. It cannot be denied that, to some extent, the elderly of today are living well at the expense of the elderly of tomorrow, particularly members of generation X, the baby bust generation. According to the Social Security Administration, an average worker retiring in 1995 will receive back everything that both he and his employer paid in Social Security taxes in less than five years.[159] Millions of baby bust generation retirees will never recover what they paid in Social Security "contributions." That isn't fair.

The question about Social Security is no longer whether it will become bankrupt, but how soon. In a field where there isn't agreement on anything, economists agree that the current system cannot remain solvent. Paul Magnusson writes that there are two competing views of the future of Social Security, depending on whether one is optimistic or pessimistic. "Apocalyse soon—or sooner."[160] Politicians, actuaries, and activists all agree that the assumptions of 1935 about old age will not be adequate to meet the realities of the next century. Yet nothing gets done.

Democracies are not well suited to making difficult political choices. Politicians do not get elected by promising sacrifice, except in the broadest, most abstract terms. It is easier to postpone action until crisis compels it. The longer the delay, the less pleasant the alternatives when action must be taken. "The longer you wait," warns Brookings Institution economist Barry Bosworth, "the bigger the required changes will get, and it won't be possible to do anything sensible."[161] Senator Kerrey, one of the few politicians to attempt to confront the AARP (albeit with little result), agrees. "I've heard colleagues [in Congress] say 'We're not in a crisis now; let's wait till the crisis arises to take action.' . . . Americans will pay the price for our delay."[162]

The federal entitlement programs for the elderly, begun out of society's commitment to achieve justice between generations, are now being criticized for a new type of injustice. Where once they lightly taxed workers to help support struggling seniors, they are now under attack for heavily taxing struggling workers to subsidize prosperous seniors. Americans are grappling, once again, with the perennial question of what one generation owes another. It will become the most important political question of our time.

Notes

INTRODUCTION

1. Cited in W. Andrew Achenbaum and Peggy Ann Kusnerz, *Images of Old Age in America, 1790 to the Present*. Institute of Gerontology, The University of Michigan-Wayne State University, 1978, p. 25.
2. Ralph Waldo Emerson, "Old Age," *Atlantic Monthly*. January 1862, p. 135.

CHAPTER 1: FROM VENERATION TO BURDEN

1. Cited in W. Andrew Achenbaum, *Old Age in the New Land*. Baltimore: Johns Hopkins University Press, 1978, p. 18.
2. Ibid., p. 19.
3. David Hackett Fischer, *Growing Old in America*. Oxford: Oxford University Press, 1978, p. 52.
4. *Historical Statistics of the United States from Colonial Times to 1970*. U.S. Department of Commerce, Bureau of the Census, 1975, Part 1, Sect. A.
5. Hace Sorel Tischler, *Self-Reliance and Social Security, 1870-1917*. Port Washington, NY: Kennikat Press, 1971, pp. 13-14.
6. *Historical Statistics*, Part A, Chapter A, pp. 43-56.
7. Gary M. Walton and Ross M. Robertson, *History of the American Economy*. New York: Harcourt Brace Jovanovich, 1983, pp. 401-403.
8. *Statistical Yearbook of the Immigration and Naturalization Service*. Washington, DC: INS, 1986. Table IMM, 1.1.
9. James MacGregor Burns, *The Workshop of Democracy*. New York: Vintage Books, 1985, p. 247.
10. *World Almanac and Book of Facts*. New York: Pharos Books, 1990, p. 553.
11. Burns, p. 247.
12. Achenbaum, p. 39.

13. Dr. Joseph Richardson, "Old Age and How to Meet It," in S.G. Lathrop (ed.), *Fifty Years and Beyond*. Chicago: Fleming H. Revell, 1881, p. 35.

14. Lathrop, p. 193.

15. Ibid., p. 249.

16. Ibid., p. 283.

17. Oliver Wendell Holmes, "The Old Man Dreams," in L. Maria Child (ed.), *Looking Toward Sunset*. New York: Houghton Mifflin, 1891, p. 44.

18. Henry Ward Beecher, "November," in Child, p. 341.

19. L. Maria Child, in Child, pp. 164-171.

20. Reverend W.X. Ninde, "Characteristics Which Adorn Old Age," in Lathrop, p. 239.

21. Arnold Lorand, *Old Age Deferred*. Philadelphia: F.A. Davis Co., 1923, pp. vii-xix.

22. Ibid., p. xxiv.

23. Ibid.

24. Ibid., p. 450.

25. Ralph Waldo Emerson, "Old Age," *Atlantic Monthly*, January 1862, pp. 134-138.

26. Oscar Wilde, *The Complete World of Oscar Wilde*. New York: Barnes & Noble, 1994, p. 436.

27. Achenbaum, p. 51.

28. Stanley G. Hall, *Senescence: The Last Half of Life*. New York: D. Appleton and Company, 1923, pp. 428-431.

29. Lillien J. Martin and Clare DeGrouchy, *Salvaging Old Age*. New York: The Macmillan Company, 1936, p. 16.

30. Ibid., p. 176.

31. Robert Hunter, *Poverty*. New York: Harper & Row, 1965 (originally published 1904), p. 97.

32. Ibid., pp. 100-101.

33. Ibid., p. xv.

34. Maurice Parmelee, *Poverty and Social Progress*. New York, 1916, p. 324.

35. Robert W. Kelso, *Poverty*. New York: Longman's, Green and Co., 1929, p. v.

36. Ibid., p. 146.

37. Ibid., p. 147.

38. Ibid., p. 151.

39. Ibid., p. 156.

40. Robert S. Lynd and Helen Merrell Lynd, *Middletown*. New York: Harcourt, Brace and Company, 1929, p. 33.

41. Ibid.

42. Ibid., p. 35.

CHAPTER 2: VOICES IN THE WILDERNESS

1. Carolyn Weaver, *The Crisis in Social Security*, Durham: NC: Duke Press Policy Studies, 1982, p. 20.

2. Ibid., p. 21.

3. Walter I. Trattner, *From Poor Law to Welfare State*, New York: Free Press, 1979, p. 15.

4. Quoted in Hace Sorel Tischler, *Self-Reliance and Social Security, 1870-1917.* Port Washington, NY: Kennikat Press, 1971, p. 16.

5. Cited in Robert H. Brenner, "'Scientific Philanthropy,' 1873-1893," *Social Service Review*, June, 1956, p. 168.

6. Ibid.

7. Ibid., pp. 171-173.

8. Weaver, pp. 25-27.

9. Ibid., p. 26.

10. Trattner, p. 178.

11. Ibid, p. 181.

12. Ibid., pp. 183-184.

13. Tischler, pp. 140-145; Trattner, pp. 186-188.

14. Cited in Vaughn Davis Bornet, "The Quest for Social Security," in John Schacht (ed.), *The Quest for Security.* Iowa City: Center for the Study of Recent History of the United States, 1982, p. 46.

15. Abraham Epstein, *Facing Old Age.* New York: Arno Press & The New York Times, 1972, p. 1.

16. Ibid., pp. 3, 9.

17. Ibid.

18. Abraham Epstein, *Insecurity: A Challenge to America.* New York: Harrison Smith & Robert Haas, 1933, pp. 491-494, 531.

19. Isaac M. Rubinow, *The Quest for Security.* New York: Henry Holt and Company, 1934, p. 207.

20. Ibid., pp. 211-214.

21. Ibid., p. 214.

22. Ibid., pp. 595-606.

23. Arthur Mastick Hyde and Ray Lyman Wilbur, *The Hoover Policies.* New York: Charles Scribner's Sons, 1937, pp. 91-92.

24. Ibid., p. 91.

25. Ibid.

26. Bornet, p. 51.

27. Frankel to Ecker, August 6, 1930, in Bornet, p. 52.

28. Bornet, pp. 52-53.

29. Hyde and Wilbur, pp. 91-92.

CHAPTER 3: A SOCIAL CONTRACT BETWEEN GENERATIONS

1. Martin Fausold, *The Presidency of Herbert C. Hoover.* Lawrence: University of Kansas Press, 1985, pp. 63-67.

2. Ibid., p. 73.

3. For an examination of Hoover's views on the appropriate role of government, see *The State Papers and Other Public Writings of Herbert Hoover*, S. Myers (ed). Garden City, NY: Doubleday Doran & Co., 1934, pp. 572-578.

4. Jordan A. Schwartz, *The Interregnum of Despair: Hoover, Congress, and the Depression.* Urbana: University of Illinois Press, 1970, p. 12.

5. Ibid., p. 13.

6. Fausold, p. 82.

7. W. Andrew Achenbaum, *Shades of Gray*. Boston: Little, Brown & Co., 1983, p. 32.

8. Franklin D. Roosevelt, *The Roosevelt Reader*, Basil Rauch (ed.). New York: Holt, Rinehart, & Winston, 1964, pp. 72-73.

9. Franklin D. Roosevelt, *The Public Papers and Addresses of Franklin D. Roosevelt*, Samuel Rosenman (ed.). New York: Random House, 1938. Vol. II, pp. 11-15.

10. Quoted in William E. Leuchtenburg, *Franklin D. Roosevelt and the New Deal*. New York: Harper & Row, 1963, p. 61.

11. Anthony Badger, *The New Deal: The Depression Years, 1933-1940*. New York: Hill & Wang, 1989, pp. 256-257.

12. Franklin D. Roosevelt, Executive Order 6757, The White House, June 29, 1934.

13. "Statement of Purpose," Reports of the Committee on Economic Security, August 13, 1934, in Edwin Witte, *The Development of the Social Security Act*. Madison: University of Wisconsin Press, 1962, pp. 21-22.

14. Ibid.

15. Frances Perkins, *The Roosevelt I Knew*. New York: Harper & Row, 1964, p. 283.

16. Witte, p. 47.

17. Frank Freidel, *Franklin D. Roosevelt: A Rendezvous with Destiny*. Boston: Little, Brown and Co., 1990, p. 150.

18, Perkins, p. 278.

19. Friedel, p. 150.

20. "The Economic Security Act," *Congressional Record*, January 17, 1935, Vol. 79, Part 1, pp. 546-549.

21. Theodore R. Marmor, *The Politics of Medicare*. Chicago: Aldine Publishing, 1973, pp. 546-549.

22. Congressional Record, January 17, 1935, Vol. 79, Part 1, pp. 546-549.

23. "Roosevelt Offers His Security Plan for Jobless, the Aged, and Widows: Program Splits Congress Party Lines," *New York Times*, January 18, 1935, p. 1.

24. *Congressional Record*, January 17, 1935, Vol. 79, Part 1, pp. 546-549.

25. "Wagner Statement on Bill's Objectives," *New York Times*, January 18, 1935, p. 16.

26. Ibid.

27. "Roosevelt Plan Splits Party Lines," *New York Times*, January 18, 1935, pp. 1, 19.

28. "Congress Clearing Stage for Earliest Enactment of the Security Program," *New York Times*, January 19, 1935, p. A1.

29. Witte, p. 80.

30. Ibid., p. 144.

31. Ibid., pp. 151-154.

32. Roosevelt, *Public Papers and Addresses*, Vol. IV, p. 325.

CHAPTER 4: NATIONAL HEALTH CARE (FOR THE ELDERLY)

1. Harry S. Truman, Special Message to Congress, November 19, 1945, in *New York Times*, November 20, 1945, pp. 1, 13.

2. Harry S. Truman, State of the Union Address, January 7, 1948, in *New York Times*, January 8, 1948, p. 4.

3. Thomas Dewey, State of the State Address, to New York Legislature, Albany, January 1, 1950, *New York Times*, January 2, 1950, p. 1.

4. Theodore R. Marmor, *The Politics of Medicare*. Chicago: Aldine Publishing, 1973, pp. 12-14.

5. Monte M. Poen, *Harry S. Truman Versus the Medical Lobby*. Columbia: University of Missouri Press, 1979, p. 188.

6. *New York Times*, May 16, 1950, p. 3.

7. Ibid.

8. Claude Pepper, *Pepper*. New York: Harcourt Brace Jovanovich, 1987, p. 205.

9. Ibid., p. 204.

10. Ibid., p. 203.

11. Poen, p. 182.

12. *New York Times*, April 19, 1951, p. 35.

13. Poen, p. 190.

14. Robert Harootyan, "Interest Groups and Aging Policy," in Robert B. Hudson (ed.), *The Aging in Politics*. Springfield, IL: Charles C. Thomas, 1981, p. 80.

15. Richard Harris, *A Sacred Trust*. New York: New American Library, 1966, p. 55.

16. Marmor, p. 16.

17. Ibid., pp. 16-17, 20.

18. Robert Taft, Statement of Candidacy, *New York Times*, October 17, 1951, p. 6.

19. Dwight Eisenhower, Press Conference, June 5, 1952, in New York Times, June 6, 1952, p. 11.

20. Announcement of Expansion of Prudential Health Insurance Coverage, *New York Times*, June 20, 1951, p. 37.

21. Republican Party Platform, *New York Times*, July 3, 1952, p. 13.

22. Adlai Stevenson, Campaign Statement, *New York Times*, July 24, 1952, p. 11.

23. 1952 Democratic Party Platform, *New York Times*, July 24, 1952, p. 17.

24. James Howard Means, M.D., "The Doctor's Lobby," *The Atlantic*, October 1952, pp. 57-60.

25. Ibid., p. 60.

26. *New York Times*, November 30, 1952, p. 54.

27. Poen, p. 206-207.

28. James L. Sundquist, *Politics and Policy*. Washington, DC: The Brookings Institution, 1968, p. 290.

29. See Marmor for a good description of the route to enactment taken by the Medicare policy.

30. Henry J. Pratt, *The Gray Lobby*. Chicago: University of Chicago Press, 1976, p. 68.

31. Ibid., p. 71.

32. John F. Kennedy, Message to Congress, February 9, 1961, *New York Times*, February 10, 1961, p. 1.

33. Harris, pp. 153-155.

34. Marmor, p. 39.

35. Sundquist, p. 450.

36. Ibid., pp. 450-452.

37. John Kingdon, *Agendas, Alternatives, and Public Policies*. Boston: Little, Brown and Co., 1984, p. 124.

38. Congressional Report, no. 3, 1965, p. 4.

39. Lyndon B. Johnson, Remarks on the Passage of Medicare, *New York Times*, July 31, 1965, p. 19.

40. Harry S. Truman, Remarks, in ibid.

41. Cited in 1966, p. 206.

42. Theodore Lowi, *The End of Liberalism*. New York: W.W. Norton, 1969, p. 64.

CHAPTER 5: THE PROGRAMS THAT ATE THE GOVERNMENT

1. Gerald Nash et al. (eds.), *Social Security: The First Half-Century*. Albuquerque: University of New Mexico Press, 1988, p. 17.

2. Rob Nelson and Jon Cowan, *Revolution X*. New York: Penguin Books, 1994, p. 64.

3. Bill Clinton, cited in Bipartisan Commission on Entitlement and Tax Reform, "Draft Findings," August 4, 1994, (n.p.).

4. Bipartisan Commission.

5. Peter J. Ferrara, *Social Security: The Inherent Contradiction*. Washington, DC: The Cato Institute, 1980, p. 28.

6. Ibid., Appendix B, Table 7; Nash et al., p. 17.

7. Nash et al., p. 15.

8. W. Andrew Achenbaum, *Social Security: Visions and Revisions*. Cambridge: Cambridge University Press, 1986, p. 39.

9. Cited in Peter Peterson, *Facing Up*. New York: Touchstone, 1994, p. 92.

10. Ibid., p. 58.

11. *Your Medicare Handbook, 1995*. Health Care Financing Administration. Washington, DC: U.S. Government Printing Office, 1995, p. 3.

12. *Reducing the Deficit: Spending and Revenue Options*. Washington, DC: Congressional Budget Office, 1995, p. 288.

13. U.S. Senate Special Committee on Aging et al., *Aging America: Trends and Projections*. Washington, DC, 1991, p. 20.

14. *Historical Statistics of the United States, Colonial Times to 1970* (Part I). Washington, DC: U.S. Department of Commerce, 1975, Series B107-115, p. 55; *Statistical Abstract of the United States*, 114th ed. Washington, DC: U.S. Government Printing Office, 1994, p. 87.

15. Craig Karpel, *The Retirement Myth*. New York: HarperCollins, 1995, p. 9.

16. *Aging America*, p. 20.

17. *Sixty-Five Plus in America*. U.S. Department of Commerce, Bureau of the Census. Washington, DC: U.S. Government Printing Office, 1992, pp. 2-3.

18. Ferrara, Appendix B, Table 33; *Statistical Abstract of the United States*, Washington, DC: U.S. Government Printing Office, 1991, pp. 64-65; Ben J. Wattenberg, *The Birth Dearth*. New York: Pharos Books, 1987, pp. 54-55, 124-130, 174.

19. *Aging America*, p. 7.

20. U.S. Bureau of the Census, "America in Transition: An Aging Society," *Current Population Reports*, Series P-23, No. 128 (September 1983); U.S. Bureau of the Census, "Projections of the Population of the United States by Age, Sex, and Race: 1988 to 2080," *Current Population Reports*, Series P-25, No. 1018 (January 1989).

21. *Aging America*, p. 7.

22. Health Care Financing Administration, in Arsen J. Darnay (ed.), *Statistical Record of Older Americans*. Detroit: Gale Research, 1994, pp. 618-619.

23. National Center for Health Statistics, *Health: United States, 1988*. DHHS Pub. No. (PHS) 89-1232. Washington, DC: Department of Health and Human Services, 1989, p. 94.

24. *Aging America*, p. 112.

25. Ibid., p. 128.

26. National Center for Health Statistics, "Utilization of Short-Stay Hospitals." Washington, DC: Department of Health and Human Services, 1988, p. 2.

27. *Aging America*, p. 121.

28. United We Stand America, Bulletin, "Health Care Reform: Measure Twice, Cut Once," 1995, p. 3.

29. Peterson, pp. 137-138.

30. Howard Fineman, "Mediscare," *Newsweek*, September 18, 1995, p. 41.

31. Ibid., p. 138.

32. Ibid., p. 137.

33. Sara Collins, "Cutting Edge Cures," *U.S. News and World Report*, June 7, 1993, p. 58.

34. *An Aging World II*, International Population Reports. Washington, DC: U.S. Department of Commerce, Bureau of the Census, 1992, p. 20.

35. Peter Heller et al., "Aging and Social Expenditure in the Major Industrial Countries, 1980-2025," International Monetary Fund, September 1986, p. 45.

36. Janice Castro, "Condition: Critical," *Time*, November 25, 1991, pp. 34-35.

37. Ibid., p. 34.

38. United Nations Development Programme, *Human Development Report, 1991*. New York: Oxford University Press, 1991, pp. 122-124.

39. Castro, p. 35.

40. Ibid., p. 35.

41. Congressional Budget Office, "Trends in Health Care Spending: An Update." Washington, DC, June 1993, Table A-20, p. 68; U.S. Department of Commerce, "Medical Enrollees, United States, Selected Years," Washington, DC, 1991.

42. "Budget Blaster," *U.S. News and World Report*, February 20, 1995, p. 38.

43. Ibid., p. 39.

44. "The Zero Deficit Plan," Washington, DC: The Concord Coalition (n.d.), p. 27.

45. "Annual Statistical Supplement to the Social Security Bulletin," U.S. Department of Health and Human Services, Social Security Administration, January 1993, p. 194.

46. Ibid.

47. "Anti-Social Security," *The Economist*, January 21, 1995, p. 30.

48. "Annual Statistical Supplement," p. 194.

49. "Budget Blaster," pp. 38-39.

50. Bipartisan Commission, "Growth of Mandatory Spending in the Federal Government," August 4, 1994 (n.p.).

51. "Federal Entitlement Outlays by Type," Peterson, Charts 4.8 and 4.9.

52. Karpel, p. 7.

53. Bipartisan Commission, Finding #1, August 4, 1994, (n.p.).

54. Karpel, pp. 7-8.

55. Susan Dentzer, "The Grim Message on Entitlements," *U.S. News and World Report*, December 19, 1994, p. 60.

CHAPTER 6: POWER

1. U.S. Senate Special Committee on Aging et al., *Aging America: Trends and Projections*. Washington, DC, 1991, p. 7.

2. Richard Neuberger and Kelly Loe, "The Old People's Crusade," *Harper's*, Vol. 172, March 1936, p. 431.

3. "If Money," *Saturday Evening Post*, Vol. 207, May 11, 1935, p. 13.

4. Ibid., p. 127.

5. Neuberger and Loe, p. 426.

6. Ibid.

7. Ibid., p. 429.

8. "Townsend Testifies for Plan," *New York Times*, February 2, 1935, p. 2.

9. "House Chiefs Plan Gag Rule to Guard Social Measure," *New York Times*, February 4, 1935, p. 1.

10. Ibid.

11. "Townsend Testifies for Plan," p. 2.

12. "Townsend Queried on Pension Plan," *New York Times*, February 17, 1935, p. 3.

13. Edwin Witte, *The Development of the Social Security Act*. Madison: University of Wisconsin Press, 1962, p. 87.

14. Francis E. Townsend, *New Horizons*. Chicago: J.L. Stewart, 1943, p. 151.

15. "The Story of AARP," reprinted in *Modern Maturity*, August 1974, p. 57.

16. Eric Schurenburg and Lani Luciano, "The Empire Called AARP," *Money*, October, 1988, p. 133.

17. "Summary of the AARP *Public Policy Agenda*: 1995." Washington, DC: American Association of Retired Persons, 1995, p. 7.

18. Ibid., pp. 19-23, 33.

19. Ibid., p. 13.

20. Ibid., p. 69.

21. Ibid., pp. 67-69.

22. Ibid., p. 51.

23. Hank Cox, "Age Before Beauty," *Regardie's*, January 1991, p. 61.

24. David DeVoss, "Empire of the Old," *Los Angeles Times Magazine*, February 12, 1989, p. 38.

25. "Gray Panthers Flex Muscles," *Washington Post*, January 15, 1987, p. 1.

26. Maggie Kuhn, "Mobilization for Aging," Gray Panthers pamphlet. Washington, DC (n.d.) (n.p.).

27. Thomas Rosenstiel, "Buying Off the Elderly," *Newsweek*, October 2, 1995, p. 40.

28. Cox, p. 71.

29. Ibid.

30. Ibid.

31. "The Big Gray Money Machine," *Newsweek*, August 15, 1988, p. 38.

32. Rosenstiel, p. 40.

33. "Money and Politics: Special Report," *Older American Reports*, February 22, 1985, p. 5.

34. Schurenburg and Luciano, p. 140.

35. Ibid., p. 130.

36. "G.O.P. Senator Investigates Retirees' Group," *New York Times*, April 9, 1995, Sect. 1, p. 19.

37. "Powerful Senior Lobby Facing Senate Probe," *Corpus Christi Caller Times*, June 5, 1995, p. A12.

38. "Taking a Hard Look at AARP's Deals," *Money*, July 1995, p. 116.

39. Ibid., p. 117.

40. Ibid., p. 116.

41. "Senator Challenges AARP," *USA Today*, June 24, 1995, p. A8.

42. "The Big Gray Money Machine," p. 39.

43. "The AARP: Clout for the Elderly," *The Internist*, January 1987, p. 20.

44. Ronald Reagan, State of the Union Address, *New York Times*, February 5, 1986, p. A21.

45. "Curbs on Medicaid Being Sought," *Washington Post*, December 7, 1986, p. A1.

46. "White House Aide Sees Health Plan as Economic Risk," *New York Times*, December 10, 1986, p. A10.

47. Ibid., p. A26.

48. "Advisors Oppose Key Element of Health Plan," *New York Times*, December 16, 1986, p. A2.

49. "U.S. Health Care Faulted in Senate," *New York Times*, January 13, 1987, p. A1.

50. "President Endorses Catastrophic Care," *Washington Post*, February 13, 1987, p. A1.

51. "Reagan, Apostle of Less, Assures Expanded Health Care for Elderly," *New York Times*, February 15, 1987, p. A1.

52. "President Endorses Catastrophic Care," *Washington Post*, February 13, 1987, p. A1.

53. "Catastrophic Care Attacks Backers in House," *Washington Post*, February 26, 1987, p. A25.

54. "Plan Backed for Catastrophic Medical Expenses," *New York Times*, May 8, 1987, p. A8.

55. "Catastrophic Insurance Bill Near Passage," *Washington Post*, May 26, 1988, p. A1.

56. "For Many, Help Is Near on Health Costs," *New York Times*, May 31, 1988, p. B9.

57. Ibid.

58. "Catastrophic Care Measure to Raise Taxes for Elderly," *Washington Post*, July 1, 1988, p. G3.

59. Bruce C. Wolpe, *Lobbying Congress*. Washington, DC: Congressional Quarterly Press, 1990, p. 71.

60. Ibid., p. 79.

61. "New Health Insurance Plan Provokes Outcry Over Costs," *New York Times*, November 2, 1988, p. A1.

62. Ibid.

63. "Bush Opposes Cut in 'Catastrophic' Premiums," *Washington Post*, April 25, 1989, p. A4.

64. "Rostenkowski Heckled By Senior Citizens," *Washington Post*, August 18, 1989, p. A4; "House Panel Leader Jeered by Elderly in Chicago," *New York Times*, August 19, 1989, p. A8.

65. "Lawmakers Found Country Calm," *Washington Post*, September 13, 1989, p. A4.

66. "Bush Urged to Save Health Plan," *Washington Post*, September 13, 1989, p. A1.

67. *Washington Post*, September 26, 1989, p. A27.

68. "Senate Spurns Move to Cancel Long-Term Health Care Plan," *New York Times*, November 20, 1989, p. A1.

69. "Buying Off the Elderly," *Newsweek*, October 2, 1995, p. 41.

70. *Statistical Abstract of the United States, 1994*, U.S. Department of Commerce, Bureau of the Census. Washington, DC: Government Printing Office, 1994, p. 287.

71. Survey of 5000 Households Nationwide for the Conference Board, "The Public View." Washington, DC: The Conference Board, 1988 (n.p.).

72. Gerald Nash et al. (eds.), *Social Security: The First Half-Century*. Albuquerque: University of New Mexico Press, 1988, p. 14.

73. "The People's Voice," *The Economist*, February 11, 1995, p. 28.

74. U.S. Advisory Commission on Intergovernmental Relations, "Changing Public Attitudes on Government and Taxes," cited in Susan MacManus, "Taxing and Spending Politics: A Generational Perspective," *The Journal of Politics*, August 1995, p. 612.

75. Calculations on total voter turnout based on data from "Voting Age Population, Percent Reporting Registered, and Voting," *Statistical Abstract of the United States: 1994*, p. 287.

76. Robert Kerrey and John C. Danforth, memo to members of the Bipartisan Commission on Entitlement and Tax Reform, August 4, 1994.

77. Bipartisan Commission on Entitlement and Tax Reform, Draft Commission Findings, August 4, 1994.

78. Ibid.

79. Willard Hogeboom, "Social Security: 'Sacred Cow' of Entitlement Programs," *USA Today Magazine*, November 1995, p. 12.

80. "Budget Blaster," *U.S. News and World Report*, February 20, 1995, p. 39.

81. "The Voters are Angry Anyway," *Fortune*, October 4, 1993, p. 104.

82. *Newsweek*, April 6, 1992, p. 28.

83. "Can't Live With 'Em, Can't Live Without 'Em," *Business Week*, September 7, 1992, p. 75.

84. Peter Peterson, speech at "United We Stand" Conference, Dallas, Texas, August 8, 1995.

85. Elizabeth Kolbert, "Who Will Face the Music?" *New York Times Magazine*, August 27, 1995, Section 6, p. 56.

86. "Tantrums, Taxes and Tactics," *U.S. News and World Report*, November 27, 1995, pp. 34-39.

87. "Republican Bill Would Trim Aid for Poor Children Who Are Ill or Disabled," *New York Times*, December 29, 1995, p. A16.

88. "Shrinking Menus: G.O.P. Lunch Plan," *New York Times*, February 22, 1995, p. C1.

89. "Budget Blaster," p. 16.

CHAPTER 7: TRADING PLACES

1. "Money Income and Poverty Status in the United States, 1989," *Current Population Reports*, Series P-60, No. 168, in U.S. Senate Committee on Aging et al., *Aging America: Trends and Projections*. Washington, DC, 1991, p. 58.

2. Ibid.; *Population Profile of the United States: 1995*. Washington, DC: U.S. Department of Commerce, Bureau of the Census, July 1995, p. 43; and "Children Below Poverty Level, 1970 to 1992," *Statistical Abstract of the United States: 1994*, Washington, DC: U.S. Department of Commerce, September 1994, No. 728.

3. *Population Profile of the United States: 1995*, p. 43.

4. "Old, But Far From Feeble," *The Economist*, March 12, 1988, p. 30; "Get Real About Deficits and Entitlements," Published by the Concord Coalition (n.d.), p. 9.

5. Lee Smith, "The Tyranny of America's Old," *Fortune*, January 13, 1992, p. 68.

6. "Progress Elsewhere," *U.S. News and World Report*, August 28, 1995, p. 24.

7. "Low Ranking for Poor American Children," *New York Times*, August 14, 1995, p. A9.

8. Smith, p. 28.

9. *Health Care Systems in Transition*. Paris: OECD, 1990, p. 193.

10. UNICEF, *The State of the World's Children: 1991*. New York: Oxford University Press, 1991, p. 104.

11. *Starting Points: Meeting the Needs of Our Youngest Children*, Report of the Carnegie Task Force on Meeting the Needs of Small Children. New York: Carnegie Corporation, April 1994, p. 65.

12. Ibid., p. 4.

13. Harold E. Fey, "Politics and the Elderly: Toward a Sharing of Resources," *The Christian Century*, December 14, 1988.

14. Gary Blonston, "An Aging Population Will Alter the Future," *Philadelphia Enquirer*, September 6, 1987, p. H1.

15. *Great Transitions: Preparing Adolescents for a New Century*, Report of the Carnegie Council on Adolescent Development. New York: Carnegie Corporation, October 1995, p. 21.

16. *Wasting America's Future*, Report on the Costs of Child Poverty by the Children's Defense Fund. Washington, DC: The Children's Defense Fund, 1994, p. 15.

17. Ibid., pp. 13-17.

18. Ibid., p. 15.

19. *Starting Points*, pp. 65-66.

20. "Study of Poor Children Shows a Painful Choice: Heat Over Food," *New York Times*, September 9, 1992, p. A17.

21. *Wasting America's Future*, p. xvii.

22. Ibid., p. 62.

23. Smith, p. 69.

24. See, for example, *Starting Points*, pp. 3-22; *Wasting America's Future*, p. 15.

25. Thomas Rosenstiel with Rich Thomas, "Senior Power Rides Again," *Newsweek*, February 20, 1995, p. 31.

26. Jonathan Kozol, "Spare Us the Cheap Grace," *Time*, December 11, 1995, p. 96.

27. *Starting Points*, p. 66.

28. Ibid.

29. Ibid.

30. Subrata N. Chakravarty and Katherine Weisman, "Consuming Our Children?" *Forbes*, November 14, 1988, p. 222.

31. "Children Get Poorer, Nation Gets Richer," *USA Today*, November 14, 1994, p. A2.

32. Jonathan Swift, "A Modest Proposal for Preventing the Children of Poor People in Ireland from Being a Burden to their Parents or Country, and for Making Them Beneficial to the Public," in *Gulliver's Travels and Other Writings*. New York: Bantam Books, 1981, p. 487.

33. Ibid., p. 489.

34. Chakravarty and Weisman, p. 222.

35. Laurence J. Kotlikoff and Jagdeesh Gokhale, "Passing the Generational Buck," *The Public Interest*, Winter 1994, p. 79.

36. Ibid., p. 80.

37. Ibid., p. 81.

38. Juliet Schor, *The Overworked American*. New York: Basic Books, 1992, p. 29.

39. Ibid., p. 24.

40. "Slow Burn: The Middle Class Feels Betrayed," *New York Times*, January 12, 1992, p. A1.

41. *Economic Report of the President*. Washington, DC: U.S. Government Printing Office, 1995, p. 21.

42. "The 1980s: A Very Good Time for the Very Rich," *New York Times*, March 5, 1992, p. A1.

43. Kevin Phillips, *The Politics of Rich and Poor*. New York: Random House, 1990, p. 17.

44. *Economic Report of the President*, p. 21.

45. "The Rich are Richer—and America May be Poorer," *Business Week*, November 18, 1991, pp, 85, 88.

46. Chakravarty and Weisman, p. 222.

47. Alden Levy, National Planning Director, Thirteenth Generation, Speech at Coalition to Save Medicare, conference, Washington, DC, August 16, 1995.

48. "Younger Persons Made Up a Disproportionate Share of the Uninsured in 1993," *Population Profile of the United States: 1995*, p. 36.

49. *Starting Points*, p. 66.

50. Ibid.

51. *Population Profile of the United States: 1995*, p. 36.

52. *The Zero Deficit Plan*. Washington, DC: The Concord Coalition, (n.d.), p. 27.

53. Smith, p. 69.

54. Ibid.

55. Neil Howe and Bill Strauss, *Get Real About Deficits and Entitlements*. Washington, DC: The Concord Coalition (n.d.), p. 5.

56. Peter Peterson, speech at "United We Stand" Conference, Dallas, Texas, August 8, 1995.

57. Ken Dychtwald and Joe Flower, *Age Wave*. New York: Bantam Books, 1990, p. 74.

58. "Discretionary Income Per Capita," in "The Senior Boom: How It Will Change America," *Fortune*, March 27, 1989, p. 62.

59. Sylvia Nasar, "Older Americans Cited in Studies of National Savings Rate Slump," *New York Times*, February 21, 1995, p. A1.

60. *Social Security Bulletin*, vol. 55, No. 3, Fall 1992.

61. "Where Retirees Spend Less," *Money*, April 1995, p. 133.

62. *Older Americans Report*, May 12, 1989, p. 189.

63. Chakravarty and Weisman, p. 222.

64. "Old, But Far From Feeble," p. 30.

65. *The Zero Deficit Plan*, p. 27.

66. *Social Security Bulletin*, Table 5, p. 14.

67. U.S. Department of Health and Human Services, *Income of the Aged Chart Book: 1990*. Washington, DC: Government Printing Office, 1990, p. 16.

68. Rob Nelson and Jon Cowan, *Revolution X*. New York: Penguin Books, 1994, p. 60.

69. Ibid., p. 67.

70. *Wasting America's Future*, p. 113.

71. Daniel Callahan, "Why We Must Set Limits," in *A Good Old Age?*, edited by Paul Homer and Martha Holstein. New York: Touchstone, 1990, p. 23.

72. Ibid., p. 24.

73. Sarah Glazer, "Overhauling Social Security," *CQ Researcher*, May 12, 1995, p. 434.

74. Peterson, speech.

75. Gary Becker, "Cut the Greybeards a Smaller Slice of the Pie," *Business Week*, March 28, 1994, p. 20.

76. Paul Tsongas, in Howe and Strauss, p. 116.

77. Michael Tanner, "Should Congress Pass Legislation to Partially Privatize the Social Security System?" *Congressional Digest*, October 1995, p. 242.

78. "Taking Shots at the Baby Boomers," *Time*, July 19, 1993, p. 31.

79. Susan MacManus, *Young Versus Old*. Boulder, CO: Westview Press, 1996, p. 127.

80. Ibid.

81. Nelson and Cowan, pp. 16, 17.

82. Paul Magnusson, "Young America's Rallying Cry: 'Dis the Deficit,'" *Business Week*, August 9, 1993, p. 37.

83. MacManus, p. 161.

84. Susan MacManus, "Taxing and Spending Politics," *Journal of Politics*, August 1995, p. 612.

85. Paul E. Peterson, "An Immodest Proposal," *The Brookings Review*, Winter 1993, p. 19.

86. Ibid., p. 23.

87. Ibid.

88. Ibid.

CHAPTER 8: THE GRAY YEARS AHEAD

1. U.S. Senate Committee on Aging et al., *Aging America: Trends and Projections*. Washington, DC, 1991, p. 7.

2. Ken Dychtwald and Joe Flower, *Age Wave*. New York: Bantam Books, 1990, pp. 14-15.

3. Ibid., pp. 16-19.

4. Horace Deets, "Boomers Will Find AARP a Resource in the Future," *AARP Bulletin*, January 1996, p. 3.

5. *Aging America*, p. 7.

6. Ibid.

7. Paul Samuelson, "Paul Samuelson on Social Security," *Newsweek*, February 13, 1967, p. 88.

8. Katherine Newman, *Declining Fortunes*. New York: Basic Books, 1993, pp. 40-43.

9. *Aging America*, p. 6.

10. "Anti-Social Security," *The Economist*, January 21, 1995, p. 30.

11. Ben J. Wattenberg, *The Birth Dearth*. New York: Pharos Books, 1987, pp. 54-55, 174.

12. *Aging America*, p. 6.

13. "Growing Pains at Forty," *Time*, May 9, 1996, p. 23.

14. Wattenberg, pp. 124-130.

15. "America Then and Now," *Time*, January 9, 1996, p. 38.

16. *Time*, May 19, 1986, p. 23.

17. Wattenberg, pp. 54-55.

18. Peter Peterson, speech at "United We Stand" Conference, Dallas, Texas, August 8, 1995.

19. "Projections of the Population of the United States, by Age, Sex, and Race: 1988 to 2080," in *America in Transition, An Aging Society*. Washington, DC: U.S. Department of Commerce, Bureau of the Census, *Current Population Reports*, Series P-25, No. 1018, January, 1989.

20. Ibid.

21. Bipartisan Commission, Finding No. 5, August 4, 1994.

22. Ibid.

23. "The Economics of Aging," *Business Week*, September 12, 1994, p. 60.

24. *Aging America*, p. 6.

25. Christopher Byron, "The Boomers Go Bust," *Esquire*, July 1995, p. 36.

26. Matthew Greenwald, "Bad News for the Baby Boomers," *American Demographics*, February 1989, p. 34.

27. Anne Willette, "No Savings Means More Work Longer," *USA Today*, May 8, 1995, p. A4.

28. "The Financial Future of the Baby Boomers Looks Bleak," *HR Focus*, August 1994, p. 8.

29. "The Economics of Aging," p. 63.

30. Ibid.

31. "More Savings Means More Work Longer," p. A1.

32. Ibid, p. A2.

33. Ibid.

34. Douglas Kruse, "Pension Substitution in the 1980s: Why the Shift Toward Defined Contribution?" *Industrial Relations*, April 1995, pp. 218-241.

35. Mary Cooper, "Paying for Retirement," *CQ Researcher*, November 5, 1993, p. 964.

36. Sylvia Nasar, "Older Americans Cited in Studies of National Savings Slump," *New York Times*, February 21, 1995, p. A1.

37. *Time*, December 14, 1987, p. 61.

38. Ibid.

39. Patricia Braus, "The Baby Boom at Mid-Decade," *American Demographics*, April 1995, p. 43.

40. "Consumer Debt Figures Revised," *New York Times*, May 11, 1993, p. D2.

41. "The Financial Future of Baby Boomers Looks Bleak," *HR Focus*, August 1994, p. 8.

42. Peter Peterson, "The Morning After," *Atlantic Monthly*, October 1987, p. 47.

43. Byron, pp. 36-37.

44. "Assessing the Decline in the National Savings Rate," Congress of the United States, Congressional Budget Office. Washington, DC: U.S. Government Printing Office, April 1993, p. 3.

45. "Older Americans Cited in Studies of National Savings Rate Declines," *New York Times*, February 21, 1995, p. A1.

46. "Assessing the Decline in the National Saving Rate," p. xi.

47. Ibid., p. 8.

48. Van Doorn Ooms, "Budget Priorities of the Nation," *Science*, December 11, 1992, p. 1743.

49. Louis Uchitelle, "Another Day Older and Running Out of Time," *New York Times*, March 26, 1995, Section 3, p. 1.

50. "Seizing the Day," *American Demographics*, July 1995, p. 22.

51. "Percent of GDP Spent on New Assets or Other Productive Investment," in Michael Wolff et al., *Where We Stand*. New York: Bantam Books, 1992, p. 29.

52. "The Economics of Aging," p. 62.

53. *Factors Affecting the International Competitiveness of the United States*, U.S. Congress, House Committee on Ways and Means. Washington, DC: U.S. Government Printing Office, May 30, 1991, p. 17.

54. George N. Hatsopoulos, Paul Krugman, and Lawrence H. Summers, "U.S. Competitiveness: Beyond the Trade Deficit," *Science*, July 15, 1988, p. 300.

55. "Fastest Growing Occupation," *U.S.A. Today*, January 12, 1996, p. A1.

56. Neil Howe and Bill Strauss, *Get Real About Deficits and Entitlements*. Washington, DC: The Concord Coalition (n.d.), p. 3.

57. Ibid.

58. Keith Bradsher, "Greenspan Says Weak Dollar Is Caused By Federal Deficits," *New York Times*, May 17, 1995, p. D2.

59. Thomas Jefferson, *Writings*. New York: The Library of America, 1984, pp. 959-962.

60. Ibid., pp. 1280-1282.

61. Peter Peterson, *Facing Up*. New York: Touchstone, 1994, p. 234.

62. William Greider, *Who Will Tell the People?* New York: Simon & Schuster, 1992, p. 35.

63. Robert Samuelson, "The Future Be Damned," *Newsweek*, January 6, 1992, p. 36.

64. *U.S. Budget For Fiscal Year 1996*. Washington, DC: U.S. Government Printing Office, p. 1.

65. Ibid.

66. John Palmer and Barbara B. Torres, "Health Care Financing and Pension Plans," in *Aging America*, p. 242.

67. Ooms, p. 1743.

68. Wade Greene, "Overconspicuous Overconsumption," *New York Times*, August 28, 1994, Section 4, p. 15.

69. Ibid.

70. Ooms, p. 1744.

71. "Boomers Tax USA's Social Institutions," *USA Today*, May 8, 1995, p. 2.

72. Ibid.

73. George J. Church and Richard Lacayo, "The Case for Killing Social Security," *Time*, March 20, 1995, p. 24.

74. Ibid.

75. Dorcas Hardy, *Social Insecurity*. New York: Villard Books, 1991.

76. Peter Frank, "Age Wave," *Baltimore Sun*, May 28, 1989, p. C1.

77. "Overhauling Social Security," *CQ Researcher*, May 12, 1995, p. 417.

78. Paul Magnusson, "Dear Elizabeth: The Dog Ate Your Social Security," *Business Week*, May 16, 1994, p. 35.

79. Joel Achenbaum, "The Big Lie," *Miami Herald*, March 25, 1990, p. 9.

80. "Social Security: Myths and Moynihan," *Wall Street Journal*, January 15, 1990, p. A1.

81. Joseph A. Arrighi, "Hands Off My Social Security," *New York Times*, March 14, 1993, Section 3, p. 1.

82. Susan Dentzer, "You're Not As Entitled As You Think," *U.S. News and World Report*, March 29, 1995, p. 67.

83. *Flemming v. Nestor*, 363 U.S. 603, 80 S. Ct. 1367, 4 L. Ed 2d 1435 (1960).

84. Peterson, speech.

85. Howe and Strauss, p. 10.

86. Lawrence Lindsey, "The Big Black Hole," *Forbes*, November 21, 1994, p. 43; Howe and Strauss, p. 10.

87. Nationwide poll of 1,007 Americans 18 and over, plus an additional 514 Americans aged 30-40, by Yankelovich, Clancy and Shulman, *Time*, May 19, 1986, p. 35.

88. Gary Blonston, "An Aging Population Will Alter the Future," *Philadelphia Enquirer*, September 6, 1987, p. H7.

89. Gina Kolata, "Family Aid to Elderly Is Very Strong, Study Shows," *New York Times*, May 3, 1993, p. A16.

90. "Will Baby Boomers Be Too Poor to Retire at 65?" *Journal of Commerce*, November 9, 1989, p. 13.

91. "Projections of the Population of the United States by Age, Sex, and Race." Washington, DC: U.S. Department of Commerce, 1989, pp. 90-91.

92. *Aging America*, p. 242.

93. "Social Security Bill Grows," *USA Today*, January 9, 1995, p. B1.

94. "Social Security and Medicare Contribution Rates for Workers and Employers, Selected Years, 1940-1990," Henry J. Aaron, Barry P. Bosworth, and Gary Burtless, *Can America Afford to Grow Old?* Washington, DC: Brookings Institution, 1989, p. 21.

95. Peter Francese, "Publisher's Note: Social Security Solution," *American Demographics*, February 1993, p. 2.

96. Peterson, speech.

97. Bipartisan Commission, August 4, 1994, Findings No. 6 and 7 (n.p.).

98. Laurence J. Kotlikoff and Jagdeesh Gokhale, "Passing the Generational Buck," *The Public Interest*, Winter 1994, p. 81.

99. Ibid., p. 79.

100. Sarah Glazer, "Overhauling Social Security," *CQ Researcher*, May 12, 1995, p. 419.

101. Lindsey, p. 42.

102. Pete DuPont, "Shrinking Retirement Returns," *Washington Times*, October 10, 1993, p. B1.

103. Rita Koselka, "The Legal Ponzi Scheme," *Forbes*, October 9, 1995.

104. William Graebner, *A History of Retirement*. New Haven, CT: Yale University Press, 1980, pp. 18-19.

105. Ibid., p. 4.

106. Ibid., p. 10.

107. Ibid.

108. Ibid.

109. Ibid., p. 6.

110. Lydia Bronte, *The Longevity Factor*. New York: HarperCollins, 1994.

111. Ibid., p. 90.

112. Ibid., p. 91.

113. Kenneth G. Manton, Larry S. Corder, and Eric Stallard, "Estimates of Change in Chronic Disability and Institutional Incidence and Prevalence Rates in the U.S. Elderly Population From the 1982, 1984, and 1989 National Long-Term Health Care Survey," *Journal of Gerontology*, 1993, pp. S153-165.

114. Felicity Barringer, "Drop Seen in Old-Age Disability, Challenging Idea of Fading Health," *New York Times*, April 7, 1993, p. A1.

115. "Current Estimates, 1988, 1989." Washington, DC: National Center for Health Statistics, 1989, p. 114.

116. Diane Crispell and William Frey, "American Maturity," *American Demographics*, March 1993, p. 35.

117. Barringer, p. A1.

118. Stephen Pollan and Mark Levine, "The Rise and Fall of Retirement," *Worth*, December 1995, p. 73.

119. Kolata, p. A16.

120. Susan Dentzer, "Do the Elderly Want to Work?" *U.S. News and World Report*, May 14, 1990, p. 49.

121. Peterson, p. 296.

122. Mahrez Okba, "The Pros and Cons of Early Retirement," *The OECD Observer*, December 1993, pp. 34-35.

123. Eric Schine, "Take the Money and Run—or Take Your Chances," *Business Week*, August 16, 1993, pp. 28-29; Michael Quint, "Company's Buyout: Was It That Good?" *New York Times*, December 15, 1995, p. D1.

124. Pollan and Levine, p. 64.

125. Andree Brooks, "Strategies: Social Security: Better to Pass at Age 62 to Collect More At 65?" *New York Times*, September 18, 1993, Section 3, p. 1.

126. Ibid.

127. Dentzer, "Do the Elderly Want to Work?" p. 49.

128. Kolata, p. A16.

129. Richard Thau, "Should the Sacred Cow Be Slaughtered?" *Vital Speeches*, June 15, 1995, p. 525.

130. Dentzer, "Do the Elderly Want to Work?" p. 50.

131. Paula Mergenhagen, "Rethinking Retirement," *American Demographics*, June 1994, p. 30.

132. Leslie Eaton, "Cloudy Sunset," *Barron's*, July 12, 1993, pp. 8-9.

133. Ibid.

134. "Why Baby Boomers Won't Be Able to Retire," *Fortune*, September 4, 1995, p. 48.

135. Mergenhagen, pp. 28-29.

136. Anne Willette, "Boomers Tax USA's Social Institutions," *USA Today*, May 8, 1995, p. A2.

137. Ibid.

138. Peterson, speech.

139. Robert Kerrey, Statement at the hearings before the Senate Finance Subcommittee on Social Security, June 27, 1995, in *Congressional Digest*, October 1995, pp. 234-236.

140. Elizabeth Kolbert, "Who Will Face the Music?" *New York Times Magazine*, August 27, 1995, p. 56.

141. Gerald Shea, in "Should Congress Pass Legislation to Partially Privatize the Social Security System?" *Congressional Digest*, October 1995, p. 239.

142. Allan Tull, in ibid.

143. Glazer, p. 421.

144. Peterson, pp. 291-292.

145. Kotlikoff and Gokhale, p. 79.

146. *The Zero Deficit Plan*. Washington, DC: The Concord Coalition (n.d.), pp. 28-30.

147. Thau, p. 526.

148. Rob Nelson and Jon Cowan, *Revolution X*. New York: Penguin Books, 1994, pp. 123-124.

149. Ibid.

150. Thau, p. 526.

151. DuPont, p. B1.

152. Koselka, pp. 70-71.

153. Ibid.

154. James Gollin, *The Star-Spangled Retirement Dream*. New York: Scribner's, 1981, p. 127.

155. Peterson, *Facing Up*, pp. 293-294.

156. "As Baby Boomers Turn Fifty, Retirement Crisis Awaits," *USA Today*, January 2, 1996, p. A10.

157. Eaton, "Cloudy Sunset," pp. 8-9.

158. "Will Generation Xers Get Their Benefits?" *CQ Researcher*, May 12, 1995, p. 426.

159. Glazer, p. 417.

160. Paul Magnusson, "Apocalypse Soon—Or Sooner," *Business Week*, May 1, 1995, p. 138.

161. Glazer, p. 418.

162. Ibid., pp. 431-432.

Selected Bibliography

Aaron, Henry J., Barry P. Bosworth, and Gary Burtless. *Can America Afford to Grow Old?* Washington, DC: Brookings Institution, 1989.

Achenbaum, W. Andrew. *Old Age in the New Land.* Baltimore: Johns Hopkins University Press, 1978.

———. *Shades of Gray.* Boston: Little, Brown and Co., 1983.

———. *Social Security: Visions and Revisions.* Cambridge: Cambridge University Press, 1986.

Achenbaum, W. Andrew, and Peggy Ann Kusnerz. *Images of Old Age in America, 1790 to the Present.* Institute of Gerontology, The University of Michigan-Wayne State University, 1978.

Altmeyer, Arthur J. *The Formative Years of Social Security.* Madison: University of Wisconsin Press, 1966.

American Association of Retired Persons. *Toward a Just and Caring Society: AARP Public Policy Agenda for 1991.* Washington, DC: 1991.

———. "Washington Report," September-October 1989.

Armstrong, Barbara. *Insuring the Essentials.* New York: Macmillan, 1932.

Badger, Anthony J. *The New Deal: The Depression Years, 1933-1940.* New York: Hill & Wang, 1989.

Bell, John. *On Regimen and Longevity.* Philadelphia: Haswell & Johnson, 1842.

Bentley, Arthur F. *The Process of Government.* San Antonio: Principia Press, 1949.

Berlant, Jeffrey. *Profession and Monopoly.* Berkeley: University of California Press, 1975.

Berry, Jeffrey. *The Interest Group Society.* Boston: Little, Brown & Co., 1984.

Binstock, Robert H., and Ethel Shanas. *Handbook of Aging and the Social Sciences.* New York: Van Nostrand, 1985.

Bornet, Vaughn D. *The Presidency of Lyndon B. Johnson.* Lawrence: University of Kansas Press, 1983.

Bornet, Vaughn D., and Edgar Eugene Robinson. *Herbert Hoover.* Stanford, CA: Hoover Institute Press, 1975.

Bronte, Lydia, and Alan Pifer. *Our Aging Society: Paradox and Promise.* New York: W.W. Norton, 1986.

Burns, James MacGregor. *The Workshop of Democracy.* New York: Vintage Books, 1985.

Burrow, James. *A.M.A.: Voice of American Medicine.* Baltimore: Johns Hopkins University Press, 1963.

Canetti, Elias. *Crowds and Power.* Middlesex, England: Penguin Books, 1960.

Chambers, Clarke A. *Seedtime of Reform: American Social Service and Social Action 1918-1933.* Minneapolis: University of Minnesota Press, 1963.

Child, Charles Manning. *Senescence and Rejuvenescence.* Chicago: University of Chicago Press, 1915.

Child, L. Maria. *Looking Toward Sunset.* New York: Houghton Mifflin and Company, 1891.

Cigler, Allan J., and Burdett A. Loomis (eds.). *Interest Group Politics.* Washington, DC: Congressional Quarterly Press, 1983.

Clark, Robert (ed.). *Retirement Policy in an Aging Society.* Durham: Duke University Press, 1980.

Conference Board. "The Public View of Public Spending." New York, March 1988.

Congressional Quarterly. *Aging in America.* Washington, DC: Congressional Quarterly Inc., 1989.

Crystal, Stephen. *America's Old Age Crisis.* New York: Basic Books, 1982.

Davis, Richard H. (ed.). *Aging: Prospects and Issues.* Los Angeles: University of Southern California Press, 1981.

Derthick, Martha. *Agency Under Stress.* Washington, DC: Brookings Institution, 1990.

———. *Policymaking for Social Security.* Washington, DC: Brookings Institution, 1979.

Drucker, Peter. *The Age of Discontinuity.* New York: Harper & Row, 1969.

Dychtwald, Ken, and Joe Flower. *Age Wave.* New York: Bantam Books, 1990.

Epstein, Abraham. *Facing Old Age.* New York: Arno Press & The New York Times, 1972 (first published 1922).

———. *Insecurity: A Challenge to America.* New York: Harrison Smith & Robert Haas, 1933.

Estes, Carroll L., Robert J. Newcomer and Associates. *Fiscal Austerity and Aging.* Beverly Hills: Sage Publications, 1983.

Farrow, Frank, Judith Meltzer, and Harold Richman. *Policy Options in Long-Term Care.* Chicago: University of Chicago Press, 1981.

Fausold, Martin. *The Presidency of Herbert C. Hoover.* Lawrence: University of Kansas Press, 1985.

Ferrara, Peter J. *Social Security: The Inherent Contradiction.* Washington, DC: The Cato Institute, 1980.

——— (ed.). *Social Security: Prospects for Real Reform.* Washington, DC: Cato Institute, 1985.

Fischer, David Hackett. *Growing Old in America.* Oxford: Oxford University Press, 1978.

Fisher, Louis. *The Politics of Shared Power.* Washington, DC: Congressional Quarterly, 1981.

Freidel, Frank. *Franklin D. Roosevelt: A Rendezvous with Destiny.* Boston: Little, Brown and Co., 1990.

Gollin, James. *The Star-Spangled Retirement Dream.* New York: Scribner's, 1981.

Graebner, William. *A History of Retirement*. New Haven, CT: Yale University Press, 1980.

Gross, Ronald, Beatrice Gross, and Sylvia Seidman (eds). *The New Old: Struggling for Decent Aging*. Garden City, NY: Anchor Press, 1978.

Hall, G. Stanley. *Senescence: The Last Half of Life*. New York: D. Appleton and·Company, 1923.

Hamilton, Alexander, James Madison, and John Jay. *The Federalist Papers*, Garry Willis (ed.). New York: Bantam Books, 1987.

Harris, Louis. *Inside America*. New York: Random House, 1987.

——. *The Myth and Reality of Aging in America*. Washington, DC: National Council on Aging, 1975.

Harris, Richard. *A Sacred Trust*. New York: New American Library, 1966.

Hess, Beth H., and Elizabeth W. Markson (eds.). *Growing Old in America*. New Brunswick, NJ: Transaction Publishers, 1991.

Homer, Paul, and Martha Holstein (eds.). *A Good Old Age?* New York: Touchstone, 1990.

Hoover, Herbert. *The Memoirs of Herbert Hoover* (3 vols.). New York, Macmillan, 1951-1952.

——. *The State Papers and Other Public Writings of Herbert Hoover*, William S. Myers (ed.). Garden City, NY: Doubleday, Doran & Co., 1934.

Hudson, Robert B. (ed.). *The Aging in Politics*. Springfield, IL: Charles C. Thomas, 1981.

Hunter, Robert. *Poverty*. New York: Harper & Row, 1965 (originally published 1904).

Hyde, Arthur Mastick, and Ray Lyman Wilbur. *The Hoover Policies*. New York: Charles Scribner's Sons, 1937.

Johnsen, Julia E. *Old Age Pensions*. New York: H.W. Wilson Company, 1935.

Johnson, Lyndon Baines. *The Johnson Presidential Press Conferences* (2 vols.). New York: Earl M. Coleman Enterprises, 1984.

——. *The Vantage Point*. New York: Holt, Rinehart & Winston, 1971.

Karpel, Craig. *The Retirement Myth*. New York: HarperCollins, 1995.

Kelso, Robert W. *Poverty*. New York: Longman's, Green and Co., 1929.

Kernell, Samuel. *Going Public*. Washington, DC: Congressional Quarterly Press, 1986.

Kingdon, John. *Agendas, Alternatives, and Public Policies*. Boston: Little, Brown and Co. 1984.

Lammers, William W. *Public Policy and the Aging*. Washington, DC: Congressional Quarterly Press, 1983.

Lathrop, Rev. S.G. *Fifty Years and Beyond*. Chicago: Fleming H. Revell, 1881.

Lehman, Harvey C. *Age and Achievement*. Princeton, NJ: Princeton University Press, 1953.

Leiby, James. *A History of Social Welfare and Social Work in the United States*. New York: Columbia University Press, 1978.

Leuchtenburg, William E. *Franklin D. Roosevelt and the New Deal*. New York: Harper & Row, 1963.

Lockett, Betty A. *Aging, Politics, and Research*. New York: Springer Publishing Company, 1983.

Lorand, Arnold. *Old Age Deferred*. Philadelphia: F.A. Davis Company, 1923.

Lowi, Theodore. *The End of Liberalism*. New York: W.W. Norton, 1969.

Lubove, Roy (ed.). *Poverty and Social Welfare in the United States*. New York: Holt, Rinehart and Winston, 1972.

———. *The Professional Altruist*. Cambridge, MA: Harvard University Press, 1965.

———. *The Struggle for Social Security*. Cambridge, MA: Harvard University Press, 1968.

——— (ed.). *Social Welfare in Transition*. Pittsburgh: University of Pittsburgh Press, 1966.

Lynd, Robert S., and Helen Merrell Lynd. *Middletown*. New York: Harcourt, Brace and Company, 1929.

MacManus, Susan. *Young Versus Old*. Boulder, CO: Westview Press, 1996.

Malthus, Thomas. *An Essay on the Principle of Population*. Middlesex: Penguin, 1970.

Marmor, Theodore R. *The Politics of Medicare*. Chicago: Aldine Publishing, 1973.

Martin, George. *Madam Secretary: Frances Perkins*. Boston: Houghton Mifflin and Company, 1976.

Martin, Lillien J., and Clare DeGrouchy. *Salvaging Old Age*. New York: The Macmillan Company, 1930.

Mayhew, David R. *Congress: The Electoral Connection*. New Haven, CT: Yale University Press, 1974.

McClelland, Peter D., and Richard J. Zeckhauser. *Demographic Dimensions of the New Republic*. Cambridge: Cambridge University Press, 1982.

Minkler, M., and Carroll Estes (eds.). *Readings in the Political Economy of Aging*. Farmingdale, NY: Baywood Publishing, 1984.

Moley, Raymond. *The First New Deal*. New York: Harcourt Brace & World, 1966.

Myers, Robert. *Social Security*. Bryn Mawr, PA: McCahan Foundation, 1975.

Nash, Gerald, Noel H. Pugach, and Richard Tomasson (eds.). *Social Security: The First Half-Century*. Albuquerque: University of New Mexico Press, 1988.

National Center for Health Statistics. *Health, United States, 1988*. DHHS Pub. No. (PHS)89-1232. Washington, DC: Department of Health and Human Services, March 1989.

———. "Life Tables." *Vital Statistics of the United States, 1987*. Vol. II, Section 6, February 1990.

———. *Utilization of Short-Stay Hospitals, United States, 1985*. Hyattsville, MD: June 1988.

Nelson, Rob, and Jon Cowan. *Revolution X*. New York: Penguin Books, 1994.

Newman, Katherine. *Declining Fortunes*. New York: Basic Books, 1993.

Olson, Mancur. *The Logic of Collective Action*. Cambridge, MA: Harvard University Press, 1965.

Ornstein, Norman, and Shirley Elder. *Interest Groups, Lobbying, and Policy Making*. Washington, DC: Congressional Quarterly Press, 1978.

Parmelee, Maurice. *Poverty and Social Progress*. New York: The Macmillan Company, 1916.

Pepper, Claude. *Pepper*. New York: Harcourt Brace Jovanovich, 1987.

Perkins, Frances. *The Roosevelt I Knew*. New York: Harper & Row, 1964.

Perot, Ross. *Intensive Care*. New York: HarperPerennial, 1995.

Peterson, Peter G. *Facing Up*. New York: Touchstone, 1994.

Petras, Kathryn, and Ross Petras. *The Only Retirement Guide You'll Ever Need*. New York: Poseidon Press, 1991.

Pifer, Alan, and Lydia Bronte (eds.). *Our Aging Society*. New York: W.W. Norton, 1986.

Piliavin, Jane Allyn et al. *Emergency Intervention*. New York: Academic Press, 1981.

Pitkin, Walter B. *Life Begins at Forty*. New York: McGraw-Hill, 1932.

Poen, Monte M. *Harry S. Truman Versus the Medical Lobby*. Columbia: University of Missouri Press, 1979.

Polsby, Nelson. *Policy Innovation in America*. New Haven, CT: Yale University Press, 1984.

Pratt, Henry J. *The Gray Lobby*. Chicago: University of Chicago Press, 1976.

Roosevelt, Franklin D. *Complete Presidential Press Conferences*, Vols. 5-6. New York: DaCapo Press, 1972.

———. *The Public Papers and Addresses of Franklin D. Roosevelt*, Samuel Rosenman (ed.). New York: Random House, 13 vols., 1938-1950.

———. *The Roosevelt Reader*. New York: Holt Rinehart & Winston, 1964.

Rubinow, Isaac M. *The Quest for Security*. New York: Henry Holt and Company, 1934.

———. *Social Insurance*. New York: Henry Holt and Company, 1913.

Salisbury, Robert (ed.). *Interest Group Politics in America*. New York: Harper & Row, 1970.

Schacht, John (ed.). *The Quest for Security*. Iowa City: Center for the Study of Recent History of the United States, 1982.

Schlesinger, Arthur M. *The Coming of the New Deal*. Boston: Houghton Mifflin, 1958.

———. *The Crisis of the Old Order, 1919-1933*. Boston: Houghton Mifflin, 1957.

Schwarz, Jordan A. *The Interregnum of Despair: Hoover, Congress, and the Depression*. Urbana: University of Illinois Press, 1970.

Stearns, Peter N. (ed.). *Old Age in Preindustrial Society*. New York: Holmes & Meier, 1982.

Streib, Gordon F., and Clement J. Schneider. *Retirement in American Society*. Ithaca, NY: Cornell University Press, 1971.

Sundquist, James L. *Politics and Policy*. Washington, DC: The Brookings Institution, 1968.

Tishler, Hace Sorel. *Self-Reliance and Social Security, 1870-1917*. Port Washington, NY: Kennikat Press, 1971.

de Tocqueville, Alexis. *Democracy in America*, Richard D. Heffner (ed.). New York: New American Library, 1956.

Townsend, Francis E. *New Horizons*. Chicago: J.L. Stewart, 1943.

Transamerica Life Companies. "Two Generations View Their Financial Futures." Los Angeles, July 1988.

Trattner, Walter I. *From Poor Law to Welfare State*. New York: Free Press, 1979.

Truman, David B. *The Governmental Process*. New York: Alfred A. Knopf, 1951.

Truman, Harry S. *The Public Papers of the Presidents of the United States, 1945-1953*. Washington, DC: U.S. Government Printing Office, 1961-66.

Tyler, Poyntz. *Social Welfare in the United States*. New York: H.W. Wilson Co., 1955.

U.S. Bureau of the Census. "Historical Statistics of the United States, Colonial Times to 1970." Washington, DC, 1975.

———. "Household Wealth and Asset Ownership: 1988," Current Population Reports Series P-70, No. 22, December 1990.

———. "Money Income and Poverty Status in the United States: 1989," *Current Population Reports*, Series P-60, No. 168, September 1990.

————. "Projections of the Population of the United States, by Age, Sex, and Race: 1988 to 2080," *Current Population Reports*, Series P-25, No. 1018, January 1989.

U.S. Department of Commerce, Economics and Statistics Administration, and Bureau of the Census. *Statistical Abstract of the United States, 1991*. Washington, DC: U.S. Government Printing Office, 1991.

————. *Statistical Abstract of the United States, 1994*. Washington, DC: U.S. Government Printing Office, 1994.

U.S. House of Representatives, Committee on Ways and Means. *Background Material and Data on Programs Within the Jurisdiction of the Committee on Ways and Means*. Washington, DC, 1989.

U.S. House of Representatives, Select Committee on Aging. *Activities of the Aging Commitee in the 101st Congress, First Session*. Washington, DC: U.S. Government Printing Office, April 1990.

U.S. Senate Special Committee on Aging, American Association of Retired Persons, Federal Council on the Aging, and U.S. Administration on Aging. *Aging America: Trends and Projections*. Washington, DC, 1988 and 1991.

Waldo, Daniel R., Sally T. Sonnefeld, David R. McKusick, and Ross H. Arnett. "Health Expenditures by Age Group, 1977 and 1987." *Health Care Financing Review*, Vol. 10, No. 4, September 1989.

Wattenberg, Ben J. *The Birth Dearth*. New York: Pharos Books, 1987.

Weaver, Carolyn L. *The Crisis in Social Security*. Durham, NC: Duke Press Policy Studies, 1982.

Wilde, Oscar. *The Complete Works of Oscar Wilde*. New York: Barnes & Noble, 1994.

Williamson, John B., Linda Evans, and Lawrence A. Powell. *The Politics of Aging*. Springfield, IL: Charles C. Thomas, 1982.

Williamson, John B., Judith A. Shindul, and Linda Evans. *Aging and Public Policy*. Springfield, IL: Charles C. Thomas, 1985.

Witte, Edwin. *The Development of the Social Security Act*. Madison: University of Wisconsin Press, 1962.

————. *Social Security Perspectives*. Madison: University of Wisconsin Press, 1962.

Wolpe, Bruce C. *Lobbying Congress*. Washington, DC: Congressional Quarterly Press, 1990.

Young, James Sterling. *The Washington Community, 1880-1828*. New York: Columbia University Press, 1966.

Zisk, Betty H. (ed.). *American Political Interest Groups*. Belmont, CA: Wadsworth Publishing, 1969.

Index

About the Author

MATTHEW C. PRICE is Assistant Professor of Political Science at Texas A&M
University-Kingsville.

ISBN 0-275-96012-9

90000>

EAN

9 780275 960124

HARDCOVER BAR CODE